# Conversations
# with Jon Hassler

# Conversations
# with Jon Hassler

Joseph Plut

*Joseph Plut*

**NODIN PRESS**

ACKNOWLEDGMENTS
Four of these interviews first appeared in a slightly different form
in the following literary quarterlies: *Staggerford* in *South Dakota
Review* (Spring 2001), *The Love Hunter* in *North Dakota Quarterly*
(Winter 2003), and *North of Hope* (Winter 2003) and *Grand
Opening* (Spring 2005) in *Renascence*. We thank the editors of these
publications for permission to reprint.

We especially thank Barbara Bendson for her diligent work with the
manuscript and for her faith in our endeavor.        - J. H. & J. P.

I am very grateful to Norton Stillman of Nodin Press for publishing
our book of interviews and to John Toren for sensitively editing the
manuscript. Jon, who died on March 20, 2008, would have been
pleased to see *Conversations with Jon Hassler* in print.        - J. P.

Cover painting: Jon Hassler
Design: John Toren

Library of Congress Cataloging-in-Publication Data

Plut, Joseph.
Conversations with Jon Hassler / Joseph Plut ; introduction by
Jon Hassler.
p. cm.
ISBN 978-1-932472-97-4
1. Hassler, Jon--Interviews. 2. Novelists, American--20th century-
-Interviews. I. Title.
PS3558.A726Z83 2010
813'.54--dc22
[B]
                                                    2010008946

HOR          813.54
      10/8/10     PLU
Nodin Press, LLC
530 North 3rd Street
Suite 120
Minneapolis, MN
55401

*To the Kirzeder family, James and Rita, and their children, Jill, Dan, Mark, Brian, and Thomas, for all the love, affirmation, and support these many years,*

*And in memory of my close friend Mark Estrin, whose love of the arts—especially film and theatre—encouraged and inspired me for over forty years,*

*And, of course, to Jon and Gretchen Kresl Hassler, whose constant enthusiasm, encouragement, and love made this project such a joy for me from its very beginnings in 1997.*

# Contents

All towns and places are in Minnesota unless otherwise indicated, and all page number references are from the hardcover editions. The Saint John's University that appears often in the text is located in Collegeville, Minnesota, a ninety-minute drive northwest of the Twin Cities.

# *Preface*

Joseph Plut

Writer Flannery O'Connor, in a letter to her friend Cecil Hawkins, stated: "At interviews, I always feel like a dry cow being milked. There is no telling what they will get out of you." I didn't ask Jon if he felt this way about our nine interviews—I hope not.

I met Jon in 1968 at Brainerd Community College (now Central Lakes College) in Brainerd, Minnesota; we both taught English there, he from 1968 to 1980, and I from 1965 to 2001. After Jon resigned in order to teach at Saint John's University in Collegeville, Minnesota, our friendship continued by phone, mail, and visits.

While conducting these interviews, Jon and I speculated that we were involved in a unique undertaking—that never before had an author been interviewed about many of his/her novels by the same interviewer. In any case, we hoped that the interviews would retain the flavor of conversations between old friends—which is what they were. As a result, you will notice that we digress and repeat ourselves from time to time. My questions, of course, were mostly scripted; Jon hadn't received them ahead of time, however, and his answers were entirely off-the-cuff.

As I prepared for a given interview, I would reread the novel that was to be its focus, as well as Jon's correspondence to me at the time of his writing it, along with articles, other published interviews, and reviews of the book. I also reviewed, as well as I could, my personal recollections of what Jon had told me while he was writing the book. I made an effort to elicit detailed information from Jon regarding various phases of his career, such as his editors and agents, publishers, revisions, and inspirations—the things that might interest a future literary biographer. But we didn't want to stint on the "small talk" either, and the interviews contain nuggets of arcane information that we found amusing, but which also expose aspects of Jon's character and personal history that often elude more formal interrogation. I realize that some of the questions may seem trivial as a result, and some overly personal, but I'm confident that readers will appreciate learning how Jon answered such questions. I also tried to highlight symbolism and themes in my questions on occasion, especially for teachers.

As we plotted this series of interviews, Jon and I envisioned a reading audience comprised of friends, fans, librarians, teachers, and academics, among others. My goal was to help the reader to get to know Jon better—both the writer and the person.

– November 2004

# Introduction

JON HASSLER

Because I spent the first twenty years of my adult life longing to be a writer without writing a word, I devoted a lot of time to doing writerly things, such as haunting the public library, going through each new issue of *Writer's Digest* and *The Writer* from cover to cover, imagining the stories I would write and where I would send them for publication.

But my favorite reading was the author interview. I recall buying the *Paris Review Interviews* every time a new collection came out, poring over the answers to the interviewers' questions and vicariously living the life those writers were leading—every one from James Joyce to John Updike. I was particularly interested in their work habits—where and how long each day did they write? How much writing could they turn out in a good day? And, of course, where did their ideas come from?

But it was disappointing to come to the end of an interview and realize that I was seeing these writers at a single moment during their lives. I wanted more. I wanted to read a succession of interviews that spanned their whole careers. How else could I watch the writer's progression from work to work? How else could I gain a sense of their total accomplishment?

And that's why I was so pleased when my friend Joe Plut came to me with the idea of doing interviews for nine of my novels. We did this over a period of five years, beginning with *The Dean's List* because it was just coming out in paperback at the time, 1997. Then we went back to the beginning and talked about *Staggerford* (1977), moving forward from there to *The Dean's List* (1997) which ends *Conversations with Jon Hassler*—nine interviews covering twenty years.

I am often asked which of my books is my favorite, and I have to honestly say that I have no favorites. Each book, like each of my children, is precious to me in its own way, because each book has its foundation in my life. *Staggerford* was my high school teaching book. I had been a college instructor for ten years by the time I began it, but before that I had spent the first ten years of my career teaching in high schools. The fact that this has become something of a cult book among high school English teachers I take as a sign that I got it right.

Then next came my most wholly imagined book, *Simon's Night* (1979), about a seventy-six-year-old retired English professor. I was asked by one elderly reader how I, at forty-five, knew so much about the soul of an old man, and the answer is that I included quite a few scenes from my own life—my physical examination, my voting for Franklin Pierce in the election of 1976, etc.—and the reader took them for the experiences of someone much older.

The case of multiple sclerosis that plays such a prominent role in *The Love Hunter* (1981) was actually that of a friend of mine named Bob Nielsen. We were young teachers together in the late '50s in Fosston when he contracted the disease. He died of it in the mid-70s. The hunting camp and the people in it came straight out of a lengthy journal entry I made after visiting such a place for a weekend of hunting on Lake Manitoba. The love triangle I imagined.

In *A Green Journey* (1985) Agatha McGee, who'd played a secondary role in *Staggerford*, steps forth for the first time as the central character. She is a composite of three people: my mother, myself, and an unmarried schoolteacher aunt of mine who used to come and live with us in the summers during my boyhood. The prototype for her pen pal, James O'Hannon, was a priest I met during one of my first visits to Ireland.

*Grand Opening* (1987) is my boyhood book. Like the Fosters in the novel, my parents and I moved to a small town in southern Minnesota, where we owned a small grocery store and witnessed the end of World War II. There was a Dodger in my life, but only for a weekend, not for an entire school year as in the book. And it was my father, not my mother, who was defeated after two terms on the school board by the same method as the book recounts. My mother, like Catherine Foster, was never happy there, but instead of moving away after one year, as in the book, we did so after eight years.

Frank Healy's boyhood in *North of Hope* (1991) was more or less my own. Later, as a priest, he finds himself in far northern Minnesota, as I did when I was teaching in Fosston and Bemidji. While this latter part of the story is entirely imagined, the wintry settings are typical of that area, Sovereign Lake being Red Lake and the Basswood Indian Reservation being a cross between the White Earth and the Red Lake reservations.

*Dear James* (1993) brings back Agatha McGee and her friend James O'Hannon. Agatha takes part in the group tour of Italy that I went on in 1985. As usual, I came home with more observations about my fellow tourists than about Italy.

In *Rookery Blues* (1995) I finally get around to college teaching, where I spent the majority of my forty-two-year career in the classroom. The impetus for this novel came from a group of seven of us new and insecure instructors at Bemidji State College (now University) who banded together in a quasi-club called The Scholars. Unlike the Icejam Quintet, none of us played a musical instrument—we mostly drank beer and rewarded failure and punished accomplishment among our members—but we found the same sort of consolation that the five jazz musicians do at Rookery State College.

Because I had more to say about college teaching and about poetry, I next wrote *The Dean's List* (1997) about Leland Edwards, one of the musicians in *Rookery Blues*, who has risen to the deanship, and about Richard Falcon, a Robert Frost-like poet who makes an extended visit to Rookery State College. Falcon's dozen or so poems are my own, written nearly forty years ago when, for a time, I took myself seriously as a poet.

I hope that you, dear reader, enjoy these interviews half as much as I used to enjoy *The Paris Review Interviews* before I began to write the first of these nine novels.

– September 2004

# Conversations
# with Jon Hassler

# Staggerford

The paperback edition of Jon's first adult novel, *Staggerford*, has sold more copies than any of his other novels. Why is it so popular? Perhaps because the familiarity of the setting—an average American high school—immediately puts the reader at ease. Having gained our interest at the outset, Jon proceeds to explore the needs, frustrations, successes, and disappointments that his characters meet up with day-to-day. We identify not only with the teachers Miles Pruitt and Agatha McGee, but also with many of the students, especially Beverly Bingham. We know these people, and because we know them, we care about what happens to them.

Jon was amazed by how closely readers identified with Miles Pruitt. It surprised him, but it shouldn't surprise us. These are honorable and basically good people, trying to do the best they can in their circumstances.

Jon has been keeping journals since 1965, when he was teaching English at Park Rapids High School in Park Rapids, and this practice has aided him enormously in his fiction. He estimates that he has filled about thirty volumes by now, and they often serve as a sourcebook for his fiction.

Jon started to write fiction in September 1970 at Brainerd Community College (now Central Lakes College in Brainerd). He soon discovered that he could not satisfactorily teach full time and also write. Therefore, he applied for, and was granted, a year's sabbatical from teaching during the 1975-1976 school year. This sabbatical gave birth to *Staggerford*.

The journal Jon kept while writing *Staggerford* was later published as *My Staggerford Journal*. Jon got the idea of publishing it

3

when he was speaking at a Minnesota Council of Teachers of English convention. "I took along my journal about writing *Staggerford*. I read parts of it to the crowd, and the reception was so enthusiastic that it occurred to me they might enjoy reading it if I wrote it out and published it." Ballantine Books published this gem in 1999, adding an invaluable companion to *Staggerford*.

In *My Staggerford Journal*, Jon acquaints the reader with the "stuff" that went into Staggerford: descriptions of weather, people that he met, what they said and what he overheard in coffee shops. Aspiring writers might be especially interested in the sections detailing the letters, telephone calls, inquiries and telegrams that were exchanged before the novel was finally accepted for publication, and the joy that Jon felt when he learned that his agent had sold two of his novels, *Staggerford* and the young people's novel *Four Miles to Pinecone*, within ten days of each other. I asked him if that feeling would be akin to winning a lottery. "For me it was the same as my school Plainview beating St. Charles in high school football, 49 to nothing, and winning the Whitewater League Championship. It was about as exciting as anything I've done since I've played high school football."

Though Jon's novels were never reviewed in *Time*, *Newsweek*, *The Nation*, *The New Republic*, or even *People* , I sometimes wonder how such publicity might have affected his career. Jon once told me he felt grateful that he really didn't get published until he was forty-four, and that *Staggerford* proved to be a very modest success. It relieved him of the pressure to make his second novel (*Simon's Night*) big and splashy.

Jon concludes *My Staggerford Journal* with an afterword, sharing with us his writer's manifesto:

*As my finances permitted, after the publication of* Staggerford, *I began teaching a reduced load of classes in order to feed my addiction to writing. And that was more or less the pattern of my life for the next twenty years, until my retirement from the classroom in 1997—for I had discovered my reason for writing. It is to write. By this, I mean that my writing income granted me the pleasure—indeed, the privilege—of doing every day what I was born to do, namely, to sit here at my desk, picking through the language and finding the best way of expressing what's on my mind, in my memory, in my imagination.*

- J. P. January 2004

*August 15, 2000*

Q. Good morning, Jon. I'm eager to talk to you about your first novel, *Staggerford*. It's interesting that your first adult novel, *Staggerford*, and your young people's novel, *Four Miles to Pinecone*, were accepted for publication within ten days of each other in September 1976. Please fill in the details of this accomplishment.

A. *Four Miles to Pinecone* was the first novel I wrote; I wrote it over five years; I wrote it once a year for five years until I got it right. I sent it to my agent, Harriet Wasserman, in New York, and she sent it around to various places, and somebody at Frederick Warne and Company (they are the publishers of *Peter Rabbit*) got interested. An editor, Margaret Lichtenberg, whose name I haven't seen since, wouldn't buy it. She kept stalling, and a year later, when I sent Harriet *Staggerford*, she sold that to Atheneum, and I remember her saying to me, "Well, now we'll get the other one sold." Then she called up Margaret Lichtenberg, told her that *Staggerford* had been sold, so she bought that one immediately. So I had two books come out within a month of each other—my first two books at the age of forty-four. Quite an accomplishment I thought at the time.

Q. I still think so. Harriet Wasserman is one of the best literary agents, having had Saul Bellow and Reynolds Price as her clients. How did she become your agent?

A. In the early '70s I wrote a short story entitled "The Cheerleader." I sent it to Gordon Lish at *Esquire*. He liked it, and he thought he might print it. He edited it, and then he sent me a note. The entire note said, "Lost it. Hope you enjoyed the ride. Gordon." He told me on the phone later that he would send it to two agents. Harriet responded to him immediately with these two sentences: "This man can write. How do we proceed?" So when I finished *Staggerford*, I sent it to her; after two tries she sold it to Atheneum.

**Q. I assume this means that you really didn't write in college, but it's been more of a recent endeavor.**

A. That's right, I didn't write a word in college. I didn't speak about my desire to be a writer in college. I had a number of friends who were writers. They published in the *Sketchbook*—the Saint John's University [Collegeville] literary magazine. I never wrote a thing until I was thirty-seven. I began to write at the age of thirty-seven and I've been working hard at it ever since.

**Q. Teaching must have been a constraint on your writing. How did you find time to write two novels in a relatively short span of time?**

A. I used my time wisely. I used weekends. I used summers. I used evenings. I used mornings. I remember for a while getting up very early before school to write in the morning. It was very satisfying, you see, so that's what gave me the energy to do it in those days. I couldn't do it now, I don't have the energy for it, but I did then.

**Q. At one point this novel bore the title *The Willoughby Uprising*. What caused you to change this to *Staggerford*, and why Staggerford?**

A. Late, late in the writing I knew I needed another word because Willoughby was such a mild name and there are harsh things going on in this book. I needed a different name, and as I was getting up one morning, I reached for the light next to my bed, and as I switched on the light I said the word "Staggerford" before I thought it, so my subconscious had been working on this and served up the word Staggerford, which strikes me as a perfect name for this town. It describes life as I see it. We're all making progress, we're all fording a river—it's a staggering, stumbling sort of progress we make. A step back for every couple of steps forward. So Staggerford struck me as ideal.

**Q. What did you learn about the writing process when working on** *Staggerford?*

A. I learned how easy a book can be to write—it went so fast. It's the fastest book I'll ever write, of course. I finished it in the first five months, revised it in another month, and then I was finished. All my books since then have taken two years. I'd been teaching twenty years when I wrote the book, and I was so full of my subject, high school teaching, that it just came pouring out.

**Q. You picked a quotation from John Cheever to serve as an epigraph to** *Staggerford.* **"Oh, why is it that life is for some an exquisite privilege and others must pay for their seats at the play with a ransom of cholers, infections and nightmares?" Why?**

A. Because it seemed to describe the people in this book. Some seemed happy, some seemed sad. Some were evil, some were good. I still ponder that question. There's no answering why we are the way we are.

**Q. That was going to be my next question. I don't know if I've ever asked you that before. Is Cheever one of your influences or mentors?**

A. I learned from Cheever how to take care with sentences. I loved his sentences, and a lot of mine in *Staggerford* are sort of based on his sentences, the structure of them, so what I loved most about Cheever is the way he put together his sentences. I would copy those sentences and write them down in longhand, hoping that his skill with the sentence would go up my arm and into my brain.

**Q. How autobiographical is** *Staggerford?*

A. Every one of my books has its foundation in my life. I taught near an Indian reservation. I knew a lot of students like Beverly Bingham who came from deprived families, and I knew people like Jeff Norquist who jumped out the window. In fact, Jeff Norquist turned up in real life two years ago having murdered three people in a northern suburb of Minneapolis. I was at an autographing session recently, and a man came up to me. He said, "Jeff Norquist in *Staggerford*—

was he based on anybody?" I said, "Sure, he was based on Murray Bunness." He said, "I've just finished taking a deposition from him." Here was a kid I had in school in 1962—he turned up in my book first; now he turns up in prison.

Q. You wrote *Staggerford* while you were living in Brainerd and teaching at Brainerd Community College, which is how we met. How much of *Staggerford* is based on Brainerd and your experiences there?

A. Mark Bunsness [a teaching colleague] turned out to be Fred Vandergar in my book. He's the man whom Miles hugged because I didn't. I went over to his house one time and I left him without hugging him, and I wished I had. So when I wrote the book I had Miles do it for me. Sometimes, the character could act better than I do. His retirement party, too, took place in Brainerd, at Harold's Club, do you remember that? And, let's see, it was Elmer Herrmann [an instructor of English and German], who kept saying the name of the smallest fish in Hawaii. "Humuhumunukunukuapuaa," he kept saying, and so I put that in the book, too. He talked about that instead of talking about Mark and retirement because he was nervous. It was his way of covering up Mark's ill health. I don't remember much else from Brainerd; it seems to me most of it's from Park Rapids where I taught high school English.

Q. Was Park Rapids primarily the town as the model for Staggerford?

A. It was—I kept seeing the streets, the houses and the stores in Park Rapids as I was writing the book. That was my last high school teaching job.

Q. How autobiographical is Miles Pruitt?

A. I said before that my fiction is 37 percent autobiographical—I think Miles is 37 percent me, that is, about one-third of him. It's like me and about one-third of his experience is mine. Two-thirds are made up. I remember being invited across the hall, for example, to the Home-Ec room to eat what the students had prepared, the way Miles does. I remember Murray Bunness pulling a knife on an Indian kid and the reservation area responding by coming to town demanding to see him. It all ended very peacefully when he stayed in the school—the Indians got tired of waiting for him. They all went home. But anyway, that was part of the 37 percent.

**Q. Here's a question I just heard about two days ago, actually. Theanna Winkelman Grivna [a former student at Brainerd Community College] told me about the origin of the name Anna Thea. Would you explain that, please?**

A. Well, Anna Thea Workman in the book, whom Miles calls Thanatopsis, was based on Theanna Winkelman's name. I'd never heard the name Theanna before, so I used it for a while—then I turned it around, and used Anna Thea, and because it had a t-h and an a, I thought it might be fitting to call her Thanatopsis as a joke, which Miles does throughout most of the book.

**Q. Did you ever assign a "What I Wish" essay? I did in Composition 1 when I was teaching *Staggerford*; I counted this as a journal entry.**

A. I never did that actually. All my best ideas for teaching come to me when I'm writing books instead of while I'm teaching, I'm afraid.

**Q. On page 269 you write: "No wonder the briefcase was so heavy, thought Miles. He should have known better than to collect all 114 papers at one time. The wrongs and losses and near misses of 114 people, when packed together in one briefcase, took on the heaviness and solidity of rock." This passage must have come from your heart. English teachers, because of the subject matter, literature and writing, often learn more about the personal lives of their students than teachers in other disciplines. How did you deal with students who were hurting and needed someone to trust and confide in?**

A. I guess I was just like Miles. In those days I just listened. I don't know what I said. I wasn't able to offer them much consolation. But I always was willing to listen which I guess a number of them figured out because I had so many of them come to me, especially in my high school teaching days in Park Rapids.

Q. I understand that Wendell Hawk, the bride's father at the wedding that Miss McGee attends, is based on someone you knew, though you denied the fact to someone who asked you.

A. Well, I met Mrs. Hawk (whose real name was Mrs. Cook) on the street one day in Park Rapids. She said, "Jon, I read *Staggerford*. I read about myself in your book." I said what I say to all people—that all my characters are composites. "No," she replied, "I was the one whose husband came home drunk before Mary's wedding, and I hit him in the head with a beer bottle and he went down the aisle with a black eye—just like in the book." Oh dear, she was correct. I wanted to fall through the sidewalk, but she said to me, "It was fun reading about it." So bless her heart. She let me off the hook.

Q. Before you came to Brainerd, you had privately published a poetry chapbook, *The Red Oak*. In some of your novels you write poems as needed for your poet characters, for example, Richard Falcon in *The Dean's List* and Herschel Mancrief in *Staggerford*. Is this a challenge or more of a lark for you?

A. This is completely a lark. I took myself seriously as a poet in the '60s, and I wrote a lot of poems. And I finally got them published in *The Dean's List*. As for Herschel Mancrief's toilet poems, I wrote those on the spot when I needed them.

Q. Any submission invitations for Herschel Mancrief yet?

A. No, he hasn't become well enough known yet, I guess.

Q. At one point in *Staggerford* you dissect mercilessly a faculty meeting called by Principal Wayne Workman.

A. Yes, if there's anything that would drive a person out of teaching, it's the meetings. And especially in college, I found out later. The high school meetings are easy compared to those. But there's so much foolishness that goes on and you waste so much energy at them, I thought I'd take them on.

Q. Misguided education theorists and administrators have drawn your satiric eye more than once during your career, beginning with *Staggerford*, where Dr. Murphy from the State Department of Education advises Miss McGee: "Never, never burden a child with a book written earlier than the child's date of birth." Do teachers in general possess a better overall picture of education and the needs and requirements of students than administrators?

A. Students and teachers know what to do; I think it's people who aren't in the classroom that hand down these edicts, and they're always so foolish while trying to be relevant. Of course, the '60s was the time for relevance and that was what the State Department was dictating at that time.

Q. Do you find satire difficult to concoct?

A. I'm finding it quite a challenge now. I'm working on a novel about Agatha McGee [*The Staggerford Flood*]. It's all very straightforward. There's hardly any satire in it. I don't know why. I may have lost my knack for it. It didn't seem to be hard when I began.

Q. One critic, Timothy Brady in *Minnesota Monthly*, mentioned in his *Grand Opening* review that almost the only flaw was the pair of cartoonish figures, Mrs. Brask and Mrs. Kimball. In *Staggerford* Wayne Workman and Coach Gibbon are basically one-dimensional cartoon figures, although Coach Gibbon amuses me. Is it possible to create three-dimensional satirical figures?

A. Gee, that's a good question. I think Zastrow is pretty one-dimensional. I take him to task in *Rookery Blues* and *The Dean's List*. So maybe it isn't. Maybe my satirical victims are all one or two-dimensional, not three.

Q. You and Flannery O'Connor share the trait of describing your characters in non-human terms. In *Staggerford* you often use bird and animal imagery. On page 64 Coach Gibbon studied Miles "the way a woodpecker examines bark for bugs." Miss McGee is "quick as a bird" (19). Imogene "was developing the features of a turkey, a tom" (33). And Carla Carpenter Pruitt "looked like a Kodiak with a fresh wound" (153). Is this conscious or deliberate?

A. No, it isn't deliberate at all. It just happened that way, I guess.

Q. Your writing style always includes descriptions of nature, the woods, birds, the moon or sun, the breeze. Did any writer influence you in this regard?

A. I think Hemingway where he takes on nature. I admire those passages a lot, and I think by bringing nature into it, you give your novel a little more scope.

Q. You studied Hemingway in graduate school, didn't you?

A. Hemingway got me through graduate school. I read everything five times that he wrote. I loved his writing more than anything else in graduate school. My master's thesis at the University of North Dakota was "Moral Choice in the Novels of Ernest Hemingway."

Q. I really like this description on page 50: "The peach moon stood at the edge of the sloping roof and seemed about to roll off." An example of your nature writing is found early on: Miles "saw four ducks and a flock of red-winged blackbirds. He saw a garter snake, a goldfish, and a crow. He saw a bittersweet vine strangling a small maple tree" (12). Do you have any favorite passages about nature in *Staggerford*?

A. I like the description when the Stevensons drive out to the reservation and they see the little houses in the woods, and also the description of Pike Park when people gather for the confrontation with the Indians. I remember enjoying writing those. I guess more of my nature writing is in *The Love Hunter* than in any other book.

Q. Ballantine published *My Staggerford Journal* in November 1999. And in the novel Miles also kept a journal. Page 76 of *Staggerford* contains one of Miles's journal entries.

*Tomorrow I will take each of my classes to the riverbank for a year-end picnic (or, in lesson-plan jargon, a field trip). My students are eighteen and they outgrew picnics in the sixth grade, but like all graduating seniors a kind of year-end lunacy has made them silly and twelve again. Each student will bring along a short poem to read and I will supply the pop. We will have a good time because the weatherman promises sunshine and the river-bank is abloom with crocuses and we will all be full of the vacation spirit. We will do a lot of laughing and inevitably someone will be pushed into the river.*

*Then after school I will go to the dim back room of the Hub for Fred Vandergar's 'party.' I fear it will be a wake for a live corpse, too solemn to be comfortable; or it will be a staged attempt at jollity, too phony to be happy.*

*Life. The light and the dark. Those 18-year-olds sitting on the riverbank in the sun. That dying man in the back room of the Hub. And me standing (in more ways than age) exactly between them. Me, without my students' optimism and without Fred's despair. Without their fidgets and without his courage. Without their youth and without his cancer. Tomorrow, halfway between the light and the dark, I will end my eleventh year of teaching.*

**Is this entry from Jon Hassler's journal as well?**

A. I believe it is—I believe it's word for word from my journal.

**Q. And you had the combination which I like about the youth and the aging, and you write, "Me, without my students' optimism and without Fred's despair. Without their fidgets and without his courage. Without their youth and without his cancer. Tomorrow, halfway between the light and the dark, I will end my eleventh year of teaching." So you really do cover all aspects of life and ages in this.**

A. I guess I do, Joe; it's a pleasure to read that again actually.

**Q. In a detailed essay, "On the Novels of Jon Hassler" in the Spring 1994 *South Dakota Review*, C.W. Truesdale comments: "Hassler often**

interrupts the flow of his main action to address other issues, or even to provide background material from often a very long time ago, not because he enjoys teaching the reader but because his conception of character goes considerably beyond the particular moment of the action." Does this explain why you needed the long journal entry about Miles and Carla? Miles's November 1st journal covers twenty-two pages (133-155).

A. Well, I guess it does. I consider myself the king of flashbacks. You know that in my first two or three novels, *The Love Hunter* and *Simon's Night*, I've got a lot of flashbacks. This acts as a kind of flashback, although it's a journal entry in *Staggerford*. It's true that I had more detail about these people, so that's why I put it in.

Q. *Staggerford* contains the seeds of some of your future novels and themes. Have you thought about this?

A. I don't know what they are, unless it's the teaching profession.

Q. Well, I'll mention some that I found—Miles's visit to his father in Duluth at a nursing home/care center. And your next novel is *Simon's Night*. Beverly moves in with Miss McGee; in *A Green Journey* Janet Raft lives with Miss McGee. And then, of course, Miss McGee and Imogene, and her mother Lillian Kite appear in future novels.

A. It's very true—I think that's right. I felt that those things needed more written about them, so I devoted entire novels to each of those aspects.

Q. Miss McGee comes through as a crusader, especially in her visit with Wayne Workman (259-262). When you began this novel, did you expect Agatha McGee to emerge as such a strong and fascinating character?

A. When I began the novel I didn't even know she was going to be in it, but as soon as she moved into it, that's the way she is, strong and fascinating, and a highly directive person from the start.

Q. I would like to quote Mr. Truesdale again. "Hassler likes to move freely in and out of his characters, though he will usually focus on one of them at a time and view things through his or her eyes, but even then his detachment from that character is always maintained. . . . This 'in and out' technique gives him the freedom to move in and out of the immediate action of a particular narrative. This method also establishes his very strong presence in his novels, even a sense of narrative control." True, you are not always in the protagonist's mind, but sometimes in many of the other characters' minds also. Is this difficult to do?

A. No, it's more difficult to stay with one person in my opinion, although in my latest novel, *The Dean's List*, it's in the first person. And throughout that novel we stay in the head of Leland Edwards. But before that I roamed around from one character to another because it gave me freedom. I wasn't restricted to any one person so much.

Q. Have other writers influenced you in this regard?

A. No, they haven't. I've been told that this third person omniscient way of writing is old-fashioned, but it seems so natural to me, I just do it.

Q. I think the reader really appreciates it, too, because the reader then gets to know each of the characters more intimately. And now we come to the most controversial aspect of *Staggerford*, the ending. Had you always foreseen Miles's death, or did that just suddenly happen for you?

A. As I conceived the book, I thought of it as the last week in Miles's life. And as I wrote the book the first time, the reader knew it, too. And then I changed it so it surprised the reader. But I always thought of it as the last week in his life from the start.

Q. Were you prepared for the overwhelmingly negative reaction from your readers regarding Miles's death?

A. No, I wasn't. I hadn't realized people had become so fond of the man.

Q. Is this partially because Miles is similar to you and your personality? Almost like an alter-ego? And does that help explain why you're so surprised by these responses that people would care so much for someone not unlike you?

A. That's a good point, Joe. I think it's probably true. I think it's right.

Q. My students, of course, are always shocked by Miles's death. Here are a few comments from some of their papers: "Shocking is a good way to describe the ending of *Staggerford*. I thought the death of Miles Pruitt was unexpected and unnecessary" (Phillip Shogren). "I did not like the fact that Miles died at the end of the book. I actually had to read it a couple of times because I could not believe that it happened. I did not think that I had read it correctly the first time" (Etta Paulson). "I admit that when I got to the end of the book and Miles was shot dead by the Bonewoman, I was shocked and even a little mad" (Julie Heinz). "I didn't want to accept the fact that Miles had been shot; I had to go back and re-read the sentences three or four times. After all the 'good' that Miles had contributed to this novel, I wanted a happy ending for him too! But, 'what I wish' and what I receive, they are two different verbs with two very different meanings; they are like life in itself. They are *Staggerford*" (Mary Kovach). Comments?

A. The last one is very good, isn't it? Yes, a lot of people say they had to read that paragraph over several times when he died because they didn't believe it. I'm surprised, of course, but I'm sort of pleased, too, that the novel had that much impact on the reader.

Q. And, now, perhaps one of the most extreme reactions from a reader whose letter you had given me many years ago: "Want to know your readers' reaction to your killing off Miles? Annoyed. What was the point? That tragedy can strike at any moment? Life is unfair? We *already* know that—that's why there's fiction. He could have married Beverly & we'd all have been happy. . . . Don't you know any happy people? Cheer up." How would or did you answer her?

A. I guess I pointed out that that's what fiction was. And it was teaching her about life. She said that's what we have fiction for is to learn about life.

Q. And this may be really like beating a dead horse, but Mr. Truesdale writes that "Miles Pruitt is one of the most attractive and engaging characters Hassler has ever created. He was so rich a character he could easily have been used . . . in a subsequent novel had he not been killed off. I liked him—a lot" (75). Your response?

A. Well, I didn't know how appealing this guy was of course as I was writing it. But I'm sort of glad I didn't have him to use. I would have never stopped using him probably. Instead of writing *Simon's Night* as my second novel, I would've written *Staggerford* Two and Three and Four probably. When you come down to it, though, I think all of my protagonists are the same man. I think Simon is Miles when he's older. And Leland Edwards [*Rookery Blues* and *The Dean's List*] is Miles. And most of my protagonists are the same man.

Q. Miles's death catches the reader completely off guard. No doubt this effect was deliberate on your part.

A. I wanted to imitate the feeling we get when we hear of a friend dying. And that's what I guess I did.

Q. You had once told our mutual friend, Dan Lange, that teaching is a sacrificial profession. At least in a symbolic way, does that contribute to the meaning of Miles's death?

A. It certainly does. I'd been teaching twenty years when I wrote the book. I was so full of how teaching can take everything you've got if you let it. And that's what it did to Miles—it took everything he had.

Q. That's really a good point. That's probably why most teachers think *Staggerford* is their favorite Hassler novel. Of course, his death did create some positive results, i.e., the rebirth of Superintendent Stevenson who now may become a valued superintendent, and also a new beginning for Beverly.

A. That's right. I don't want the reader to think the novel ends with Miles's death. There are good things that grow out of this situation, and those are two of the best.

Q. Although it's only mid-August now, I already feel a kind of melancholy. Some leaves are starting to turn colors. *Staggerford* transpires during nine days (plus the Epilogue), October 30th through November 7th, including All Saints Day and All Souls Day. When I teach *Staggerford*, students are always amazed (once they finish reading the novel) to learn how much foreshadowing you used. What particular examples do you like of foreshadowing in the novel?

A. I like the Bonewoman coming to Miles's house looking for bones. I like Miles out there on the bleachers lying on his back with his hands crossed on his chest. I like Thanatopsis, meaning "view of death." She's one of the first who sees him after he dies, so those are three at least.

Q. Those are good ones that I didn't really discuss. We did more obvious ones—the Bonewoman's killing of the salesman, the blood on the deer hunter's hands, Miles wearing a dead man's clothes, Roxie's story about the corporal who died by eating a beer bottle. And now, we come to the English teacher part, the theme of *Staggerford*. To ease into this, please share what your *Staggerford* editor at Atheneum, Judith Kern, saw as the theme.

A. She said to me, "This book is about the ongoing quality of life." I had to agree.

Q. That sums it up, doesn't it? The Bonewoman, of course, is a figure of death, and not only because of her name. In two specific sections you make this connection: "In the darkness, the fragrance of Miss McGee's old garden, turned up and tired, seemed to be rising in faint whiffs from the Bonewoman's deep footprints—the tuberous smell of roots freshly exposed and the sour smell of tomatoes spoiled by frost and left with a few blighted potatoes to blacken and nourish the spent, gray soil" (32). Any comments?

A. Well, the Bonewoman, of course, in this novel is symbolic of death. I like the passage about the garden a lot. I've had letters from readers who have lived in Minnesota and then moved elsewhere, saying that that passage brought them back to Minnesota, that business about the garden freezing up in the fall, the smells from the tuberous plants. The Bonewoman came to me one day when I was having dinner in Jax Cafe in northeast Minneapolis. The woman in the next booth said, "We call her the Bonewoman." That's all I ever heard. That's when she was born.

Q. The gist of the novel in its larger implications seems to be Miss McGee's meditations on her ferns.

> *Rain's only value, for Miss McGee, was that it reminded her how precious was good weather. She despised rain. But she knew that to the earth, rain was as necessary as sunshine. Could it be, she wondered, that the vice and barbarism abroad in the world served, like the rain, some purpose? Did the abominations in the Sunday paper mingle somehow with the goodness in the world and together, like the rain and sun feeding the ferns, did they nourish some kind of life she was unaware of? (125)*

And then on page 126: "If you let sunshine stand for the goodness in the world and you let rain stand for evil, do goodness and evil mingle like sun and rain to produce something? To bring something to maturity, like those ferns? Does God permit sin because it's an ingredient in something he's concocting and we human beings aren't aware of what it is? Is there sprouting up somewhere a beautiful fern, as it were, composed of goodness and sin?"

Would you explain, if you care to, what you meant by these thoughts of Miss McGee?

A. As evil as Miles's death seemed, there were some good things that came out of it.

Q. And you need both good and evil—life is that, a choice, and without one, you wouldn't have the other. Yet the final image is that of an ascension or resurrection (341): "After school he [Stevenson] went home and put his arms around the heavy softness of Mrs. Stevenson's middle and lifted her, astounded, three inches off the floor." Endings beget beginnings?

A. I guess so, I guess that's what that means.

Q. One last go at the theme—Joseph Hynes, in his November 3, 1995, *Commonweal* article, "Midwestern Loneliness—The novels of Jon Hassler," posits this theme: "(1) works without faith can help others and make your life count; and (2) if you can just hold your own against all the stuff coming down on your head, that's victory enough." Do you agree with this?

A. I guess I do. I think that's true. I'm not very good about talking about theme. I don't think about it as I write, but I guess he has it there, sure.

Q. And that's Miles's philosophy, too, isn't it, that if you hold your own, meaning the tie?

A. He says a tie is as good as a win which makes the coach mad because he can't understand that.

Q. And that's what it really is, it's victory enough. Now for the easy and more factual, less theoretical questions: My students always like Beverly very much. I understand that she returns in the novel you are currently writing [*The Staggerford Flood*].

A. She does—she comes back to see Agatha after being around the world with her soldier husband. She's divorced now. She has a son who's mentally unstable and she comes to see Agatha and ends up staying three or four days because a flood comes to town and she can't get away. She stays with Agatha and six other women in the house. There are eight of them all together in this house for three days.

Q. That sounds fascinating. We'll be glad to see Beverly again. And I just thought of this a while ago; *Staggerford* almost got reviewed by *Newsweek*. Would you share that story?

A. *Newsweek* called me up the week *Staggerford* came out. They said they were going to feature it with a review. They wanted a picture of me for the magazine. So I loaded up my camera and I had Liz, my daughter, take my picture in Gregory Park in Brainerd, and I sent it off to them by Federal Express, and I bought the magazine next week and it wasn't in there. And I called and asked them if it was going to be in there, and they said probably not. They said something else had come up and they didn't have the space for it anymore.

Q. Wasn't Walter Clemons going to review it? I remember that he was *Newsweek*'s main book critic.

A. Yes, it was he.

Q. Is this a parable about reviews and critical attention, meaning that after your large body of work, some do review you but many don't?

A. Yes, I've always been unnoticed in a lot of important places and I continue to be so.

Q. *Staggerford* did receive a number of reviews, especially for a first novel. Probably the biggest "name" critic reviewed it in the *New York Times Book Review*. Please give us the details.

A. The review in the *Times Book Review* was by Joyce Carol Oates who didn't like the book very much. She thought the main character was boring and she didn't care for the humor.

Q. May I quote part of Oates's review?

A. Yes, please.

Q. "As it is, *Staggerford* begins strongly but soon wanes, fragmenting into a series of unexceptional comic scenes reminiscent of television, and its deadpan killing of its hero is a dated Black Comic device that seems curiously out of place in this particular novel." So that really coincides with what you said about her lacking a sense of humor.

A. Yes, she didn't laugh at all in the book, I don't believe.

**Q. Now, we'll go to a more positive review about both of us which appeared in the August 10, 1977, issue of** the *Christian Science Monitor,* **written by Roderick Nordell:**

*First the Mad Hugger, and now this novel of skilled tragicomedy by one of the Hugger's fellow teachers. They must be doing something right at the community college in Brainerd (pop. 11,000), Minnesota.*

*The national press understandably picked up the human interest story of amiable Joe Plut, known as the Mad Hugger because he carries out his classroom theories of warmth and openness in human relations by hugging when others might merely shake hands. He hugged just about everybody at this year's commencement.*

*Now it would be good to see Jon Hassler getting widespread attention for the human interest in his first novel. Here is a pitch for warmth and openness, too. Indeed, they happen to be symbolized by the spontaneous, compassionate hug bestowed on a doomed character by a man not known for hugging. But author Hassler's warmth is mingled with wryness, his humor touched with a bleak realism that makes a bizarre climax the more jarring for its understatement.*

**Did my hugging influence the scene of Miles visiting Fred Vandergar?**

A. It certainly must have because you were hugging all over the place. I was impressed by that. And I saw what a hug could do, so that's why I had Miles do it to Fred.

**Q. That's gratifying to know. In 1978 Andre Deutsch published** *Staggerford* **in England. That must have been affirming and exciting for you.**

A. Yes, that was very good. I got a letter from an editor at Andre Deutsch telling me what a good book it was.

**Q. I only saw one British review, but it's a good one. Hermione Lee, who recently wrote a biography of Virginia Woolf, I believe, is that right?— reviewed** *Staggerford* **in the June 25, 1978, issue of the** *Observer.* **"***Staggerford* **is a surprise. It looks at first like an undemanding provincial satire, in**

'Main Street' tradition. . . . But Jon Hassler is more interesting than this. . . . the blighted lives of some of the schoolchildren, and the difficulties of the sympathetic, unheroic hero introduce an unexpectedly stern, hard-edged quality, and allow for a startling and perfectly controlled tragic outcome." What do you say?

A. I like that review a lot.

Q. I do, too. I wish we were on television so that I could illustrate this next question visually. The book jackets for the American and British *Staggerford* editions are radically different. Could you describe each, and then state your preference?

A. Well, I never cared for the American edition because it's so expressionistic. This is not an expressionistic book, you know. It's very realistic and I thought it should have a realistic cover. But it has some very strange art on the cover; the top one has, I think, the marching band which isn't too bad, the American flag flying over it, the marching band at halftime of the football game. But then there's a picture of what must be the Bonewoman who doesn't look like the Bonewoman in my mind. Then there's a picture of a chicken pecking at Miles Pruitt's bullet hole in his head. I think it took me a long time to figure out what that was, but I think that's what it is. Now on the British edition you have Miles Pruitt, who's lost a lot of weight, of course, coming out of a house—it looks a lot like Agatha McGee's house.

Q. True, the British one is really far better. Do you have any say in the artwork used for your book jackets?

A. I do now, but I didn't then.

Q. *Staggerford's* pedigree—any awards?

A. Well, let's see. I was awarded Friends of American Writers Novel of the Year Award in 1978. I went there with my daughter Liz to Chicago to receive that award. Also, *Staggerford* was selected to be the Book of the Month Club Alternate.

**Q. Were any of these chapters first written as short stories?**

A. Yes, the hippie poet's visit to Miss McGee's class was a short story entitled "The Undistinguished Poet," which was published in the *South Dakota Review* in 1972. It was in 1971 that my elder son Michael, an eighth grader, caused Miss McGee to be conceived in my imagination. Michael came home from school one day and said that a poet had visited his class. I asked, "Well, what's his poetry like?" He answered, "Sort of strange. He said 'shit' and 'screw' and stuff like that." I was enraged. Open the classroom to culture and in rush the barbarians. Who did this so-called poet think he was, scandalizing eighth graders? I complained about the poet's profanities for a day or two, until it dawned on me that I was behaving like some rigid old spinster, and at that point Agatha McGee, a 6th-grade teacher in a parochial school, stepped into my life and unburdened me. Writing the story, I had *South Dakota Review* in mind, because [editor] John Milton's rejection letters were more detailed and diplomatic than those of the dozen other editors I'd been trying to interest in my work. When John, a month or two later, accepted "The Undistinguished Poet," my reaction was deeply satisfying. I was about to see my powerful ally, Agatha McGee, come to life on the printed page. For I sensed that Miss McGee, validated now by John Milton, would be given license to enter several more stories and four novels and fight countless battles for me. Indeed, she took on bigger battles than mine. Last I heard, she'd brought peace to Northern Ireland. There was also an unpublished story entitled "Two Weddings," which details Miss McGee's attempt to retire (from the "Tuesday" chapter).

**Q. When did *Staggerford* appear in paperback?**

A. It appeared in paperback in 1986, nine years after its first publication in hardback; it came out as the first of Ballantine's paperback editions of my work.

**Q. Is it still selling well?**

A. I believe it is. We're up to fifteen or sixteen printings since 1986 which is a good sign.

**Q. Is it partially because teachers often use this in their classrooms?**

A. I'm sure that's the reason.

**Q. Any movie nibbles during these last twenty-some years? I know of one from your postcard dated May 19, 1989, from Saint John's: "Another party interested in *Staggerford*—one Patrick Lynch, husband of Jane Curtin, offering $5000 for an 18-mo. Option—with American Playhouse in mind."**

A. I remember the nibble from Lynch. He wrote me a letter of apology after he failed to interest producers in the movie version. He said: "The story and the characters are wonderful, and people need to see more films dealing with these very human issues. I'm looking forward to reading your *Green Journey* sequel, and the new book you are working on now. If I didn't get to make a film for you, I've certainly introduced your work to a number of grateful friends." There were also movie nibbles in the early eighties, but they came to nothing. It was optioned once or twice for a year or so, but the option was dropped and it reverted to me. So it's out there—it's available for anybody who wants it.

**Q. How many copies did Atheneum print in the one and only printing of the hardcover edition?**

A. I think they printed 7,500.

**Q. You have a classic story about remaindered copies of the hardcover *Staggerford* and B. Dalton's.**

A. Yes, I went into B. Dalton's in Minneapolis and found *Staggerford* on the remainder table—fifteen copies. I took all fifteen up to the counter, and the clerk said to me, "You must like this book." I said, "I did. I like it a lot. I wrote it," and I showed her my picture on the back jacket flap. She looked at it and she called up the manager from the back room. I thought she wanted him to meet me. When he got up there, she said to him, "Would you okay the check this man is writing?"

Q. I understand that hardback copies of *Staggerford* are now in great demand. What is the going rate for a book in good condition?

A. An autographed copy in good condition goes for about $400 right now, and I've seen some unautographed for $300 on the Net.

Q. That must astonish you and must also gratify you.

A. Yes, it means that I'm not forgotten, at least that's good.

Q. I think many people wish to have their whole collection in hardcover. Well, I feel as if I'm back in grad school. I hope that I passed this test. You certainly did, Jon. At our next session we'll discuss the 1979 *Simon's Night* and the 1981 *The Love Hunter*. I'm really eager to reread both of these.

A. That's great, Joe, it's been a pleasure. Thanks so much.

# Simon's Night

Jon had given me his "My Simon's Night Journal" manuscript many months ago, and now that I finally have read it, I find it as intriguing and worthwhile as his published *My Staggerford Journal*. Once again, the reader is privy to Jon's thoughts, daily routines, creative roadblocks, successes, and doubts in the birthing of *Simon's Night* with entries beginning January 8, 1977, and ending on November 22, 1978.

From the entry of September 2, 1977, I learned that the protagonist's original name had been Simon Peter Venables and the novel's title "Venables the King." On October 30, 1977, Jon wrote that "I've decided to go with an Irish name. Callihan or O'Malley or some such name. Both strike me as much more colorful than Venables." Then, on November 12th, "Callahan is now my hero's name; 'Callahan the King' is now the title."

Some months later, April 20, 1978, with Jon in Brainerd, the entry reads:

*Then out and away with my dog on a leash, down to the river along a muddy trail and past a young man with a bb gun shooting beer cans and uphill to the cemetery, where I read the short names as I pass, needing as I do a name for Callahan; I'm looking for something Irish and of one syllable. Quinn? Lynch? Dunn? Shea?*

And, finally, the July 31, 1978, entry gives us the final title: "Novel Four, entitled *Simon's Night*, stands five-sixths finished."

I would like to quote a paragraph from August 27, 1978:

*I took up and rejected lots of titles before I hit on* Simon's Night. *I hit on* Simon's Night *while driving in my car. I put on a hell of a lot of miles in a year's time and I try to think about my writing as I drive but I seldom succeed; I'm lucky if I have one profitable thought about my writing in 10,000 miles. But coming home from the cabin [Nevis] about three weeks ago (as I made the turn from hiway 33 to hiway 64, as I looked across the hayfield of the farmer who cuts his hay with a team of horses) I thought of* Simon's Night. *If the book is publishable, and I have no assurance that it is, I'd be surprised if the editor requested a different title.*

In Jon's fiction he uses similes (and metaphors) to enlarge the novel's canvas and scope whereas his journal writing is somewhat more matter-of-fact and spare.

Another detail from Jon's life concerns the birth date of Simon. The reader learns immediately on page 3: "Simon lacked five days of being as old as the century (born: 5 January 1900) and in his seventy-six years . . ." In a letter dated January 5, 1988, Jon wrote me that "Grandfather Callinan was born 122 years ago on this day. I used his birthday for Simon, who is 'five days younger than the century.'" One rarely learns about biographical information encoded in a writer's creation, but I am fortunate in finding out more and more about the origins and reasons for some of Jon's artistic choices. That probably constitutes one of the main reasons this project has been so rewarding for me. I hope that similar revelations scattered throughout this interview will also intrigue you.

- J. P. August 2004

*September 15, 2000*

Q. Jon, *Simon's Night*, your second adult novel, was published in 1979 by Atheneum with the same agent, Harriet Wasserman, and editor, Judith Kern, as for *Staggerford*. Is that correct?

A. That's right. It was my second novel. I remember writing it, wondering if I was a flash in the pan or if I had a second novel in me. So I was very pleased to finish this novel. I took it to New York and Judith Kern picked it up right away.

Q. How many hardcover copies of *Simon's Night* were printed?

A. They printed 6,000 to start with, and then, when the good reviews came out, after the book was out of print, it went back to print with 3,000 more, but it came too late to take advantage of the good reviews. I think we sold 9,000 in all.

Q. And how many is that in comparison to *Staggerford's* hardcover printing?

A. They printed 7,500 of *Staggerford*.

Q. How many Ballantine paperbacks of *Simon* are in print currently?

A. I have no idea. It's gone through about twelve printings.

Q. Andre Deutsch, your English publisher of *Staggerford*, indicated interest via editor Esther Whitby in publishing *Simon's Night*. Did an English edition come about?

A. Yes, they published an English edition, and that was almost the last the English were ever interested in me, *Staggerford* and *Simon's Night*. Then, when *Green Journey* came out ten years later, they did that, but that was all they've done for me. [*The Love Hunter* was also published in England.]

Q. Jon, a section of *Simon's Night* first appeared as a short story, "Small-eye's Last Hunt," in *Prairie Schooner* (Summer 1972). Was this your first published story?

A. It was. It appeared in '72 as you say. It was the fourteenth story I wrote and I sent it to *Prairie Schooner* and they published it. Then I thought I would turn it into a novel, and so I began to write about this Indian Smalleye in an old folks' home. I realized I didn't know anything about Indians, so I put in the retired teacher because I knew about English teachers. Simon, therefore, became the main subject and Smalleye became secondary.

Q. I think another issue, too, had one of your stories. Please tell about your attempts to place your short stories in magazines.

A. After I wrote five or six stories, I began to send them out. I tried to keep two or three in the mail at one time, so when I got a rejection back, I wasn't too discouraged. I kept sending them out over a period of five years. I published six stories in the quarterlies and collected eighty-five rejection slips. It's hard to get published.

Q. "Smalleye's Last Hunt" ends with this coda: "The next afternoon as Nelson wandered about the yard dragging his lawn chair, he found near the street a dead snow goose. On the white down were small rusty spots of dried blood where shotgun pellets had penetrated its throat." Why did you omit Smalleye's success in shooting a goose? I thought it would be included in *Simon's Night*.

A. I don't know why. I guess I didn't want to distract from the main idea of it. He got hurt in the process. He was trying for success, and I found it hard to believe that he could shoot a goose actually at night, and if he did, that he could find it at night, so I don't know exactly why. It might have been that I didn't believe it.

Q. That's as good a reason as any. Nelson, of course, was the forerunner of Simon Shea.

A. Yes, Nelson was Smalleye's companion and he helped him up on the roof, and then he became Simon when I brought the English professor into the book.

**Q. Simon's attempt to enlist in the military in 1918 reads almost like a short story. Was it?**

A. That wasn't a short story, but it could have been certainly. That was a story I got from two sources. One, I used my own physical exams in the Army as an example and as a prototype for Simon's exam. And then, when he was turned down, I used an experience of my mother's cousin I met one time in South Dakota. He told me the story about his getting through high school early in order to join the army in World War I and they had a big send-off. The band played and everything, they got on the train, they went to Sioux Falls for their physicals. He flunked. He couldn't go home, of course, because he was given this great send-off. So that was an interesting dilemma for him. I put that in the book. My uncle went to Minneapolis and stayed with my grandfather and grandmother who fed him bananas and got his weight up so that he was accepted by the Navy finally.

**Q. So most of it was actually true except for the bananas. I see some basic similarities between *Simon's Night* and *Staggerford*, your first novel. Do you?**

A. I don't know, Joe; you'd have to point some out to me. I can't think of any.

**Q. The main character of each is an English instructor.**

A. Yes, I think most of my main characters are the same person actually. I think Simon is Miles if he'd have lived and grown old. I believe that's true.

**Q. Each, of course, has a Catholic background; each novel covers a short time period (six days in *Simon's Night* and eight days in *Staggerford*); both take place in late fall; Simon has memory flashbacks and Miles has**

journals; each ends with a catharsis, one positive in *Simon* and one negative with Miles's death in *Staggerford*.

A. I guess that's very true, Joseph. It's fascinating. I guess I thought of all those at one time or another; they slip my mind now.

Q. **Referring to the short time span of both these novels, is this a technique to help illustrate your theme that lives can change dramatically in a matter of days?**

A. No, I did it mainly for formal reasons, I think. You see, when I originally wrote *Staggerford*, it took place during the school year and then I reduced it to a month and that seemed better, it seemed more powerful, so I reduced it to a few days, and it seemed more powerful yet. It's like compression in a gasoline engine. It seems to me the compression produces power and so I decided to do that. Then I wrote *The Love Hunter* that takes place in three days. If I'd kept that up I'd be down to about an hour and a half now. So I expanded after that. It was very good training for my early writing, I think, to write about short time periods.

Q. **You almost out-Beckett Samuel Beckett. I think his last play was a cry at birth changing into a death gasp, and it takes less than a minute to perform. You said that Simon is Miles if he'd have lived. Is Simon, in part, Jon Hassler thirty-some years later? Of course, all three are Catholic English instructors. But it really seems that Simon is perhaps also you down the road.**

A. That's true, I wrote *Simon* and published it when I was forty-five. People said how could you have written about an old man at that age. I didn't find it hard because I just imagined what I would do in that situation. So I guess he must be me; he is a lot like Miles, too. All my main characters are like me.

Q. **Now that you're sixty-seven, do you think you accurately captured Simon as a seventy-six-year-old man?**

A. I guess I did, except for energy. He has more energy than I do.

Q. What would you change or do differently if you were developing the character today?

A. Now it would have been harder to make a case for his being faithful to his wife after twenty-three years because of annulments and such things in the Catholic Church. He might have gotten one of those and been free to marry Linda. Another change I would have made is I would have had his wife Barbara tell him she was coming back before he left his home on the river. I mean, it's such a coincidence that she would come back just as he moved into the Norman Home. I think I would eliminate that coincidence by having her threaten to come back, and his being scared into the Norman Home by her return.

Q. At one point in *Simon's Night*, Simon receives the "Midcentury Award," and honored along with him was "a preacher from Plainview." I immediately thought of Paul Dimmitburg from Plum (*Grand Opening*) who would be roughly in his fifties in 1976. Wouldn't that have been interesting!

A. It certainly would have been, though I hadn't thought of Paul at that point in my writing.

Q. That's what's fun, I think, about being a Hassler reader. One makes connections from one novel to another. Did Agatha's experience with the fake wedding at the Senior Citizens' Center in *Staggerford* help plant the seeds for the older characters in *Simon's Night* and, of course, the Norman Home?

A. Yes, it certainly did; when she went to that fake wedding, it was all those foolish old people that convinced me I could write about foolish old people more. That's why I put them into the Norman Home. They're foolish and they're old.

Q. What were your other influences or inspirations for *Simon's Night* or for rendering old people?

A. I remember the influence of a buried leg. When I was a kid working in the cemetery in Plainview, a car drove up and a priest got out on one side and a guy got out of the other. Somebody grabbed a newspaper from the trunk, and they dropped it into a hole they dug in the ground. Turned out to be Mrs Welp's leg. Mrs. Welp had had her leg amputated in Wabasha; the family was down there. A nun came out of the operating room with a leg and said, "You have to bury this in consecrated ground," so one of the people took it and drove to Plainview and got the priest, and they blessed it and put it in the ground. That's where I got the idea for burying the leg in the story.

**Q. The Badbattle River flows through Rookery and Staggerford. It's an evocative name. How did you conceive of it?**

A. I don't know. It just seemed like a good name to me. I remember a librarian in Minneapolis asking me where it was. She looked on maps all over the place and she couldn't find it. That's because it doesn't exist. It exists only in my head, but it flows through all but one of my novels [*Grand Opening*].

**Q. And that brings us to the next question. Simon doesn't care for the plains around Ithaca Mills, preferring, instead, the hills of Rookery. I remember reading Faulkner and finding a map of Yoknapatawpha County. Would you visually describe your map of Hassler's Minnesota, the locations of Ithaca Mills, Staggerford, Rookery, St. Andrew's College, the Badbattle River? Do these represent existing towns and cities in Minnesota?**

A. I think they do. I think *Staggerford* is about Park Rapids, Walker, that area. Let's see, Ithaca Mills would be west of there out in the plains at the edge of the Red River Valley probably, and the Badbattle flows into the Red River and flows north. Rookery would be up near Bemidji. St. Andrew's would be Saint John's, of course. Yes, that's the way I think of my places in Minnesota.

**Q. I know that you say that 37 percent of your writing is autobiographical. What percentage is autobiographical in *Simon's Night*?**

A. Let's see. I guess 37 percent. A lot of *Simon's Night* came out of my journal—his going to the polls, for example, voting for Franklin

Pierce. I voted for Pierce in the Carter-Ford election that year. And Simon's earliest memory, of being pulled along the sidewalk by his mother and the sled, is my earliest memory.

Q. I remember your telling me the story about Franklin Pierce and Nathaniel Hawthorne at Pierce's wife's funeral. Would you share this story, please?

A. As I was writing *Simon's Night*, I was reading a book called *Yesterdays with Authors* by James T. Fields. He was a friend of Hawthorne's. He was writing about his memory of Hawthorne and Emerson and Thoreau and those people. He told about the death of Franklin Pierce's wife. Franklin Pierce had been president, of course, and he was a lifelong friend of Hawthorne's. They met in college. Standing at the graveside, he looked over at Hawthorne, who was very sick at that point, and he went over and turned up Hawthorne's collar against the wind. I was always impressed by that gesture.

Q. And then going through my voluminous Hassler file, I noticed there was a profile published of you in the *Minneapolis Tribune* January 19, 1986, and one question asked you was this. "If I had thirty minutes to talk to anyone in history, it would be _____," and you answered, Nathaniel Hawthorne. I think that's a fascinating answer. Would you expand on that, please?

A. Well, I've often thought I would like to be able to write the way he does, for his stories seem to mean more than just the story. They seem to have reverberations beyond the end of the book. Also, I was interested in his life since he was alone a lot of the time the way I had been at that point in my life. And there's a period in his life that's unaccounted for. After he got out of college, he stayed home for a year or two. Nothing is known about that year, what he did. I'd love to ask him about that. So it's part mystery and part admiration.

Q. Returning to a previous question, I know that at least one section of *Simon's Night*—the Ireland flashback—is autobiographical. Would you like to tell us which parts are based on fact?

A. Yes, that comes out of my journal. You and I went to Ireland in 1976, right? We left in May and came back in June, and we had a great time. It was my first time abroad. I was so impressed with Ireland and the sights we saw along the way, so I took a lot of that out of my journal and I also put Linda Mayo in it—I made her up as a lover for Simon. Other than that, those were the sights we saw. We went to Dingle and we went to Galway. We went to Dublin. We went to the Shrine at Knock, places like that. We stayed in Tipperary, I remember—had a great time.

Q. Of course, when reading about our trip, I was re-living our trip. One example is "Tell me *left*."

A. "Left, left," Joe would have to say, and I'd go back to driving on the left-hand side of the road where I belonged.

Q. And on the flight over you were looking out the window and I think Simon does the same thing.

A. This was my first time in an airplane. I looked out the window. I saw all these trees perfectly spaced. And I thought, where is such an orchard in Minnesota. I pointed them out to the woman sitting next to me. I said, "Look at that orchard down there." She looked and she turned to me with disgust. "Those are the rivets on the wing."

Q. And then James Joyce's Martello Tower. We were there on Bloomsday, June 16th. And did we go to Davy Byrne's Pub? I think we did. I noticed that Simon and Linda meet there.

A. We stopped in to look at the place because we were there on the 16th, I remember. There wasn't anything going on when we were there.

Q. Now it's become big, but I was disappointed then. And, of course, the Aran Islands which Simon and Linda visited and "the slow and farting horse." I remember that for three straight hours "Charlie" the horse pulling our jaunting car farted. And the man's name was Brown. Did we learn as they do that we had eaten at his home or did we just surmise it?

A. I think we learned or I think I was certain of that, I don't remember, but I think he took us to his own house to eat lunch.

Q. And a fine lunch, too—brown bread and ham, baked beans. While I went to plays in London, you sat in Russell Square and wrote in your journal. But when did you write in your journal in Ireland when I didn't go to the theatre? You very vividly and accurately described the places we visited in Ireland.

A. I guess maybe while you were writing Christmas cards from the year before, I was writing in my journal.

Q. That's a good answer, Jon. As a footnote, would you discuss the article about Ireland published in the Travel Section of the *New York Times* on May 15, 1977?

A. Yes, that was entitled "Dingle Drenched and Dingle Dry." It was about our stay in Dingle and we were there on a Saturday. It was rainy—we went out to Slea Head, and then our landlady, who looked like Marjorie Main in the Ma and Pa Kettle movies, told us we must go out there again the next day and see it in the sunshine, so when the sunshine came out on Sunday, we went out again—it was just glorious out there. I'll never forget how glorious it looked in the sun, so she was right.

Q. More autobiography: Is Simon's creative writing class based on a Brainerd Community College class that you taught (201-204)? This is the one with Linda Mayo and Mrs. Hamilton.

A. It certainly is. It's a composite of classes I taught in Brainerd which were zany.

Q. At one point in *Simon's Night* you refer to Simon's habit of looking out the window:

*And what, [the students] wondered, went on in his head during those long pauses in the classroom? Midway through a lecture you would see his thoughts suddenly swerve from the topic at hand*

*and his eyes stray from his notes and come to rest on the rolling woodland outside the window. He would stand there transfixed for several seconds—for half a minute sometimes—as though he saw among the branches of the trees, as in a child's picture puzzle, the lines of a human face.*

**Many students have told me over the years about your pausing to look out the window during class. Any comment?**

A. That's right. I didn't know I did that, but students told me I did it, so I had Simon do it. And that describes myself, looking out those windows at Brainerd to a rolling woodland, a very pretty area. I'm always drawn to windows anyway. I remember in Brainerd I was given an office without a window, and I kept leaving it and going out in the hallway and looking out the window. Unconsciously, I'd find myself standing there looking out the window.

**Q. On pages 87 and 88, when Simon applied for a savings account and Barbara was the person helping him, one reads: "Ordinarily Simon's eyes were helplessly drawn to any window and to the rectangle of life it afforded." That reminds me of you. I remember the booth or table you favored by the storefront window at the Park Rapids cafes.**

A. I guess that's true. I've always loved looking out windows. My eyes were always drawn outside.

**Q. In that same section (99) Simon decided to be young again, to change his method of teaching. I think this happened at St. Andrew's. Was this based on anything in your life? I would think this didn't happen. You were a fine and concerned teacher when we first met in 1968.**

A. Well, thank you. That's true, I was always a pretty good teacher. I always related to my students pretty well. I had Simon change from a stodgy teacher to a good one. I just had to bring him around and make him more sympathetic.

**Q. At one point Simon observes that "young people are among the brightest beacons in the world" (85). Was this part of the attraction for teaching for you? I'm sure it is for me.**

A. Young people lead the way for a lot of us, including myself. We look to them for direction.

**Q. On page 91 we read about Doctor Franklin who "was toiling mightily—and in vain, thought Simon—to make this college in the jackpines the Princeton of the West." Where did this come from?**

A. This came from the University of North Dakota where they were indeed trying to be the Princeton of the West, and they were trying to make English studies so hard and they were just so discouraging. I disliked graduate school anyway. That's why I pictured those people at Rookery State as being so ugly.

**Q. Was Simon's college teaching experiences at Rookery State based on your three years teaching at Bemidji State University (1965-1968)?**

A. Yes, that's what I thought of as Bemidji State. I thought of myself teaching there. I imagined Bemidji when I imagined the town, the bank where Barbara worked and things like that.

**Q. *Simon's Night* is dedicated to James Casper, a teaching colleague of ours during our Brainerd years. Both of you had also taught together at Bemidji. Is Simon's close friend, Jay Johnson, loosely based on Jim Casper or any other colleague of yours at Bemidji?**

A. I guess it's loosely based on Jim. I dedicated the book to Jim; I don't think Jim's ever read it. He told me one time he never read the book. He read a page and it was so good, he didn't want to read any more.

**Q. Is Linda Mayo partially based on one of your former students? I don't mean about the romance obviously, but the appearance and demeanor and enthusiasm.**

A. She's a composite of girls I've had in class. I wasn't thinking of anyone in particular. I was thinking more of girls I had in high school when I was teaching in Park Rapids.

Q. Simon takes walks as you always would do. You wrote on page 141: "The alarmed cows walked stiffly away, and when they judged they were safe they stopped and looked stupidly back at the dog. Was there a more dim-witted look in the world than that of a puzzled cow?" I remember our walks when I would visit you at your cabin on Belle Taine Lake. I believe that you quoted A. E. Housman to the goats, and I think at least one seemed interested. Is this little vignette with Simon and the cows based on your walks by your cabin?

A. Yes, it is certainly, and the cabin is like Simon's cabin. My cabin, like Simon's, was about the same number of miles from town, and his also faced water. It had long walks to take nearby. I would recite poetry to the goats, but there were cows along the way, too. One goat stood on top of an abandoned car and watched us go by. He always listened to me recite poetry as I went by in the evening.

Q. Like you, Simon Shea was an only child. Did that fact influence your conception of Simon?

A. Yes, it did. Also, his father ran a store which my father did. His mother was a lot like my mother.

Q. On page 137, "for a married man he [Simon] had certainly spent a lot of his life alone." Would that be an accurate assessment of much of your married life?

A. That's true, too. I think about all the towns I taught in. I have a lot of bachelor friends including you because I felt myself as single a lot of the time.

Q. Still personal—on pages 131-134 you write about Simon and Barbara's isolation from others. "Like most unhappy couples, they were left alone ... What was the flaw that kept the Sheas on the sidelines throughout the social season?" I feel that these pages were based on personal experience.

A. Yes, years would go by between visitors.

Q. Now the questions lighten up for a while. Obviously, William Butler Yeats is a favorite poet of yours as well as of Simon's. How about Anne Sexton and Sylvia Plath that Simon liked or used to like?

A. Yes, I was reading them a lot as I was writing that book. I guess they haven't endured the way Yeats has in my memory or my interest, but I was reading them at that point.

Q. At one point Simon reminisces about when he was seven and his father was chopping wood and Simon threw the sticks down the coal chute into the basement. Immediately I thought about my father and me harvesting potatoes in the fall. Dad would spade the potato hill, and I, on my knees, would dig in the dirt to retrieve the potatoes. Do other readers comment on how passages from your books evoke childhood memories?

A. That one in particular I read in Mankato when I was down there for a radio show, and Professor Robert Wright told me that it was a very evocative passage for him, too. I guess that's about the last time—that was twenty years ago or so.

Q. Simon reviewed books for a number of years. Had you reviewed any yet in the 1970s? I know that you did in the 1980s.

A. At that time I had probably reviewed only one or two.

Q. Simon reviewed books by Scott Fitzgerald and Hilaire Belloc in the same review. He wrote, "If the serious reader is going to find fault with these two otherwise estimable masters of English prose, he will find it in the tendency of Fitzgerald to be unnecessarily complex and in the tendency of Belloc to be unnecessarily simple" (129). This passage brought back elusive memories of something witty you wrote about Saul Bellow which your agent asked you to change. Could you tell me about that?

A. Simon comes across a review of a book by Saul Bellow. He says Saul Bellow is fascinating for five pages, interesting for ten, boring for fifteen, any five, any ten, any fifteen. Well, as soon as Harriet read that, she called me up and she said, "Would you mind taking that out? Saul would be so insulted to read that." So I took it out, as though Bellow would read my book.

Q. Again, as in *Staggerford*, you use bird imagery: "an elderly woman with a beak like a buzzard's" (89) and "Spinner and Leep reminded Simon of sparrows" (6). Is it easier to characterize people physically by using such imagery?

A. I guess it must have been then. I don't do that so much anymore.

Q. Each chapter ends with Simon reciting part of a Psalm and then continuing with his own meditation and examination of conscience, as it were. Your first volume of memoirs, which probably comes out next year, has its title from a Psalm, *Days Like Smoke*. [It hasn't been published yet.] How did you decide to use this device?

A. I don't know. I wanted to get Simon's prayers into this book, and I wanted him to have a springboard for his prayers, so I used the Psalms. I guess I'd been going to Blue Cloud Abbey in South Dakota quite a bit around that time where they recited the Psalms, so I used them.

Q. Joseph Hynes, in the November 3, 1995, *Commonweal*, "Midwestern Loneliness—The Novels of Jon Hassler," writes:

*Indeed, one of the creative joys of the novel is Simon's praying. The manner is always that of personal conversations with God as both superior and friend. Simon is alternately grateful, loving, needful, contrite, puzzled, and inquiring. Notably, he is not angry, maudlin, despairing, self-pitying, or demanding. That is, he believes in God and feels close to Him, but knows his own place as creature. To pull this off without being cute or slavish or drippingly pious seems to me one of Hassler's remarkable achievements. (10)*

I agree. Your comments?

A. That's a very gratifying passage of criticism. I have to say that I never reached that point in prayer. It was easier for Simon to do it than me.

**Q. You almost prayed through Simon.**

A. I guess I did actually.

**Q. Now comes the most challenging part for me in the novel, Simon's two days at the Olympus Mall. Grotesque, phantasmagoric, mythological are some of the words that spring to mind to describe my reactions. I believe that this section is perhaps the most difficult to comprehend and assimilate of all your writing. What did you intend to achieve with these chapters, "Thursday" and "Friday"?**

A. This is where Simon turns his life around. It's while eating a hot-dog at a small stand there. He comes to the conclusion that he can go home and he can invigorate the people in the old folks' home. He decides to do that because he's been visited by these people who are so discouraged and there they treat him as a confessor. Because of that he decides to turn his life around and be useful again.

**Q. This section reminds me of novels immersed in mythology, such as Updike's _The Centaur_. Does understanding the mythology used help to explain the story and theme?**

A. I have no idea. I know Updike referred to the fable or the myth throughout his book. I don't refer to it at all. I just named the place Olympus and then I let it go.

**Q. How about Ithaca Mills? Ithaca was the homeland of Odysseus, and Penelope was his wife who waited twenty years for his return. Barbara in a sense waited thirty-three years.**

A. I named Ithaca Mills after Ithaca, New York.

**Q. And then we have Jupiter, the vehicle place. We have Diana, the sales clerk at the Five and Dime. These all seem classical allusions and, of course, Olympus itself.**

A. You're right. I don't know if I had that in mind.

Q. This is more for the reader then, too. These help to place the novel as an odyssey of a soul or Orpheus in the underworld. The tone is different, I think, from the rest of the novel. This is going to be a very long question with probably not much of an answer. Simon's time in the Olympus Mall, it seems to me, is equated with a visit to Hades or hell or the underworld. Instead of being ferried to Hades by Charon (who would transport souls of the dead over the river Styx), Simon comically is transported to Hades (Olympus Mall) and the Jupiter Service (garage) in his defective Ford, backwards. Is this his ride to hell?

A. Gee, I don't know. It's his ride to the Olympus Mall. To the gods—yes, perhaps it is to the underworld. I like that interpretation, Joe.

Q. Simon's encounters in the Olympus Mall prove eerie and nightmarish, like a German expressionistic film: security guard, old man in tennis shoes whose mother died, father of the bride with her "pink asshole," a grandmother distraught. Are these the living dead of America, isolated and hurting?

A. They are certainly, and the fact that you get so much out of this proves what I say, that the book is not finished until the reader reads it.

Q. Then—to continue the dead and/or hell motif—before the resurrection, Simon inadvertently visits two funeral homes with comic and bizarre results.

A. Yes, that was to steer him into action to convince him he should do something before he died.

Q. You really capture, by the way, the fashions of the 1970s on page 253, like a garishly Technicolored piece of film: "The fashion this season was the layered look: red, white, and blue polyester; all the women wore it. The men wore leisure suits, mostly lime green or amber, and the children displayed large numerals and other printed material across their shirts." You really bring that vividly to life. I can picture people, friends and acquaintances wearing those styles.

A. Yes, I remember that in particular from the Bicentennial year, a lot of red, white and blue—people were wearing that.

Q. Barbara also undergoes a journey through hell. Neither has experienced rain (cleansing, purification) for some time (a drought in El Paso as well as in Rookery and Ithaca Mills); each carries the fire of hell—i.e., loneliness, incompleteness, possible decrepitude in the case of Simon. Two striking passages convey Barbara's torture. One describes the oval moon, and the reader is led to associate this with Barbara since she has always been described as having ovals or being oval.

> *Barbara . . . stopped and peered over the rail just as the moon came out from behind a cloud and cast its reflection onto the water. She stood for a minute looking down at the bright oval. . . . Now and again a fitful breeze raised tiny waves that tore at the edges of the oval and threatened to pull it to pieces, but the moon was too cohesive to come apart—though rippled at the edges, it kept itself whole. . . . She looked back at the water where now a sudden gust of wind kicked up waves that shattered the reflection of the moon and scattered its pieces across the black water like chips of ice. (194)*

Is this rather intense passage a reflection of Barbara's mental and psychological state of mind?

A. Yes, I wanted that to stand for her desperation.

Q. And the next two pages continue Barbara's interior journey, even repeating the word "ice."

> *Barbara was standing up to her knees in a river. It was night [night in the other passage also] and the river was covered with slivers of ice. It was her impossible task to keep the ice from slipping past her, for if the slivers floated further downstream they would surely be the death of many people. . . . Ice floated past her and people died. Where did all this ice come from, and why did the terrible responsibility for stopping it fall upon her? Why was there ice in the world at all? She sensed that someone she knew*

*had introduced ice into the world, but she couldn't think who it was. (195)*

Would you turn psychiatrist and analyze Barbara's dream for us?

A. This seems to be a typical nightmare. I don't know, Joe. You're better in interpreting than I am, certainly.

Q. But it makes her ready, then, for reconciliation, doesn't it? They both go through their own hell in a sense. Barbara's is nightmares and Simon's is hearing these people at the Mall. And both provide them with the openness for each other.

A. They both go out into the desert and have their experience and come back and heal themselves more or less.

Q. John Cheever provided your epigraph for *Staggerford*, and here it's lines from Wallace Stevens: "After the final no there comes a yes / And on that yes the future world depends. / No was the night." After these detailed questions, the meaning is probably self-explanatory, but would you comment anyway?

A. It's a book about affirmation, and if you deny life, there's no life there. That's what Simon did when he went into the Home. But then he decided to leave and face the world, that's yes, "and on that yes, the future of the world depends," says Wallace Stevens. "No was the night"—this was Simon's night which he went through—and came out the other end a better man.

Q. And that leads us to the long night of Simon (nineteen years if not longer) ending with Barbara, rain, cleansing, rebirth, completion. Is that the meaning of the title—I'm sure it is—as we discussed?

A. Yes, it is. He says in the book somewhere that when night comes on, you want to make your bed, lie in it, and so that's why he goes into the Home, but see, then he comes out the other side.

Q. I think we've probably already done the theme to death, but if there's anything else that we could discuss, I'm sure it is his rebirth and resurrection.

A. I remember that's why I put the Psalm in at the beginning. "At nightfall weeping enters in." At the end of the book, I add the next line, "but with the dawn rejoicing. At nightfall weeping enters in, but with the dawn rejoicing."

Q. The final grand passage (311-312) concludes *Simon's Night* with

> *the sound of rain . . . falling on the slope under his yard light. And beyond the light it was raining into the Badbattle, a bubble where each drop of rain struck the moving water. . . . Rain fell onto hillsides and it ran brimming into streams, and water rose to a great depth in ditches where culverts were plugged. Rain fell across the land as unbidden and broad as the hope for good harvest, it fell onto everyone's roof like a blessing, it fell into everyone's life like the promise of love.*

Of course, this brings to mind the conclusion to James Joyce's story "The Dead" with snow falling and covering everything. Surely, this must have influenced you.

A. That's right. I remember reading that passage in Joyce. I remember driving home from Blue Cloud Abbey [SD] one time through rain like that. So I stopped the car and wrote some of those details down, like the rain falling in garbage cans and things like that. And it seems to me that stood for rejuvenation, the coming back of life.

Q. When I was reading J. F. Powers's *Wheat That Springeth Green*, I heard a theory that the last word of a novel could serve as its summation. For *Wheat That Springeth Green*, "cross" is the last word which really sums up Father Joe Hackett's mission, to pick up his cross and become a good priest. The last word in *Simon's Night* is "love." Could that serve as a summation of your theme and story?

A. It certainly could. That's a theory of Bob Wyatt, who told me that the last word of a novel contains the novel, and I guess it works in that case, doesn't it, unconsciously? Bob Wyatt was my editor for *North of Hope*, and it ends with the word "once." I don't know what that means. But *Dear James* ends with the word "again," which I didn't see any significance in, and he said perfect, it's a sequel to *Green Journey*, so you're revisiting it again. So the next two novels, I consciously made the last word stand for the novel. In *The Dean's List* the last word is "poem" having to do with the poet. I forget the last word of *Rookery Blues*, I'll have to look that up [it's "music"].

**Q. I'm glad you told me it was from Bob Wyatt. That comes full circle since it was from you I heard it. You had more media exposure with the publication of *Simon's Night* than with *Staggerford*. Would you describe some of the outlandish aspects of your television appearances?**

A. I was asked to go to Minneapolis's WTCN Television in those days to promote *Simon's Night*. I showed up there as requested one morning about 9:00 or 10:00. I was one of several guests. The main guest was Horst the hairdresser who had a woman on stage with her hair wet. He was going to make her over. Between each guest we'd go back to Horst and see how she was coming. She got to be there by answering a question in twenty-five words or less why she wanted her hair done by Horst. She looked a terrible mess at the beginning, but he did bring her around. Another one was an exercise lady in purple tights who showed us how to exercise. The Astonishing Neal was there. He was psychic—he brought his own mirror and hung it on the wall. He made up his face before he appeared. There were two gentlemen from the Society of the Blind. And there was myself.

I was the last one, and when I came on, there was a minute or two before the commercial ended, and the host said to me, "Where's the book?" I said, "They sent you a book." He said, "No, they didn't. You have to have a book. This is television." I said, "I don't have a book. I didn't think to bring a book with me." So he talked about *Simon's Night* without the benefit of seeing it on the screen. His first question was, "What are we going to do about the problems of old folks' homes?" Because he was emcee, that's the way he got a handle on a book, of course. The hook about *Simon's Night* must be problems about old folks' homes. So he asked me what we were going to do about that. I don't know what I said. I was interested in seeing what I said, so when I left, I asked when the program would be on—I knew it was being recorded. They told me it would be on at 5:30 in the morning. Well, hell, who would watch that. I looked in the paper when I got back to the hotel. Sure enough, there was *What's New* at 5:30 every morning, no other time. I can't imagine who would watch that program. It was awful.

**Q. That was probably the low point of your media exposure. Critics and reviewers overall embraced *Simon's Night*. Do you read the reviews, and do they matter to you or influence you?**

A. I'm interested in them. Of course, I read them. If they're bad I don't believe them unless two or more reviewers agree on one point which they seldom do. But people come up to me. More readers tell me it's their favorite book, more than any other. I don't know what it has, but it has something they like a lot.

**Q. In the *New York Times Book Review*, dated October 28, 1979, Richard Bradford, author of the novel *Red Sky at Morning*, offered a glowing review of *Simon's Night*:**

> . . . *upon Simon's error hinges one of the most delightful novels I have read in years, a work of manifold virtues, felicitous, intelligent and very funny. . . . Thank you for* Simon's Night, *Mr. Hassler. If you have any more novels in the works that are this good, or even a fraction as good, you'll oblige us all by sending them out into the world as briskly as possible.*

**That certainly is a 180° turnaround from Joyce Carol Oates's review of *Staggerford* two years before in the *New York Times Book Review*. Do you have any idea why?**

A. I don't know why except he was really struck by this book. When I spoke earlier about the novel being out of print for a while, it was when that review appeared, there weren't any books in the bookstore for a period of three or four weeks, so I suppose that held down the sale of the novel.

Q. It's too bad that the commercial aspects are so important. Going through the reviews of *Simon's Night*, I discovered that you and Scott Spencer were both reviewed in the same "Recent Fiction" column for the London *Daily Telegraph* (April 17, 1980).

A. That is quite a coincidence since Spencer wrote the screenplay for *The Love Hunter*. [It was never filmed.]

Q. Eugenia Thornton opened her review with "*Simon's Night* is a marvel. Out of Old Age, which our peculiar times have determined to view as a sort of generational sin, Jon Hassler has drawn forth a poignant, funny, wise novel about Eternal Youth."

A. She wrote reviews for the *Plain Dealer* in Cleveland, and she supported my early work with enthusiastic mention.

Q. As recently as October 24, 1997, in *Commonweal*, Stephen Schloesser, a doctoral candidate in modern European history at Stanford University, included in his essay a discussion of *Simon's Night*:

> The novel turns on a contest between two forces: life's incalculability, and Simon's obstinacy. It takes a powerful moment of grace—a startling visit after forty years—to make Simon see, suddenly, not so much what he has done, but rather what he has become. In the event, he repents of his self-wounding willfulness and opens himself to the violence of grace—so that it might fill him with new life. (31)

Are you pleased that this novel is still getting critical reactions?

A. Yes, of course I am. It has an element that I'm not aware of. Perhaps it's the character of Simon and the intractability of vows.

Q. One more excerpted review: This is from the *McAllen* [Texas] *Monitor* (September 16, 1979) written by Judy Rigler:

*The opening paragraphs of this novel promise a depth of character and sensitivity of plot not often seen in modern fiction. In a time when so many contemporary novels are literally thrown together, it is a pleasant discovery that this novel lives up to its early promise. . . .Besides being an affirmation of the richness that life can hold for everyone, not just the young,* Simon's Night *is a fine novel. There are several beautiful love stories within its pages, two involving man and woman, one involving man and the written word, and one involving man and life. All contribute to the positive, touching quality of the story. Hassler's characters are filled with the mixture of eccentricity and intelligence that makes us whole, intriguing human beings. Written in a prose that borders on poetic, with compassion and wit, this novel is a joy to read and reflect upon.*

A. All my novels are accessible; that's what makes them appealing to readers.

**Q. Movie producers sporadically have shown interest in** Simon's Night. **Could you give a brief history of this?**

A. It's currently under option to Kate Lehmann, a Minneapolis producer who hopes to film it for cable television. My stepson Emil wrote the screenplay. [The option ran out in the fall of 2005.]

**Q. A more recent fan of yours, Anthony Low, Professor of English at New York University, expressed his opinion in** Renascence, **Fall 1994: "If I have a favorite among Hassler's novels, it is probably** Simon's Night." **I know what he means.** Simon **proves to be even richer in my second reading twenty-one years later. I hope that for me your subsequent novels don't pale in comparison. Thank you very much, Jon, for another enlightening interview.**

A. Thank you, Joe, it's been fun.

# The Love Hunter

The Love Hunter was the first of Jon's novels to be published by William Morrow, the first to be published in paperback, and the first to be optioned—and then bought—by a movie company. Alas, these promising events did not propel The Love Hunter to commercial success as you will learn in our interview. The Love Hunter was also the first of Jon's novels to take for its subject matter a love triangle. Rather than merely repeat the success of his earlier novels, Jon made a quantum leap into the hitherto uncharted territory of male/female relationships. His new editor at Morrow, Harvey Ginsberg, believed that The Love Hunter could be Jon's "breakthrough" novel, but that proved not to be the case. Bantam Books published a limited quantity of the paperback and chose not to reprint when the initial printing sold out. Robert Redford purchased the film rights, yet The Love Hunter remains simply one more title in Hollywood's cemetery of bought but unfilmed properties.

In a St. Cloud Times interview (October 20, 1980), Jon described why The Love Hunter took longer to complete than his earlier works:

> I think I got deeper into relationships, more subtle kinds of relationships and thinking them through took more time. I discovered as I was writing that I wasn't turning out as much per day. I'd write for five or six hours and have a page and a half or two pages, maybe not even that much.
>
> At first I began to worry. I thought I was beginning to lose my ability. But after a while I came to see that what I was turning out, even though it was fairly meager per day, stood up very well. I was satisfied with it. So then I quit worrying.

The interviewer, Beth Linnen, commented that moral dilemmas, such as that Chris faced in *The Love Hunter*, recurred in Jon's writing. Jon responded: "I didn't realize this as I was writing them, but it seems to me that all these books are about faithfulness or infidelity, constancy or inconstancy, relationships between friends and lovers."

Though the book was not universally adored by the critics, the majority of the reviews were highly laudatory. Writing in the *New York Times Book Review* (August 16, 1981) Randolph Hogan delivered the line that has appeared as a blurb on most of Jon's subsequent novels: "Jon Hassler is a writer good enough to restore your faith in fiction." He also observed: "Perhaps what's most striking about Mr. Hassler's writing is the voice. It makes you want to keep on reading just to remain in the company of such a wise man."

Eugenia Thornton in *Cleveland Plain Dealer* (June 28, 1981), always a fan of Jon's writing, praised Jon and this novel:

> *Jon Hassler is one of America's most completely satisfying novelists. Ever since his remarkable first novel,* Staggerford, *he has moved surely forward in the perfection of his art. His prose is flawless, his characters are decent, believable people about whom you care immensely, his stories are strong. He writes about what he knows so that we may know it too and find therein a power of understanding.* The Love Hunter *is his third novel and his best. ....*
>
> The Love Hunter *is an exciting novel about love and life and death and the terrible hazards involved in being a vulnerable human being. It is informed by an awe-inspiring ability to understand those parts of all of us which we think we keep well hidden from the world.*
>
> *If you read only one novel this summer, read* The Love Hunter.

And Bruce Allen (*Chicago Tribune Book World*, December 13, 1981) noted:

> The Love Hunter *is a work of scrupulous realism, attentive to significant detail, finding credible symbolic relevance in everyday objects and natural actions and gestures. You know you're in good hands immediately, from Hassler's masterly handling of the*

*exposition: The first five pages of this novel should be required reading for aspiring writers. . . . What distinguishes Jon Hassler from most of his contemporaries is his ability to make decent people both complicated and interesting....I consider him one of our very best novelists.*

Weidenfeld and Nicolson published *The Love Hunter* in England in 1982, making this the third of Jon's novels, following *Staggerford* and *Simon's Night*, to appear in the United Kingdom. The four English reviews that I read were all positive. For example, the *Books & Bookmen* critic (April 1982) described the book as "a finely wrought and compelling piece of story-telling," and went on to say, "Jon Hassler's prose is wry and elegant, his handling of a difficult theme delicate but assured, and there is a great deal of exceedingly sharp, and often very funny, dialogue."

Thus, Jon's third novel achieved a literary bull's-eye on all fronts—publication in the United States with a larger publishing house, a paperback edition, a British edition, and the option and sale to a major movie personage/company. Still, widespread commercial success remained elusive. With some Ballantine paperbacks yet in print, I am still hopeful that *The Love Hunter*, like the phoenix, will rise once more to a wider readership and to a committed movie producer. This novel deserves nothing less.

- J. P. July 2004

*September 17, 2000*

Q. We're at your and Gretchen's townhouse in Minneapolis. Today, we're discussing *The Love Hunter*. Between the appearance of *Simon's Night* in 1979 and the publication of *The Love Hunter* in 1981, you received two fellowships, one especially prestigious. Would you tell us about them?

A. First I received a Minnesota State Arts Board grant for writing fiction, and then in the spring of 1980 I received a Guggenheim Fellowship, and that was very important to me. It allowed me to take a year off and just work on nothing but my fiction. Bob Spaeth, the dean from Saint John's University in Collegeville, came to Brainerd and invited me to come to the University for the year, so I went to Saint John's and never went home again. I loved it too much there, and I stayed for seventeen years until I retired as a teacher.

Q. I went through a change then, too. I really missed seeing you every teaching day at Brainerd Community College, catching up on school gossip and literary news and having our frequent lunches. Now, in regard to your leaving Brainerd, on page 299 of *The Love Hunter*, Bruce Quinn is not eager to attend Rookery State College because of "its shabby treatment of Larry." Could this be an accurate statement of Brainerd Community College's treatment of you at this time?

A. No, I think it was a reflection of Bemidji State's treatment of me twelve years earlier when I lost my job there because I didn't get a doctorate. Brainerd was always good to me, although it became stultifying after a while. I remember when I won the Guggenheim, nobody understood what it was except you and a student who came along one day and said, "Congratulations on that thing with a G."

Q. For *The Love Hunter* you still had the same agent, Harriet Wasserman, but a different editor and a different publisher.

A. I told Harriet, my agent, I wanted a different publisher because Atheneum had not promoted *Staggerford* and *Simon's Night* very much, so she sold my book to Harper & Row where Harvey Ginsberg was my editor, and then, before it was published, Harvey Ginsberg suddenly moved over to William Morrow and Company, and I was faced with a choice of going with him or staying there and having my book being an orphan, as they call it, and I wouldn't have anybody cheering for it. So I went to Morrow with him, and he became my editor for the next three books. He was altogether different from Judith Kern—he was a fussy man, very fussy, and he kept saying things like, "We have to make the reader worry more," that was always one of his themes. He didn't like the title of *The Love Hunter* although he loved the book itself. He wanted to call it *Old Friends* which wasn't much of a title, it seemed to me. I stuck to my guns there.

**Q. I agree—I think *Old Friends* is a very lame title. Could you compare your working relationship with him to yours with Judith Kern at Atheneum? Was she more a "hands off" kind of editor?**

A. Yes, she was. She let me write more freely, and he objected to very small things a lot of the time. He had a secretary I remember who was just like him. This was a young man who worked for him in the office. I remember I went to New York one time. I phoned and I said, "I'll be at the office by 4:00," and the secretary said, "At or by?" So that's the sort of guys they both were, very fussy.

**Q. What strengths did each of them have as an editor?**

A. Well, of course, Judith Kern, I saw her strength as letting me go, giving me a wide rein. And Harvey was good at knowing what the public wanted. He knew that the public wanted things like *The Love Hunter*, and so he fit Morrow's style pretty well because Morrow was used to publishing blockbusters. I thought maybe I'd sell a lot of books if I went with Morrow. As it turned out, *The Love Hunter* didn't sell all that many because when my book came out, Morrow was feuding with B. Dalton and they weren't sending them any books. B. Dalton at the time was the biggest retailer in the country, so that was a problem. Anyhow, I went on to publish two more books with him, *A Green Journey* and *Grand Opening*. Then in 1990 I left with *North of Hope* and went to Ballantine.

**Q. Yes, your agent, Harriet, and your editor, Harvey, both did perceive *The Love Hunter* as your "breakthrough" novel, didn't they?**

A. That's what they called it, my breakthrough book, and by that they meant it was going to sell a lot of copies, and it sold somewhat more than the other two. I guess it may have sold 20,000, which sounds like a lot, but you don't get on to the bottom of the *New York Times* bestseller list without selling 50,000 in a country of 250 million people which at the time didn't seem like very many. I remember my main competitor at that time was *Thin Thighs in Thirty Days*. That was the book everybody was buying in 1981.

Q. How many were printed in hardcover of *The Love Hunter*?

A. I never heard. I expect it was 20,000 or maybe a few more than that.

Q. I think I saw an article in maybe *Publishers Weekly* that said 25,000. So that figure would be in the ballpark then. I was wondering what weaknesses did each of your editors, Judith and Harvey, exhibit?

A. Well, it wasn't a weakness actually with Judy, but I had a hard time talking to her. She was so hip—she was such a New York type. I remember going out to lunch with her one time. She waded across the street and didn't even look at the oncoming taxis. I stayed on the curb afraid I was going to get hit. She got out on the street and she turned to me. She hollered, "C'mon. They don't hit you, it's too much paperwork." See, that's the kind of person she was. Also, one time she called me at home to ask me a question. We'd discussed this before. She said, "I forgot the answer. I had a stroke." It was only a figure of speech, I learned after I had sent her a get-well card. So you see, we weren't on the same wavelength. Harvey, on the other hand, was so attuned to what the public wanted that he didn't care much for my second and third books that I gave him.

Q. How did you decide on the title *The Love Hunter*? I think it's an incredible title.

A. It came to me at a movie. I went to *The Deer Hunter* which didn't have anything to do with my novel, but I thought of *The Love Hunter* and I was afraid somebody would use it before I published it. Nobody has used it yet. Harvey didn't like the title, nor did Jeanne Fischer, the book reviewer from St. Paul. She said, "What a terrible title. It sounds just like a romance." But I thought it was a good title. It still seems good enough to me.

Q. Did *The Love Hunter* have any foreign reprints?

A. *The Love Hunter* had two—Finland, yes, and Germany, both.

**Q. Any awards for *The Love Hunter*?**

A. No awards that I can think of—nothing. It got some pretty good reviews, but that's about it.

**Q. You acknowledge the fellowship provided by the Minnesota State Arts Board and funded by the Minnesota Legislature. Please tell us more.**

A. This was the first of three awards I got from the Minnesota State Arts Board. They gave it to me in about 1979 or '80, and I finished *The Love Hunter*; I took time off from teaching in order to do it with the money that they gave me, so that was very good. It was a $10,000 award.

**Q. That is sizeable. I did find in a copy of a letter you had given me from Harvey Ginsberg to you, dated March 31, 1980, in which he praises what you had written thus far. "The first thing that I want to say is what enormous pleasure your prose gives me. I strode through the pages with hardly a pause for marginal jottings, merely absorption in what you were saying and how you were saying it." And he concluded with this sentence: "Truly, the questions you have raised and the questions I am raising seem almost peripheral at this stage when juxtaposed with the skill and beauty of what you have so far accomplished." Was that gratifying?**

A. I had forgotten he praised me that much. It is very gratifying to hear that again. Yes, he liked that book a lot.

**Q. Did you like the book jacket art? I found it striking and perhaps you could describe it for the reader.**

A. It pictured a flying duck losing one feather. The feather was falling from the duck. It was very well done. The colors were green—a muted green. It was a very impressive color, I thought.

**Q. And the feather is symbolic?**

A. I guess it is since no one in the story is whole. Everyone suffers some sort of loss. Chris and Larry and Rachel are the three main characters. Larry has MS, Chris is lonely, and Rachel loses Larry eventually.

Q. Also, the size of the book is larger compared to the others. I measured your first two novels in hardcover, and each is 8½ inches tall whereas *The Love Hunter* (and all of your subsequent novels in hardback) is 9½ inches tall. Do you prefer this larger format for hardcover?

A. Yes, I think it is more impressive on the shelf, at least.

Q. This novel caused the biggest stir in Hollywood of all your novels. Please share all the juicy and gory details.

A. In February of 1981 Robert Redford bought *The Love Hunter*. I remember when I told you that, Joe, you had to go home and take half a Valium you were so excited. Then the producer, a man named Richard Roth [producer of *Julia*, starring Jane Fonda and Vanessa Redgrave] called me up some time later. He said, "Did you ever have another idea for a disease for this book?" I said, "No, it was MS all along." He said, "But we're thinking on the big screen, you know; Robert doesn't want to look sick." Robert, meaning Robert Redford. Well, I told that to my class. They suggested herpes.

I bought a house with the money I earned on that book. The day I bought it I called up Richard Roth to thank him. He said I was the first person ever to call him to thank him for money. Anyway, one time they decided they were going to film it at Saint John's. Saint John's was going to be the campus because the book is about a college campus in Rookery. And so there was a movie crew going to come up to talk to me and buy me lunch, and they called up at the last minute and said they weren't coming to Saint John's. Would I come down to Minneapolis and join them for lunch. So I went to Minneapolis, the Marquette Hotel, and there Bill Pohlad was. He was interested in film. There were a still photographer sent by Robert Redford and the screenwriter also sent by Redford. His name was Scott Spencer. The man who was in charge of the Minnesota Film Board, he *was* the Minnesota Film Board—Nick Edwards. Anyway, we sat at the Marquette having lunch, and it became Scott Spencer's job to tell me that they weren't going to film it at Saint John's. They were going to film at Carleton in Northfield, and they weren't going to make it Rookery Playhouse. They were going to make it the Guthrie Theater in Minneapolis. They weren't going to make it a town which was like Bemidji. They were going to make it Minneapolis.

Well, it didn't take me long to figure out why—because Nick Edwards had gone to Carleton. He lived in Minneapolis. He'd shown Scott all these places and so Scott wrote them into the script. And then, when I got the script, it was mostly about Jesse James Days [annual celebration in Northfield]. And there were about ten minutes at the end of the film when they decided to go hunting. That was the extent of the hunting which is central to the book. Anyway, it never got made because the screenplay was so poor, I thought.

When lunch was over the waiter left the check on the table. Nobody would pick it up. The still photographer didn't want it, and Nick Edwards said, "We don't have a budget for lunches." So Scott Spencer said very magnanimously, "Let me buy Jon's lunch at least," as though he'd been trying to buy everybody's, and he paid for mine, and everybody else paid their own. They called the waiter over, and he made a lot of squiggles and circles on the bill, and they added it up separately. It was very cheap. That was Hollywood. That was as close as I'd ever gotten to Hollywood lunches. The movie never got made. It was put on the shelf, never used; it belongs to TriStar Studios to this day, and it's never been filmed. It strikes me as my best movie idea. The love triangle. The duck hunting and so forth.

**Q. Had you registered your disapproval with the screenplay to the producer Richard Roth?**

A. Yes, I had; I wrote him a letter.

**Q. By chance, did you have any contact with Redford?**

A. I have a letter from him telling me how difficult the story is to film and how much he likes it. He says, "I hope things will actually get underway very soon." That was twenty years ago.

Q. Had you been in Los Angeles at all during this time?

A. Yes, I went to California in 1983. I visited Mr. Ziegler, the agent who sold *The Love Hunter* to Roth.

Q. I have a postcard from you dated January 19, 1983: "While learning very little about TLH I've learned a lot about the principals. Ziggy is a lascivious wretch, Roth is a man after my own heart and Redford is acting strange. As for Roth's secretary, when I told her my name she said, 'Are you calling about *The Mary Pickford Story*?'"

A. Ziegler's secretary was named Patty Detroit. She was a forty-year-old woman who had gone west with a Polish last name and changed it in commemoration of her hometown.

Q. I have a xeroxed copy of an interview with Scott Spencer that you probably sent to me; neither the magazine nor the date is included. I quote:

> The screenwriting project Spencer learned most from was one for Robert Redford. 'It was an interesting experience because he's so smart about movies, and I got to see how a real movie person thinks. On the other hand, it was a real exercise in frustration. Redford had bought this book called The Love Hunter *about a guy with multiple sclerosis, his wife, and their best friend, who falls in love with the wife. Originally, Redford wanted to play the guy with MS, and I wrote it like that. When I finished, he said he liked the script very much, but he didn't think he could play a guy with MS, and could I write it again so he could be the other guy? So I wrote it again, and he still didn't want to do it.'*

I think this fits in with your memories also.

A. It certainly does. That's exactly what I remember about it. Yes.

Q. Some years ago, when I was visiting you in Minneapolis, I suggested that we see Redford's movie, *Quiz Show*, which he directed, and you refused. Would you explain, although the reason seems obvious, why you boycott Redford's films?

A. Well, because he still has *The Love Hunter* under contract and he bought it. It's his property, so I can't sell it to anybody else. Nobody else can make a movie out of it, and so that's why I boycott his films.

Q. So it's really in limbo. Didn't Paul Newman also want to buy the screen rights after reading the *New York Times Book Review*?

A. He did. He contacted Harriet, my agent, and said he wanted the book. By that time we'd sold it to Redford. Harriet told me that a screenwriter named Ron Buck called her from Florida where his Paul Newman script was being filmed, and he said (with Newman prompting him in the background), "Paul wants to play the sick guy."

Q. Weren't there rumors rife in Hollywood and even in the *National Enquirer* that Newman and Redford would be in the movie?

A. I think that was Redford's idea to start with, but Newman didn't want to work with him again. That's what I heard.

Q. *The Love Hunter* was the first of your novels to be reprinted in paperback.

A. Bantam Books came out with a very small printing in 1982. It pictured a man and a woman with red faces on the cover. It was embarrassing. It looked like a romance and the print looked like a romance. And it was even called a sizzling romance. It looked to me like it was about two people who got sunburned under a sunlamp.

Q. I remember you saying that it looked almost like third-degree burns. In an interview at about this time (*Minneapolis Tribune*, October 2, 1981), you discussed your writing in a fresh and revealing way. I would like to quote three paragraphs:

> *A novel—you get so absorbed; it takes up all your days. When one is done, you have to start afresh with the next. Things that succeeded in a previous book tend to intimidate you. You have to take a new idea and run with it.*

*There's a point in there when the whole thing changes. You're so delighted to get into it (the story) for a good long ways, a couple hundred pages—then you discover you can't turn around and get out. You're trapped in there. You've invested a year. It can get pretty scary; you're never sure if you're going to lose it.*

*I think of when I was a kid and I'd carry these big washtubs of water for washing clothes. They were so bulky and the handles were so far apart; if you tipped it a little bit, the water'd start spilling out. That's the way I feel about the novel; it keeps filling and filling and you've got to be careful.*

I believe that is the only interview I've read in which you express yourself in quite this way. Have you changed your attitude in almost twenty years?

A. My attitudes are mainly the same. Each book just feels like you're trapped in the book. You wait until the day you're done with it, and the day you're done with it, you can't wait to get started on the next one. It's sort of a circle that way. Also, the thing about the washtubs is true. You fill up and you fill up. If you write something on page 100, it can't contradict something you wrote on page 22, so you have to keep everything in mind. You can't spill any of it out. You can't forget any of it. So that's very demanding, too.

Q. In *The Love Hunter,* Rookery, Minnesota, which had been a partial setting for *Simon's Night,* is now a main setting, at least for flashbacks. Rookery means a colony of rooks, birds of the crow family. Please explain how that title fits in.

A. Well, great blue herons also nest in rookeries. They're such ungainly creatures. I thought of the faculty at Rookery State in *Simon's Night*—it was such an ungainly faculty. I thought I would call it Rookery State. Then I just stayed with that. It seemed like a good name for a town, too.

Q. And later on, isn't the name of the athletic team the Blue Herons?

A. Yes, it is. In *The Dean's List*, that's the name of the varsity teams.

Q. Also, "to rook" means winning money from a person at cards, especially by swindling. Is this part of the theme also? Are the professors, both active and retired, being swindled by Rookery State and the system? Larry got fired because of his illness. And then Larry is being swindled, in a sense, of Rachel's love by Chris.

A. That's right, and he sums up his life by his disease.

Q. On pages 205-206 you write: "Chris had heard that in accordance with the residents' distorted view of things (surely not as an aid to rationality) the [Rookery State] mental hospital grounds were called a campus, the officer in charge of each building was addressed as the dean and the admitting clerk's nameplate said 'Registrar.' Maybe not so foolish, thought Chris, recalling certain mad days at Rookery State College." That's delicious satire; comments?

A. That was a mental hospital, right? Yes, I enjoyed that.

Q. Sticking with Rookery and Rookery State College, one finds on page 303: "September 9, 1980. Letter from president to all department chairmen: college staff to be reduced by 14½ professors, effective at end of academic year." Of course, the "½" gives the punchline. I know that this is not fiction but fact; would you explain?

A. At Brainerd, we lived through a downsizing, Joseph. It was very hard on morale. We went through those very things where they reduced us by 2½ faculty and then 3½ —things like that for three or four years running.

Q. And weren't fourteen or fifteen people given layoff notices?

A. Yes, I think I was one of them, actually. Then they signed us up again.

Q. More Hassler geography: Owl Brook is based on what town or city? I know that the Owl Brook Owls tied the Staggerford Stags in a football game in *Staggerford*.

A. It's just a neighboring town based on Owl Brook Creek in New Hampshire. The fall of 1975, when I went out to New England, I walked along a creek called Owl Brook Creek. I thought that would be a good name for a town.

Q. I find that *The Love Hunter* is strikingly different from your two previous novels and, in fact, from almost all of your other novels. What happened?

A. When I started to write *The Love Hunter*, I decided to write a thriller. With the idea of the love triangle and the hunting trip, I'd write a thriller in a few days. And the deeper I got into the book, the more I couldn't write a thriller, and I wrote the first half of it in six weeks—it took me two years to finish it. I got my characters in such hot water, it took me two years to get them out.

Q. So artistry triumphed over the thriller. Barton Sutter began his *Minneapolis Tribune* review (June 28, 1981) with "In literature as in architecture, the triangle has proved one of the strongest principles of design, and a triangle provides the tension that supports *The Love Hunter*." This novel is a love story, almost a *menage à trois*. Very early on, you tip your hand and tell what Chris plans to do: "Which was precisely where Chris's mind had been for the past sixty days—the Manitoba bogland, where Larry, between now and Sunday, would die" (20).

> Sometimes a counselor had to counsel himself:
> You love Rachel? Yes, yes. Then you shall have her. Ah.
> And you love Larry? He is my closest friend. My only friend.
> Then you must kill him. (24)

This seems very audacious of you, having your protagonist announce such a dastardly mission and right at the beginning of the novel.

A. That was part of the thriller of course—the thriller idea. Also, Larry had asked for death. As his MS got worse he had asked more than once for deliverance from it, and so Chris thinks he's going to be doing him a favor.

Q. Because of Chris's intention, regardless of motives, was it difficult to identify with him? Sutter in his review thought that "As the novel develops, Chris becomes less likable and remains disappointingly passive at some crucial points."

A. Well, I guess I sympathize with him because his wife had left him. He was living alone and he was very lonely. I was able to sympathize with that. Also, we saw the entire story through his eyes, so that also kept me on his side throughout.

Q. Miles, too, in *Staggerford* seemed passive in ways. In the January 12, 1976, entry in *My Staggerford Journal*, you wrote: "Why are they [the feelings] lacking in the Pruitt sections? Because Pruitt is me? Because I am habitually reluctant to express my feelings? Yes." Was it even more of a challenge to create Chris with all of his ambiguities?

A. Yes, I remember that. I remember thinking that very thing. He was a hard guy to get a handle on. I suppose because he was planning to murder for one thing. I think I succeeded.

Q. I do, too. Is Chris more you or is Larry, or are you a combination of the two?

A. I don't know if Chris is me. I certainly was hunting in those days with my son David; we went to Manitoba. And we went to the hunting camp which turned out to be the one in the book, so that part is certainly autobiographical. Other than that, I guess not.

Q. I believe that Larry, at least his physical condition with MS, is based on a friend of yours?

A. Yes, when I was a young teacher, I had a friend named Bob Nielsen in Fosston, and he got MS and it took him fifteen years to die. Every year I'd drive to his home where he lived with his parents. He was unmarried, and I'd see his decline, and I remember thinking if I ever became a novelist, that would be an interesting idea for a book. We'd have two people start out together and one go into decline and the other keep on teaching. When I came to write the book, I had that in my background. It wasn't enough, however, to start a book. It wasn't until I got the idea for the love triangle that I could start it.

Q. Did your friend also get fired because of his MS?

A. He wasn't fired. He quit, though, after the second year since his eyesight was going bad.

Q. Did you do any research on MS?

A. No, I didn't do any research. I just remembered his condition.

Q. What were the general comments from readers about this?

A. I heard from nurses and a couple doctors. They were amazed that a novelist would portray MS so accurately. I was very pleased about that. Then, when I moved to Saint John's, there was a guy on the staff who had MS. I was afraid of his reading it. He read the book and told me the same thing.

Q. Weren't you even asked to address an MS convention one time?

A. I was. Yes. I didn't do it, but I was asked.

Q. Now that you have a Parkinsonian disease [later diagnosed as Progressive Supranuclear Palsy], do you experience some of what Larry went through in his life?

A. I think I'm beginning to now. I've had it for six years and the first several years were very, very mild. But I'm beginning to be immobilized by it, so I can feel what he felt more.

Q. Do you think that you were rather accurate in conveying the physical and emotional and mental challenges that a life-changing disease effects?

A. Yes, I was and am. However, my emotional makeup is different from Larry's. I'm much more passive than he was.

Q. There's a description on page 143 of a wounded mallard: "Across the bay the wounded mallard was struggling toward Teal Point. As it swam, it beat the water with its good wing, trying to fly." Could that be a symbol for Larry?

A. Yes, he's the same way.

Q. Chris "rested his eyes on the various shades of blue-gray that never failed to soothe him, the muted color of hazy distance, the hazy color of Rachel's eyes" (150). And on page 152, Chris "brought up the glasses and held them on the plane of the world's edge and saw the color he loved—gray veiled by the blue of airy distance: precisely the color he saw in Rachel's eyes when she was wistful. Or weary. Or gorging herself on his love." Nature and Rachel here seem to become intertwined. Does this signify that Rachel, like nature, is restorative?

A. I guess it does. I don't know if I thought of it at the time, Joe. But I think it does.

Q. "Love was a trap. If you loved, you doubled your chances of sorrow" (169). Did you write this, or did you borrow it? It's a fascinating statement, Jon.

A. I invented that line. I think I believed it at the time actually, but I don't anymore.

Q. May I ask why you don't anymore?

A. For many years I used to say to people that I've been lucky with everything in life except love. Then I finally got lucky in love in finding my current wife, Gretchen.

Q. That's a beautiful compliment. Now, for an abrupt transition—Chris's recollection of his first hunting trip when he was six ends with the half-naked farmer retrieving the duck from the pond:

*So this was hunting. It struck Chris as an extraordinary business indeed—the dark day, the dead bird, the farmer's genitals, the blind enclosure of grass. There was more to it than a child could understand, but he carried away (and he kept it all these years) the notion that entangled in the urge to hunt was a sexual impulse vying with the desire to kill. So it had been when he was six. And so it was today. (227)*

**Could you explain the psychological implications of this?**

A. I don't know. I think it's part of the male psyche—the part that wants to kill and have sex—the male sort of assertion. I think they go together.

**Q. This leads to Chris's dream of attempting to kill Larry, but Chris can't breathe, he is dying, and he wakes to find the gray cat lying across his face (239-241). How did you discover the literary means to convey these rather Freudian and psychological states of Chris's mind?**

A. I don't know. I just wrote them. I don't remember. I don't remember thinking in Freudian terms, but they turn out to be that way.

**Q. Newspaper articles and headlines and TV in your books enlighten readers about current events. Sometimes, these are informative, satirical, or symbolic. What do you hope to accomplish with this technique used in all three novels thus far?**

A. I don't remember what I had in *The Love Hunter*, but I remember thinking I wanted to place it in time, and that was the easiest way to do it.

**Q. I think one was about the Pope in Iowa, and of course Agatha in *Staggerford* was reading about all the Goths and Visigoths in the Sunday paper when she had a whole meditation on the ferns. You also use composers and artists, such as Beethoven, Mahler, Van Dyck, and Goya, to comment on and illuminate characters and their mental states. Does this help you to get a "handle" on your people?**

A. Yes, it does. It tells me about their emotional life, their reaction to this art and music.

**Q. I have more autobiographical elements to check out. Larry and Chris had been observed drinking beer outdoors in a park (44). Did any of your superintendents tell your faculty not to be seen drinking in public?**

A. Yes, the setting there was Fosston in the late '50s when I taught there. We were forbidden to even go down to the liquor store and buy beer. We couldn't drink in town. We had to go to Erskine which was twelve miles away where there was a little night club. We could have dinner and have drinks there. We couldn't gamble, couldn't play poker. It was a very strict town—we couldn't dance. In fact, the girls' phy-ed teacher had started a course in square dancing. The school board held a special meeting to decide whether to fire her or not. The vote was 3-3, so they decided to keep her. She remained there the rest of her teaching career.

**Q. Rachel's comment, "And to think only a few weeks ago I was calling him Mr. Quinn" (44), derives from Brainerd. Would you explain?**

A. I heard that very line at your house. One time you had a picnic at your house, and Steve Long's [Brainerd Community College biology instructor] new wife, who had been a student, said, "And to think only a few weeks ago I was calling him Mr. Long."

**Q. Please tell the real life story about receiving a father's day card from a student (34-40), as Chris does.**

A. Yes, I get a lot of mileage out of that in this book. Chris tells the story to Larry about his own children who forget to send him a Father's Day card, but he gets one from a former student who asked him one time if she could call him Dad—she didn't have a dad—she said it would just do her good to be able to say Dad when she met him in the hallway. He gave her permission to do that and he got a card from her. It was the only Father's Day card he got, and that was based on a girl in Brainerd who had asked if she could call me Dad. I gave her permission. The following Father's Day she was the only one I got a card from. My kids forgot to send me one. I was at the cabin, alone at that point.

Q. I remember her—Vicker Avery. She was in theatre, I believe. Karen "gives as good as she gets in debating with the argumentative chairman of the village council . . . who can't put the fluoridation of drinking water out of his mind" (55). That surely must be a Brainerd reference.

A. It certainly is. All twelve years I lived there, that was a big issue in Brainerd, whether to let fluoride in the water or not. And finally, the State Court decided that it had to fluoridate its water, so they did, but they kept the faucet open for those who didn't like fluoride so that they could get their water. I don't think anybody ever used it.

Q. Will Jones years ago wrote a *Minneapolis Tribune* article (June 26, 1982) about the drink of tequila, soy sauce, and lime juice served by Sam, the husband of Rachel's mother (298). Had you ever tried this, or is this just fiction?

A. That was just fiction. Will Jones must have been an alcoholic—he took to that so quickly. He wrote an entire article about it.

Q. Yes, he did. Were the illness and death of Peter Ellis, Chris's boyhood friend, based on an actual childhood friendship of yours (266-272)? It's very effective.

A. Yes, that's based on Jackie Harlan who was a boyhood friend of mine. I use him again in my *Good People* book which is to be published next year. I tell the story over again about how he died, how I went to visit him. He had rheumatic fever. I put that in the book as sort of the calm before the storm because that's before the storm strikes up. I got the idea from *Othello* where Desdemona and Emilia sing the "Willow Song," and they have this quiet conversation before Othello comes in to murder Desdemona. I thought that would be a good sort of contrast for the violence that follows.

Q. "But more than that, what really bothered him [Chris] was the great number of students with whom he had no meaningful contact" (57-58). I know that you never went into counseling students, but had you had this feeling during your teaching career?

A. I don't think I needed more meaningful contact with students. I just thought it would be a good deal if he did. It would be more interesting for my book if he did.

Q. And I know you've alluded to this earlier today, Jon; was Blackie LaVoi's hunting camp fictional or based on actual experience? You've already indicated that, but would you explain more?

A. Blackie LaVoi was a guy named Rod DuCharme who had a hunting camp on Lake Manitoba, and when my son David was a senior in high school, I told him, "For your graduation present, Dave, we're going to a real hunting camp." We heard about this from other people—they told us how wonderful it was. We went up there—it was a dump. We slept on corn shucks. We ate duck twice a day, underdone duck. We didn't get any ducks because the weather was fine. David loved it and I hated it because Rod charged us so much money for it. I came home and I wrote thirty pages about it in my journal, so that when I got around to writing the novel, all I had to do was lift it out of the journal and put it in the book—it was all there.

Q. This leads to Blackie's long speech acknowledging the sham involved; "that's what they pay me for—that feeling that they've conquered nature" (231). Is this part of what you thought Rod was going through, too?

A. Sure, I knew that he knew better than to think this was the end—all of life up there, but he ran this operation—he kept us hunters out in the field—he kept us thinking we were conquering nature.

Q. Was the relationship of the two couples, the Quinns and the MacKensies, loosely based on your faculty experiences?

A. Yes, it sure was. That was the Nelsons. Dennis Nelson was a friend I made in Fosston as soon as I moved up there. He was the one who taught me how to hunt ducks. And I went hunting with him, and then I went hunting with him and his wife, and then they had a baby and we became very close as couples. I remember one time there was a blizzard—school was called off—we were over at their house, and it was so blizzardy, we decided we had to sleep at their house. We didn't have our pajamas, so I drove home and got our pajamas, and we slept at their house because we couldn't go home. That was funny. Dennis left Fosston the year before I did. He went to UMD [U of MN at Duluth] and became head of the Economics Department there. I haven't seen him since.

Q. The dedication page for *The Love Hunter* reads: "For Lavina and Ray." Would you explain?

A. Lavina and Ray Erickson in Brainerd were close friends of mine at that point in my life, so I went over to their house a lot in the evenings—spent a lot of time there with them.

Q. Lavina had been active at the Brainerd Community College theatre. Did she serve, in a way, as a model for Rachel with her community theatre participation?

A. Yes, she did—exactly.

Q. Of course, the cliché, "It's a small world," fits here. Lavina had the role of Barbara in your adaptation of *Simon's Night*, produced by the Lyric Theatre in Minneapolis in April 1991.

A. Yes, it is a small world, isn't it? She turned up in my life again.

Q. The epigraph for *The Love Hunter* is from Shakespeare's *Othello*: "That death's unnatural that kills for loving." How does this fit in with the theme and story of the novel?

A. Well, of course, Chris intends to kill Larry because he loves Rachel and yet, it's an unnatural sort of death.

Q. *The Love Hunter* concludes: "For too long, as a safeguard against disappointment, he [Chris] had been wary of life, had kept his distance from it, had been entering it and leaving it like a bit player with stage fright. But now, with Rachel, he saw the possibility of stepping out of the wings and embracing it again. So much depended on what role she would choose for herself. What role for him. What play." Shakespeare and theatre figure prominently in *The Love Hunter*. Could the theme partially be the famous quote from *As You Like It*: "All the world's a stage, / And all the men and women merely players"?

A. Yes, that seemed to make sense to me at the time.

Q. Why did you pick *Twelfth Night* as Rachel's play for the Rookery Playhouse?

A. Because I had recently seen it in Brainerd directed by our colleague Robert Dryden. I loved it so much I'd thought it would work as a play in the book.

Q. Is Larry's mental breakdown at the opening night of *Twelfth Night* all imagination? It's very convincingly written.

A. Yes, that was before I knew anybody who had psychosis like that, actually. But his son Bruce is playing Feste. He gets confused as he sees his son on the stage.

Q. I had to read Feste's song in Act IV of *Twelfth Night* to be sure that the line, "Pare thy nails, Dad," was accurate. It is. That fit in perfectly with Larry's deterioration. Was it difficult to have all of this coalesce in this scene?

A. I don't remember that as difficult at all. It seemed to fit right in. Each part—the play and then real-life drama.

Q. You had mentioned yesterday something about Bruce and the origins of him and his Christian singing group. I was wondering if you could comment on that?

A. That's based on a group that my son Mike was in with Guy Doud, who was a theatre director and actor for a while from Brainerd. They were in this Christian group; I went to a couple of their concerts, so I understood that mentality—as far as the songs they sang.

Q. While I was typing these questions, I suddenly realized that the whole novel is based on theatre. Not only do I mean the obvious setting of Rachel and the Playhouse, but Blackie's camp is pure theatre. Blackie is the director, costumes are worn (rubber ponchos, camouflage clothing), props are used, the hunters recite their well-rehearsed yearly hunting stories for the script, even the plumber's son could be Feste, and Blackie orchestrates everything.

A. You outdo yourself as a literary critic, Joseph.

Q. Mrs. LaVoi keeps talking about the comic relief in life. What is the comic relief in *The Love Hunter* in your view?

A. Well, the characters up there at that hunting camp I thought they'd be funny if they weren't so tragic. There was a young woman, Poo Poo, who worked there, Larry called her Knockers of the North. And then there were the hunters themselves who were such braggarts—I got such a kick out of them and they were so macho— they bragged all the time. There was a pecking order at the camp, you see; when you were at the top, you knew Blackie the longest. Chris, having gone up there for the first time, was at the bottom of the pecking order.

Q. Were Jon and David at the bottom of the pecking order in the actual camp?

A. Yes, we were, along with my friend Chuck Pettit, who went up there with us.

Q. Simon Shea from *Simon's Night* shows up twice (177, 201). I was glad about that. Is this device used to help connect the novels with each other?

A. Yes, I thought I'd put Simon in there in a walk-on part. It's fun to do that. In the novel I'm working on now [*The Staggerford Flood*], I have a character from each one of the novels who comes in and out.

Q. I think the readers enjoy that, too. Chris listened to *Grand Central*

*Station* when he was a boy, and, obviously, so did you. This was one of my favorite radio programs; it helped whet my appetite for New York.

A. I'm sure it did. It was on around noon on Saturday, wasn't it? I remember the musical theme. I remember the advertising. They'd say, "You're on the right track with Pillsbury pancake flour."

Q. I didn't remember that. But I remember the program well—GRAND CENTRAL STATION. Rachel on page 159 shares how she feels when she had "an absolutely brilliant rehearsal," and everything came together. Is this how you felt when you conducted a really good class or when you write three or four hundred usable words of fiction?

A. Of course, it's the same thing. "Grand Central Station. You're on the right track with Pillsbury pancake flour." (laughter from both)

Q. Rachel continues with her enthusiasm on page 183, telling about her work:

> You know what's so fascinating about plays, Chris? It's making harmony out of chaos. You start with a bunch of mismatched actors and an empty stage and an auditorium with five hundred empty seats and a mess of threadbare props and costumes and this impossible deadline and you go to work—and suddenly it's opening night, and if you've done your job, everything comes together, including the audience.

Could this be what writing a novel is?

A. It certainly is—it's just like that. How about *Let's Pretend*, Joe? Did you listen to *Let's Pretend*? That was wonderful. "Cream of Wheat is so good to eat we have it every day."

Q. That also was Saturday morning radio. I think we listened to the same weekend programs. And then I think *Blondie* was Sunday night. It's fun to talk about our radio listening, but I guess we need to return to *The Love Hunter*. Rachel's enthusiasm for theatre, when everything comes together, is this mystique part of what drew you to writing for the theatre?

A. I guess it was. It was about then that I started to write *Simon's Night* for the stage.

Q. *The Love Hunter* begins on October 4, 1979, the third in a row for a fall setting. Is this just coincidence?

A. I guess it is, although this had to be fall because of hunting season.

Q. Your novel is peppered with memorable patches of writing and gripping scenes. One well-written (and humorous) scene concerns Bernard Beckwith and his CB handle, Saint Bernard; he gave the wrong directions to about thirty truckers who sat "bumper to bumper in the wilderness with the nearest crossroad for turning around three miles behind them" (293-295). This provided a great catharsis of laughter for dying Larry, Chris, Rachel, and Bruce [Larry and Rachel's son]. How did the germ of this scene come about?

A. That happened in Staples one time. A guy on a CB sent a whole bunch of trucks along a road because of smoke across the highway— there were fires then, so he sent out this general alarm to truckers coming through town. They all turned north—they went on a different road, and they came to an unpassable bridge. And they were stuck there. I don't know if the bridge was out or if it was too weak to hold a big truck. It took a long time to get straightened out.

Q. Chapter 6 contains another vivid episode, the brutal storm, in which you employ superb description and action, almost like a movie screenplay; the reader can follow well what is happening to all of the principals. Did such scenes require extensive plotting and rewriting?

A. No, they didn't. I remember how fast I wrote that scene. I remember how it went—the culminating scene often does. I remember I worried about the poet's visit to Rookery State in *The Dean's List*, and yet when the time came to write it, his presentation in the auditorium, it came off without a hitch. It must be because I'd been preparing all the way for it.

Q. Your writing style continues to impress me. Karl Molstad, a former student of mine, reviewed *The Love Hunter* for the *Minnesota Daily* (July 24, 1981): "Hassler's writing never becomes chaotic. It has, rather, an exquisite shapeliness. Individual sentences and paragraphs show a meticulous craftsmanship." There are so many examples that I would like to quote, but I'll limit these to two. "The sun was high enough now to warm the air; soft breezes moved back and forth over the water. Along the far shore of the lagoon each wavelet was a chip of silver, each blade of swamp grass a stalk of gold" (135). The other is found on page 147: "The duck, absorbing the nine shots, spun and sank and came up again, dead. Its downy gray underside lay stonelike on the roiling water; one of its feet stood up like a flower on a short stalk—a flat, webbed foot slowly contracting like a blossom going shut." I believe that you have something to add about this last description.

A. Oh, yes, there's a printer from Minneapolis who wanted to print that passage and did, on a broadsheet. I have that framed upstairs on the wall. He thought that was a good description of a duck.

Q. Do you have any favorite passages in *The Love Hunter*, either in what you wrote or what you conveyed?

A. Like you, I admired the storm scene and the two men surviving that. I remember writing that and I remember being thrilled by it as I wrote.

Q. On page 132 you included a passage which made me think of *Simon's Night*. Chris and Larry are following Blackie through the tall swamp grass. Larry asks, "He's leading us into the underworld, isn't he?" And shortly thereafter, Larry continues: "He's leading us down to the river of forgetfulness." Of course, in Greek mythology, the Lethe is the river in Hades producing forgetfulness. Simon spent time in the Olympus Mall which seemed to be hell or Hades before he experienced a resurrection. Christ, after His crucifixion, descended into hell for three days. And Larry and Chris are on a three day trip to Hades or hell—lodgings, food, weather all are horrid. And then this experience renews Larry; he experiences a resurrection to life for at least a time. What is your comment about all of this?

A. I've often thought of *The Love Hunter*, even though there aren't any priests or nuns in it, as my most Catholic novel, my most Christian novel, and the idea of three days in hell and then resurrection was certainly part of my thinking as I went into this book.

**Q. And then you mention the protagonist's name—Chris.**

A. Yes, there were a number of Christian symbols in this book including Chris's name. I don't remember what else there was at the present time. But I remember thinking it as I wrote it.

**Q. Before we get to the critics, what would you say that the theme or overall meaning of *The Love Hunter* is.**

A. Well, it's the resilience of the human spirit, I think, and how Larry comes back—the resilience of love and the importance of love in life. You know the way in all my novels how somebody goes through a bad time and comes out the other end—except Miles Pruitt, of course—resurrected, more or less.

**Q. Bart Sutter winds up his *Minneapolis Tribune* review (June 28, 1981) with this accolade: "Already a better stylist than either Sherwood Anderson or Sinclair Lewis, Hassler, if he continues to improve and to produce at the pace he's set so far, may finally furnish us with a shelf of fiction more valuable than the collected works of either of those earlier Midwestern authors." I guess you can live with that review.**

A. Yes, you see that's the sort of review I believe.

**Q. I don't blame you. Amazing—when Ballantine published *The Love Hunter* in paperback in 1988, the *New York Times Book Review* included it in the weekly column "New & Noteworthy." Is this the only time that one of your novels, either hardcover or paperback, made it in "New & Noteworthy"?**

A. It is, it's the only time. [The paperback of *North of Hope* was also included in the "New & Noteworthy" section in the November 24, 1991, issue of the *New York Times Book Review*.]

Q. And now comes the jackpot—and the most famous quote from any critic of your work. Randolph Hogan, a member of the cultural news staff of the *New York Times*, reviewed *The Love Hunter* in the August 16, 1981, issue of the *New York Times Book Review*. The first sentence is plastered on most of your paperback editions, and the rest of the first paragraph is pretty good, too.

> *Jon Hassler is a writer good enough to restore your faith in fiction. Unlike so many contemporary writers, he creates characters you come to care about and believe in. His subjects are life, love and death—what the best novels have always been about—and he writes with wisdom and grace. His third novel (the previous two,* Staggerford *and* Simon's Night, *received high praise) is the kind of book that makes you want to buttonhole someone and say, 'Read this.'*

I suppose that you were almost tempted to give up writing after this; it's hard to surpass such praise and from the *New York Times*!

A. Yes, that was very gratifying. Also, I've said more than once that on my tombstone is going to be the sentence, "He's a writer good enough to restore your faith in fiction." That's been repeated so much it's memorialized.

Q. And it's become part of the Jon Hassler lore. Does *The Love Hunter* still hold up for you?

A. Yes, very much. I was reading it the other day. I dipped into it and read passages; it seemed very good to me.

Q. Have there been any other movie nibbles, or is this novel pretty well dead in regard to the film world because of Redford's purchase?

A. Every once in a while somebody comes to me and wants to film the book, and I say you have to get it from TriStar Studios, and they check in and they find it's too expensive and they drop it. So they're having other nibbles, but nobody's interested.

**Q. Would you explain the expense?**

A. Well, Redford paid quite a bit for screenwriting. He had Scott Spencer write two drafts. I guess he had other people write drafts; I don't know who they were, so he wants to get all his money back for that.

**Q. Thank you, Jon, for providing your many readers, including me, with an astonishingly good read. It holds up as well this time, too.**

A. Glad to hear that, Joe. It's a pleasure talking to you.

# A Green Journey

I'm sure that Jon had no idea, when he created Agatha McGee as
a supporting character in *Staggerford*, that she would capture not
only his imagination but also that of countless readers. Yet Miss
McGee became the protagonist in four of Jon's subsequent novels
beginning with *A Green Journey*. And she also became an alter ego
for Jon himself.

In an article by James Engel in the *St. Cloud Visitor*, a Catholic
newspaper, dated August 8, 1985, Jon is quoted as saying: "Nobody
was troubled by the changes in the Church (during Vatican II) like
I was. Boy, did I fight against them." In *A Green Journey*, Agatha
McGee became his stand-in in this struggle. "'It was amazing the
change that came over me when I got her as a substitute for myself.
As she did the fighting, I didn't have to anymore," Hassler said.

Whatever the origins of Agatha's personality, she certainly out-
grows the somewhat rigid constraints of a small-town Catholic
grade school teacher. Her forthrightness coupled with her concern
makes her a very human and believable person. Agatha does possess a heart; her isolation even in her beloved Staggerford creates
a loneliness, an unfulfillment. And when she writes to, and then
meets, James, she lowers her barriers, risking the hurts and disappointments by not being in control.

In an article by Dave Wood, who was then the book editor of the
*Minneapolis Tribune* (January 13, 1985), Jon said:

> I write every morning until my mind gives out, which is usually
> at lunch. That time includes a lot of coffee, looking out the window,
> reading my journals. I don't plot my novels ahead of time. I let the plot
> discover itself. I try to put two or three characters in an unstable situa-
> tion and go from there.

In this novel the two or three characters "in an unstable situation"
would certainly include Agatha and James and perhaps Bishop Baker.

All three become intertwined, none knowing the final outcome. Agatha is unstable in relationships with both James and the Bishop, especially after finding out that James is a priest. Her whole emotional framework has been shattered. Also, she isn't sure about trying to save St. Isidore's and "working" for the Bishop. James, astonished that Agatha flew to Ireland, dreads Agatha's learning the truth; when she does, his situation with both Agatha and the American bishop is in jeopardy. And Bishop Baker, always uncomfortable with Agatha, finds himself in the middle of this. Not one of the three is in charge of what's happening or even comfortable with the events.

Jon strikes a universality with these characters. Though *A Green Journey* is one of his more Catholic novels, one doesn't have to be Catholic—or live in Minnesota—to appreciate the conflicts and challenges confronting each person. Dave Wood makes this point in the article cited earlier: "It rings true, this novel of small but important people concerned with their small but important concerns who behave in pretty much the same way people would almost anywhere on this big green earth." These concerns just happen to be Catholic in *A Green Journey*. Agatha, James, and the Bishop, although united in faith, struggle with that faith and themselves. For Agatha, can she allow a blueprint for her life different from what she had envisioned and desired? She loves James as a man, as a kindred spirit; will she be able to accept James as a man and as a priest? Will she learn to accept the Bishop as a person and not as an enemy, the embodiment of all that she distrusts and even fears? Since Agatha is the protagonist of *A Green Journey*, the onus is on her to change, to grow, somehow to forge a positive relationship with both of these men of God. She accepts a temporary truce with the Bishop, accepting the position of principal at St. Isidore's while knowing full well that her precious school is on the Bishop's "hit list" for closing.

Agatha's resolution regarding James is more oblique and uncertain. As with many of Jon's characters, Agatha, after enduring her biggest crisis in life, chooses living; life will not defeat her. The reader is less sure about what direction James and the Bishop will take after their seismic experience. We can be grateful that Jon resurrects all three for *Dear James*.

A fan of Jon's writing, a former Latin teacher and a Lutheran, wrote a letter to "Miss McGee" dated February 7, 1997:

*Since you don't know me as I haven't lived in Staggerford, I won't be informal in my address and call you by your first name; however, I've known you for many years beginning with your having Miles Pruitt as a roomer in your home. I suffered with you when you went to Ireland; I loved its blues and greens, the skies, the Ocean, the people when I myself went to that interesting country. I liked meeting dear James and have cherished your relationship. . . .*

*Why am I writing to you? Because I love Jon Hassler's writing and I have just reread all except* North of Hope, *which will be my next re-reading pleasure.*

*When I first read* Grand Opening *I kept wondering what I was missing. It was you, of course, Miss McGee.*

I thought this to be a really fine example of Agatha's effect (and, of course, Jon's) on readers. Jon's characters become real and none more so than Agatha. They live and breathe, and we, the readers, are privy to their thoughts, doubts, beliefs, successes, and failures. We are pleased when they reappear in subsequent Hassler novels. They are old friends, and we are eager to see what has been happening in their lives.

Jon uses Agatha to write letters to the Twin Cities newspapers regarding his health, particularly his Parkinsonian disease [later diagnosed as Progressive Supranuclear Palsy] and this is what is referred to. I think that using this oblique manner to talk about his health is a wonderful literary device. People who are concerned know what is happening, yet the information isn't presented in a mawkish manner. I would like to quote further from the fan's letter.

*I'm pleased the Mpls.* Star Tribune *published your letter. It is important to Hassler readers to know how he is.*

*With you, Agatha (if I dare) he will keep his sense of humor and perhaps have another of God's putting him at ease when he needs that. Of course, he's never known, he says, God to be a nagger.*

*Keep walking with your dear friend. We all need you and him.* I add "Amen."

- J. P. August 2002

*October 28, 2000*

Q. Good morning, Jon. It's a Saturday, and again we're meeting at your Minneapolis home. *A Green Journey*, published by Morrow, came out in 1985. Up to now, you had a novel published every two years, *Staggerford* (1977), *Simon's Night* (1979), and *The Love Hunter* (1981). What happened?

A. In the early '80s I was writing "The Book of Brendan," but it didn't succeed as a novel, so I put it away and wrote *A Green Journey*. I remember I'd moved to Saint John's at that point, and when *A Green Journey* came out, one of the monks said, "Gee, we thought you had taken on Powers's [J. F. Powers] silent ways."

Q. You had been working on this novel for some time. A postcard from Albuquerque [NM] postmarked January 14, 1983, says: "Working a little each day on Green Journey—150 pp. will go to NY in March."

A. I remember that's about where it started, I think, in Albuquerque. I might have written some of it at Saint John's before I went to Albuquerque. I spent a month down there, the month of January 1983, with my cousin Ellen. That's when I wrote a lot of it.

Q. Did you have the same team, Harriet Wasserman as agent and Harvey Ginsberg as editor, for *A Green Journey*?

A. Yes.

Q. I remember your saying that Harvey was not as enthusiastic about this follow-up novel as he had been about *The Love Hunter*.

A. No, he didn't like it as much because it didn't have as much, oh, I don't know, didn't have as much dirt in it. He told me after *Grand Opening*, "Nobody wants to read about a seventy-year-old woman or a twelve-year-old boy." I didn't know that, see—and he told me that after *Grand Opening*, but I proved that people wanted to read about Agatha McGee. Now she's eighty and they still want to read about her, they say.

Q. Yet, in a letter he had written you, dated April 6, 1983, at least initially, he was very polite and positive. He writes, "I am delighted we are back in business again and even more delighted that it is with a novel that everyone is enthusiastic about." He does have almost two pages of suggestions and questions, but he signs off with "Forgive me if I have gone on at length. I can only hope you may find some of what I've written helpful instead of intrusive. In any case, Agatha is a great creation and we both want to do her justice."

A. See, I think he forgot that he liked the book when he told me that not a lot of people liked to read about a seventy-year-old woman. I think he liked it just fine when it came out.

Q. What was Harriet's reaction to *A Green Journey*?

A. Harriet, of course, loved it. She's always been on my side. She loves everything I write.

Q. You had dedicated your first novel, *Staggerford*, to your parents. *A Green Journey* bears this inscription: "To my mother Ellen Callinan Hassler / And to the memory of my father Leo B. Hassler 1896-1984." Why did you decide to dedicate a second novel to your parents?

A. I remember I worked on this novel at my father's deathbed, so I decided that he needed more recognition. I wanted it for my mother also, so I dedicated it to them. I guess it was his death that brought that to mind more than anything.

Q. You also acknowledge the John Simon Guggenheim Foundation "for the generous award of a fellowship in connection with this work." Had you submitted parts of this novel with your application, or did the fellowship enable you to devote full-time to writing it?

A. I had submitted *Simon's Night* to the Guggenheim board and they liked it a lot, and they gave me $20,000, which at that point was a year's salary, so I took a year off, went to Saint John's in 1980. I stayed and never went home again, I liked it so much there. So it changed my life—that Guggenheim award.

**Q. Did you have any tentative titles before you chose the final one?**

A. I thought I should call it *Irish Light*, but Harriet, my agent, said, "It sounds like a lite beer."

**Q. You chose another pertinent epigraph for *A Green Journey*: "Things throw light on things, / And all the stones have wings" by Theodore Roethke. I'll ask you later what this means in relation to the novel, but my question now is: why didn't you choose epigraphs for the five subsequent novels? The first four had superb ones.**

A. I remember looking for epigraphs for the next couple novels, but it seemed like nothing was quite a fit, so I gave up because it seemed so contrived.

**Q. I believe that a couple of chapters from *A Green Journey* appeared first as short stories in *McCall's*. Would you elaborate?**

A. The short story, "The Holy War of Agatha McGee," did appear in *McCall's*, and then they printed "The Midnight Vigil of Agatha McGee." That story had been the origin of this book actually. I wrote that before I wrote the book. So *McCall's* had two short stories about Agatha McGee. I sent a third one that they never did print, which is in my latest *Rufus at the Door* collection, called "Agatha McGee and the St. Isidore Seven."

**Q. Please discuss the evolution and transformation of Miss McGee from a secondary character in *Staggerford* to the protagonist in *A Green Journey*.**

A. Well, she's been with me so long, she's sort of an alter ego for me. She was formerly known as Miss McGee in *Staggerford*. Then I got to know her better, when I went over to *A Green Journey*, so I began to call her Agatha. Not many people do, but I had to. She's been on my mind a lot because she's so much like my mother, I think. Also a maiden aunt I had who used to teach school. Also myself—she's partly myself, and she's the conservative side of me which permits me to go ahead and be more liberal because she's taking care of the conservative issues for me these days.

Q. Francis Raft tells Agatha, "If I'm ever in doubt about how much credit to give a thing, I always give it more, to be on the safe side. . . . And you, Miss McGee, you always give it less, ain't I right?" (44). Is this consistent with your models for Agatha?

A. It sure is, yes, she's always been very strict. She expects a lot from people, and when they fail her, she flunks them.

Q. Also, could this be part of the meaning of *A Green Journey*, i.e., Agatha is forced to give something—or someone—more credit than less?

A. Yes, it was my purpose to present her with a problem that was bigger than herself. That's why I had her fall in love at the age of sixty-eight for the first time in her life because I wanted to test her and see how far she'd go.

Q. And in line with that, things and people are no longer looked at as only black or only white from Agatha's point of view.

A. That's right, she had learning to do, you see. I think I wanted to educate my mother, too, in writing this book. I think it was an attempt to get my mother to do the same thing.

Q. Why do readers like Agatha, do you think? I know that they do.

A. I sometimes think it's because of this world where so much is ambiguous. Agatha is so definite about things. They like definiteness, and they don't mind the strictness on her part as it's only fictional. They think she's quite a character.

Q. I'm sure that part of Agatha's appeal is her no-nonsense approach to life as you indicated. A young farmer named Preston Warner had asked her to marry him in 1938. "'But I can't marry a farmer,' she had told him at the annual Grange picnic the summer she was twenty-five, and along with Preston Warner she rejected a house, a barn, a herd of Guernseys and a hundred acres of fertile soil. 'I was born to teach, not to churn,' she had said, not realizing that he was her last chance, though it's doubtful that realizing it would have changed her mind. She loved classrooms. Barns made her sneeze" (18). In two sentences you summed up the pro and con of Agatha's marrying Preston.

A. Yes, I always thought that was an interesting relationship, although it doesn't have much in it. Later in the book she sees him on the street. He's sitting in his car watching people go by. I guess he remained single the rest of his life as she did.

Q. In fact, that was my very next question. As a pathetic postscript on pages 151 and 152, we meet Preston again: "These days Preston Warner ... devoted his life to nothing more than sitting in his car on Main Street and watching people walk by. Every day, empty-eyed and emaciated, he drove into town ... and sat motionless and stone-faced behind the wheel ... Very little of what he watched registered in his mind—you could see that through the windshield when you walked past his car and tried to engage his eyes and failed." Is Preston in this condition because of Agatha's refusal of marriage many, many years ago, or is this an inevitable end for him, regardless of being married or not?

A. I don't think it had anything to do with Agatha's rejection of him. It's just the way he turned out. Then, when she sees him, of course, she doesn't regret turning him down. It's based on a guy in Plainview I used to see who would do that very thing. He'd drive to town and look at people walk by.

Q. How did you decide on this name, Agatha McGee?

A. Well, as I said before, I needed an Irish name because Irish names inspire me. Agatha was old-fashioned, and McGee seemed to be, and I hadn't heard of a McGee since Fibber McGee. I figured people wouldn't know about him very much anymore, a radio personality in the 1940's, so I went with Agatha McGee.

Q. Ah, yes, Fibber McGee and Molly. On page 151 Agatha learns that her surname McGee is derived from the word *gaoth* or *wind*. Is there any symbolic meaning in her name to help explain her character?

A. Well, I tried to make it symbolic, but you know, when I went to Ireland in 1981, I decided I'd go to the records and look up the Hassler or Callinan name, my mother's Irish name, and instead I didn't do that—I looked up Agatha's name. That's what it said, and so that's why I used that. She's a force of nature, though, like the wind, I think.

Q. Upon learning that the Bishop no longer will visit individual parishes for confirmation, Agatha arranges to have twelve confirmands with their parents and sponsors travel to the Bishop's residence in Berrington for their confirmation. How much of this is based on fact?

A. A similar event took place in the Duluth diocese when I lived in Brainerd. The Bishop in Duluth decided that he wouldn't confirm kids until they asked for it—I thought that was foolish, and so I threatened to take my daughter, who was an eighth grader at that point, up to Duluth, and I guess a lot of parents objected because he did send his representative to Brainerd to confirm them.

Q. By the way, what Minnesota town or city is Berrington based on, Duluth?

A. I think Berrington is more like Bemidji. Berrington and Rookery are both combinations of Bemidji, I think.

Q. "For a hundred years the diocese of Berrington had been blessed with a trickle of priests from Ireland, three or four every decade, but now with the worldwide shortage of seminarians this foreign supply was drying up." Is this observation based on the Duluth diocese? You had lived in the Duluth diocese for twelve years when you lived in Brainerd.

A. That's right, and Brainerd always had a pastor from Ireland, and there were several of them in the diocese, I know. The pastor in Brainerd began to bemoan the fact that they started not coming any more, so I knew that was a fact.

Q. "Hardscrabble girls. That was Agatha's term for the daughters of improvident or missing parents who lived on the stony farms in the forest north of town" (41). This refers to Janet Raft, but it could equally apply to Beverly Bingham from *Staggerford*. Is this an actual word, or did you make it up?

A. Hardscrabble is a word actually—I have heard it a number of times. Also, I keep writing about that girl. And although she changes her name, she's Laura Connor [*Rookery Blues*, *The Dean's List*] later and she was Jemmy Stott [*Jemmy*] earlier.

Q. Janet's first boyfriend, Eddie, the father of Stephen, was stationed at the air base. Beverly Bingham [*Staggerford*] talked about Gary Olson and his air force uniform. Does a man in uniform in your novels signify a kind of escape for these young women in small towns, a one-way ticket out?

A. Yes, it proved to be that for Beverly. She married Gary Olson, and he took her as far as Australia. Agatha used to get postcards from her from Australia. Then she divorced him in my current book. She was divorced a second time in my current book, actually [*The Staggerford Flood*].

Q. Where did Randy come from, observation or imagination, or a combination?

A. I suppose it's a combination like all my characters, except I remember that I really let my imagination run with him, and I was very pleased with him. He was such a loser.

Q. "Randy liked beer. Beer lowered his spirits. He had come dangerously close to being happy this evening" (107). That seems an excellent psychological observation. Is this based on a person or people that you've known?

A. I don't remember. All I know is that it's Randy.

Q. Your editor Harvey Ginsberg had misgivings about Randy. "Right at the head of that list is wanting to know how I, the reader, am supposed to feel about Randy. I think he's a jerk; Harriet, kinder by far than I, thinks he's sympathetic. For example, she thinks the scene with Eugene

Westerman is touching as well as comic. I think it's wonderful and comic but, again if this were a movie, Randy would be Andy Devine, the strictly comic sidekick, and no kind of romantic interest at all. If I'm right, are we supposed to want Janet to go back to him?" Comments?

A. Well, he forgets how much Janet loved him, and he was from a wealthy family, had a great singing voice. He'd pick up the microphone, and he'd sing at this awful night club they were in. He was romantic, so Harvey never understood that side of him. And it's like my editor Bob Wyatt later with *Dear James*. He never liked French. He kept saying, he's such a low life.

Q. Yet Randy is the one that provided her rescue from being a hardscrabble woman. You and I had a meal at the restaurant near Park Rapids that served as a model for the Brass Fox. It was a hamburger place, and I believe you pointed out the table that Randy would usually sit at.

A. Yes, it was called Paulette's. It was out in the country north of Park Rapids.

Q. Agatha and James really meet through the Catholic weekly, *The Fortress*. Is this a code name for *The Wanderer* in St. Paul?

A. Yes. *The Wanderer* is a very conservative Catholic newspaper—it's been published in St. Paul for a hundred years. And *The Fortress* was that type.

Q. I remember when we first met at Brainerd Community College, you asked me if I knew about *The Wanderer*, and I said it wasn't my favorite newspaper, and you said it was yours. I think that little exchange postponed our friendship for a couple years.

A. That said so much about us in those days. Your liberal leanings and my conservative leanings.

Q. Now on to Ireland—you and I had gone to England and Ireland during the summer of 1976. How many other times, approximately, have you been to Ireland?

A. I've been there seven more times. I think I was there twice more before I began to write *A Green Journey*.

Q. I have never flown, nor been, to Shannon. Is the airport adjacent to a pasture as it is in *A Green Journey*?

A. It is. The first Irish beings you see are cows as the plane lands.

Q. The Bishop brought with him (and buys another one on this trip) a penny whistle. Didn't you buy one in Ireland? I remember hearing you play some tunes on it at your Nevis cabin.

A. Yes, I did.

Q. The Plunketts' B & B in Knob reminds me of the O'Connors' B & B that we stayed at in Dingle. Did our B & B help provide the atmosphere and characterization for the Plunketts and their B & B?

A. Yes, it did—particularly the husband of the woman who ran the place.

Q. I remember that you thought our Mr. O'Connor looked like Percy Kilbride, the Pa Kettle of the Ma and Pa Kettle movies. Then Mr. Plunkett's first name is Percy. Is that the reason?

A. I guess it is.

Q. The Bishop and Agatha drive through the Wicklow Hills to the valley of Glendelough [Glendelack for pronunciation]. Jon, we had done the same trip, hadn't we?

A. That was a wonderful trip. That was our first time out of the city of Dublin. That was where we saw the magnificent Irish countryside for the first time.

Q. Chapters 20 and 22 fascinate the reader with comparisons and contrasts of the two men of God, the bishop and James, and the climax of their time together with both needing their stomachs pumped provides hilarity, all because of the supposed death of the cat, Lady Wellington.

Afterwards, James discovers the truth, that Lady Wellington had given birth to four kittens. C. W. Truesdale in his long analysis, "On the Novels of Jon Hassler" (September 1994 issue of *South Dakota Review*), labels this scene "a comic masterpiece," and I agree. Had you heard this story in some form, or did you create it?

A. I heard this story when I first moved to Saint John's. My friend Lee Hanley told it to me about a monk in the Abbey who was out on parish duty. He picked mushrooms and served them to two friends who came to dinner, but the friends were leery of eating them, so they fed some to the cat with butter. The cat then stiffened up and looked dead, so the three monks got in the car and they went to the St. Cloud Hospital, had their stomachs pumped, and then they went back and they discovered that the cat had given birth to kittens. And that was the source of the episode in the book.

Q. We probably shouldn't be doing these interviews. Your stature as a novelist will be lowered a few notches when the reader learns that Mrs. Welp's leg from *Simon's Night* and this incident are from real life. Paintings again play a rather important role in your characters' lives. I am thinking particularly of Brueghel's *Peasant Wedding*. I assume that you had viewed this at the National Gallery in Dublin?

A. Yes, I did.

Q. Would you explain in greater detail the meaning of the painting in relation to the meaning of the novel? James is struck by its depiction of life.

A. Yes, there's a party going on among the peasants. It's a rollicking day—they're picnicking, they're dancing, they're kissing, they're eating—they're having a great time under the autumn trees, and James points this out to Agatha—he loves the life here. And she finds it too chaotic for her own taste. This points out the difference between them.

Q. And also the fact that neither of them has a life such as depicted in the painting. I discovered in my *A Green Journey* file folder a Teacher's

**Guide you had prepared for Ballantine Books. How did this come about?**

A. I guess they decided to sell this to high schools and asked me to write a Teacher's Guide. I made a very complete description of the plot—much too complete, much too long for their purposes, I think, although they printed it.

Q. **Have you written any additional teacher's guides for any of your other novels?**

A. No, I was never asked to write another one.

Q. **In this Guide you include passages from your journals, written during your visits to Ireland. I would like to quote one: "I find a Last Supper by a painter I never heard of. It's more human than Leonardo's. It's huge. I sit before it quite a while studying the apostles. I count only 11. I search for the 12th and find the hint of a face in the upper right corner. Is this Judas and is he all but rubbed out by reason of his intended betrayal?" This painting shows up in** *A Green Journey* **(150):**

> *Their [Agatha and James's] last stop was in a mammoth room containing a mammoth Last Supper painted by someone Agatha had never heard of. There was a bench before it, and they sat. She studied Christ. He was intent on the bread he was breaking. . . . She felt a sudden desire to attend Mass with James. Tomorrow was Sunday. But she didn't bring it up, and she didn't know why she didn't bring it up. Her eyes roamed over the faces. She counted them.*
> *'James, why are there only eleven?'*
> *'Eleven? I hadn't noticed.'*
> *They counted together.*
> *'Look.' She found the hint of a face in the upper right corner, a man standing behind the others. 'Is that Judas, do you suppose?'*
> *'Yes, indeed, all but erased by reason of the betrayal he's planning. I never noticed him before.'*
> *Because the painting was not brightly lit, the face was hard to hold in view.*

Undoubtedly the hint of Judas's face suggests James's imminent (the next day) betrayal of Agatha's trust in him when she learns that he is a priest.

A. That's very good, Joseph. I don't know if I knew that at the time because I remember viewing the picture just as I described it.

Q. **But it is in there then, isn't it? That works very well. Now for the longest question thus far of our interviews, I would like to quote another of your journal entries from the Guide:**

> I get off the bus on a narrow, steep street and find my way to a pier curving out into the sea. I sit on a bench and make a sketchy sketch of the high rocky coast that bends around to the east. It isn't a very satisfactory sketch. With a quick stroke of my pen I place a gull above the outermost point of land, and it's better. For a reason I don't understand the gull puts the whole sketch into perspective, gives it dimension it didn't otherwise have. Have I hit upon some principle of art that says we ought to provide the viewer with some slight distraction from the core of the work and give the subject, by contrast, clearer definition?

This, too, has its counterpart in the novel (188-189):

> Taking the tablet from Janet, Agatha coiled herself into her sketching posture, crossing her legs and sitting forward over the tablet on her knee. She uncapped her pen and faced off to her right, away from Janet. Her head bobbed, eyes up, eyes down, as she began drawing a rocky headland in the distance. . . .
>
> They said no more for a time. Agatha completed her drawing. She held it at arm's length.
>
> 'It isn't very good, is it, Janet? The cliffs haven't any depth to them. That was always my problem, I could never achieve the illusion of the third dimension.'
>
> 'I see what you mean.' Janet took the tablet and pen and with an impulsive stroke she put a gliding gull high in the sky over the headland.
>
> Suddenly the sketch was better. The bird for some reason gave depth to the scene. She looked at Agatha, who nodded.

> *'Now answer me this, Janet: Why should that bird make such a difference? It's only a tiny scratch of ink. It draws the eye away from the land, and yet it improves the looks of the land. How can that be?'*
>
> *Janet handed back the tablet. 'I don't know, but it sure helps.'*
>
> *Agatha wondered if there was an artistic principle about providing the viewer with some distraction in order for the core of the work to come into focus. She recalled the tantalizing, elusive image of Judas in the Last Supper painting, drawing the eye away from Christ while heightening the drama that Christ was at the center of. In the night sky didn't you see a dim star better if you looked slightly to one side of it? In the past four years hadn't she come to a fuller understanding of her own life by concentrating on the life of James O'Hannon?*

I find this fascinating, and I'm sure our readers will, too, reading your journal entry and then reading the fictional equivalent. Artists often in the past had a role similar to priests and prophets, and in this definition of your role as writer, we have witnessed a kind of literary alchemy—changing your real life journals into their fictional manifestation. Is this one of your literary trademarks, searching through journals for what would be the appropriate response or action or thoughts for a certain character in a certain situation?

A. Yes, I draw a lot on my journals although I don't do it with characters in mind. I do it between novels before I begin a novel, but I set aside passages that I think will work. And then when I come to them, I put them in the book.

Q. The passage just quoted leads directly to the use of your epigraph from Theodore Roethke: "Things throw light on things, / And all the stones have wings." I'll quote again the last line from the previous quote: "In the past four years hadn't she come to a fuller understanding of her own life by concentrating on the life of James O'Hannon?"

> *'Things throw light on things,' she said.*
>
> *'And all the stones have wings,' Janet replied automatically. (189)*

Jon, would you please explicate this quote and its relation to the theme and meaning of *A Green Journey*?

A. Yes, I guess she'd been living a very isolated life, you know. She got out and she saw what it was like elsewhere. She went to Ireland. She opened up horizons, and she began to understand herself better. So the things she saw threw light on her own life. I think that's what the poem means—one thing throws light on the other by comparison. And then all the stones have wings. Of course, that has application later when Janet sees what she thinks are stones get up from the beach and fly away because they're gulls.

Q. In your next novel, *Grand Opening*, you include a character Rufus that is an idiot ("a person deficient in mind and permanently incapable of rational conduct"). In this novel Agatha encounters an idiot girl. Brendan is twelve when he meets Rufus, and Agatha is nine. Do these characters somehow imply the unexpected, unknowable, unconventional, extraordinary, even the mystical in life? Both Rufus and the girl impact the lives of Brendan and Agatha.

A. That's right. I remember the experience of my own youth when I witnessed the Dickman girl in her house in Plainview. And Rufus went uptown a lot with his mother; his name wasn't Rufus—it was Clarence. Anyway, I remember what an impact it had on me to see both of them. And I remember Agatha going away from the site wondering about God and her place in life and things like that.

Q. Seeing the Quimby idiot girl introduced Agatha to chaos for the first time in her life. Is chaos something incomprehensible, out of one's control, in a sense? After seeing James in his priestly vestments for the 11:30 A.M. Mass at Ballybegs, Agatha's mind returns to her first encounter with irrational chaos, almost the horror of life.

A. Yes, she doesn't know what to do with chaos—it doesn't make any sense to her. She's been going through life making sense of things, and this doesn't make any sense to her at all.

Q. The reader gets two footnotes, in a sense, about Miles and Beverly from *Staggerford* (155-156 and 244-245). Also, Simon Shea made two brief appearances in your previous novel *The Love Hunter*. Here, however, the characters are more organic to the novel. In the first one Agatha relates to James the whole episode about Miles, and I suppose this foreshadows her second major blow in her life when she learns that James is a priest. The second incident reinforces this; she tells the story about Miles's death to the Bishop, and he realizes that more is being said than appears on the surface: "When she finished, she lifted her eyes to the bishop. Her hands lay limp on the table. He knew that the emotion in her voice was too fresh to be traced all the way back to Miles Pruitt. It was the pain of a newer wound" (245). The past prepares Agatha—and the reader—for the present. Is that right?

A. It's very true—things throw light on things.

Q. In your Teacher's Guide, you have a question: "Explain the symbolic effect of the following," and, of course, I was very amused. We both know that you have a great deal of symbolism in your novels; it's just that you aren't conscious of the symbolism as you are writing. You list three—the Quimby idiot, which we've just discussed; *Buried Child*, which we will discuss soon; and seagulls. Seagulls did not jump out at me. Would you explain the symbolism involving seagulls?

A. Well, they fly—they're buoyant. I think that signals the point in the book where Agatha begins to recover and Janet does, too.

Q. Agatha says on page 152, "The sea then. I can't seem to get enough of it." Is that you also?

A. It certainly was in those days. I loved the ocean.

Q. Another sea passage with Agatha on page 161:

> *Sitting there, she became conscious of a strange sound carrying to her from the end of the street. It was like nothing she had ever heard before, a steady moaning, low and mysterious; a choir of bass voices in agony; an organ in a deep cave. . . . Panting a little,*

*she climbed to the crest of the ridge and beheld, to her surprise, the sea. Waves roared as they curled and spilled onto the beach and frothed at the foot of the dune she was on.*

I suppose that this is used as a kind of foreshadowing of her state of mind when, on the next page, she sees Father James in his priestly vestments at Mass.

A. Yes, it is. It's chaotic—it's very impressive—it's larger than she is.

Q. Like Barbara in *Simon's Night,* Agatha has dreams about water: "For the past two weeks cascading water had been showing up repeatedly in her dreams and she had awakened each morning with a deep yearning for something she couldn't identify" (68). I know that this is connected with the above passage, but would you do the connecting?

A. I guess this is carrying her out beyond her limited life the way the sea does. It's not placid water—it's wild water. It suggests the passion of her love for James and the passion of her disappointment at the chaos when she discovers he's a priest.

Q. I thought that you had seen Sam Shepard's *Buried Child* at the Peacock Theatre in Dublin, and I find confirmation in a Yeats country postcard from you, dated May 18, 1981:

> *It's the same Ireland it was 5 years ago, rain, on the hour, cows in the road and rumors of war from the North. Saw Shepard's Buried Child at the Peacock the other night (the Abbey basement)— pretty good play, marvelous cast; also saw 200 cops in front of the GPO expecting trouble—riot helmets and bulletproof shields.*

Had you kept a journal to imprint these scenes in your mind?

A. Yes, I had, and I used everything from that evening to write the culmination of this book.

Q. Could you discuss the symbolism of *Buried Child* as applied to the characters and theme of *A Green Journey?*

A. Well, I used *Buried Child* as a metaphor for what had been going on in Ireland because *Buried Child* is sort of a skeleton in the closet. It's a problem from the past in this family that's ignored and then brought out every once in a while. And that's what the troubles are in Ireland. They go back so far and yet people keep bringing them out, bringing them up—they never get over their grudges. So I used *Buried Child* as a metaphor for the Irish grudge.

Q. On pages 183-185 Janet and then Agatha listen to IRA speakers in front of the General Post Office. Had you been there also, or is this the power of imagination?

A. I had been there in the afternoon when they were speaking, and everybody was asked to sign a book of condolence for this family in the north that had been killed. They had black flags and they dressed in black—the people who came down from the north to do this, so I saw all this.

Q. Are the death of Paddy Creely, a supposed IRA sympathizer, and then the outcry based on news reports?

A. Yes, they are.

Q. Had you gone to Belfast for a day on one of your trips? I thought that you were planning to.

A. I went to Belfast on the 1981 trip. I got on the train in Dublin and went to Belfast, got off the train, and the first thing that greeted me was the scrawl on the wall that said, "F**k the Pope." Then I went outside and saw a soldier pointing a gun at me, and then I went down to the shops. I was frisked before I was let into the center of the city. I went into a bookstore to buy a book and gave the clerk some Irish money. The clerk wouldn't take Irish money, so I went out and got on the train and back to Dublin.

Q. So that's really what happened to Janet then. Chapter 23 contains short, almost cinematic scenes, alternating between the Bishop and Agatha driving to the Wicklow Hills and Janet and Jack Scully traveling to Belfast. Are these meant to illuminate or complement each other? Both Agatha and Janet gain self-knowledge as a result of these trips.

A. It's very true. They're both on their way somewhere. They're both traveling, so I just contrasted them and compared them.

Q. Does the beauty and mystery of Ireland itself challenge your talent for description?

A. Yes, it evidently did then. I don't know now. I was there two summers ago and I didn't write as much about it, but it certainly was beautiful.

Q. The meaning of the title *A Green Journey*, I assume, is somewhat obvious, but would you explain the different meanings inherent in that title?

A. Well, I saw two when I used it. I saw Ireland being the green part, and then I saw the greening of Agatha McGee when she fell in love as an older lady.

Q. How many copies were printed by Morrow?

A. I believe 25,000.

Q. I read that a Catholic book club purchased 6,000 copies when the novel came out.

A. I heard that. I never heard from them again.

Q. I know some readers have felt that *A Green Journey* is a somewhat lightweight novel, especially coming after the powerhouse *The Love Hunter*. I suppose that could be because *A Green Journey* is more a novel of character than of plot. Does that make sense?

A. Yes, I guess the plot isn't quite as graphic or quite as exciting, although I like it just as much as *The Love Hunter* myself.

Q. The *New York Times Book Review*, source of astonishingly positive quotes for *Simon's Night* and *The Love Hunter*, only devoted one paragraph to *A Green Journey*. In the March 24, 1985, issue, Janice Eidus wrote that "*A Green Journey* . . . contains a palatable cast of well-meaning characters and offers the reassurance that those three old standbys of faith, hope and charity still matter. Unfortunately, Jon Hassler's well-meaning characters are only superficially rendered, and those old standbys have been dealt with more originally and profoundly elsewhere." What happened?

A. I don't know—they gave it to somebody who didn't like it.

Q. The *Record*, Saint John's student newspaper dated February 21, 1985, thought that the greatest weakness of *A Green Journey* was its opening chapters. "In the first seventy pages of the book, Hassler covers four years in the lives of several of his characters. For this reason much of his exposition must take the form of a summary. . . . Though starting the novel four years in advance of the main action was necessary in order to tell Agatha's story properly, the texture of the opening chapters and the characterization of Janet Meers have suffered as a result." Your answer?

A. I don't agree with that because I think Janet is given quite a bit of print in the first two chapters when she goes to Agatha's house to have her baby. Also, I remember how much I enjoyed writing those first four chapters.

Q. The *Record* reviewer, Greg Machacek, posits an interesting point: in your classes you "stress the importance of characterization over all other aspects of fiction." Obviously, characterization is one of your main strengths as a writer. Does the character come first for you and then the situation?

A. Yes, it's always character first for me.

Q. You and author Judith Guest (*Ordinary People, Second Heaven, Errands*) appeared together at the Minneapolis Writers' Workshop at Saint John's University on August 3, 1985. I'll quote from Dave Wood's account (*Minneapolis Tribune*, August 11, 1985):

> Guest started the show by saying she admires Hassler's brevity and his depth of characterization. 'I love Agatha McGee (a Hassler

*character) and I always have, but Jon's minor characters are just*
*wonderful. Like Lillian Kite (a character in both* Staggerford *and*
A Green Journey*). I read about her and I think, isn't she ridicu-*
*lous and then I think, 'God, I'm just like her!' And then she read*
*a passage from* A Green Journey *in which Hassler speaks of Lil-*
*lian Kite's traveling habits. (God, I thought, I'm just like her, too.)*
*Guest continued with a startlingly effective and brief passage from*
*the same book in which Agatha McGee goes picking chokecherries*
*with Francis Raft, the hardscrabble farmer who just can't seem to*
*Get Ahead.*

**Have other writers of fiction shared what they admire about your**
**writing?**

A. I guess not. I guess I haven't known all that many writers of fiction,
except in reviews. In several of those passages, she quoted from the
first four chapters of that book.

**Q Including the** *Record* **critique, which is basically affirming, I have in**
**my files nine positive reviews to offset the** *New York Times Book Review*. **I**
**would like to quote a few. Playwright Marisha Chamberlain (***Mpls. St. Paul***
*Magazine*, **February 1986) begins with "Jon Hassler has done it again. His**
**new novel,** *A Green Journey*, **repeats the success of his stunning first book,**
*Staggerford*. **Both draw unsurpassing beauty from ordinary lives." And**
**she concludes: "'Throughout her life,' Hassler writes, 'whenever she was**
**bowled over, Agatha invariably got to her feet again by finding the precise**
**words and the proper listener to hear them.' Something bowled Jon Has-**
**sler over, and once again he's found the precise words. May he have many**
**proper listeners." What do you say about that?**

A. That's very nice. I had forgotten Marisha wrote that.

**Q. I have a few more to quote.** *National Catholic Reporter* **(November 22,**
**1991) reports that** *A Green Journey* **"is a novel about personal discovery and**
**transformation. Before it ends, Agatha is surprised by love. The character-**
**ization is pure J. F. Powers." That is lovely. How do you feel being compared**
**to Powers? I know you both taught at Saint John's and knew each other.**

A. Yes, he's always been admired for his style, and what I try to do is make my style worthy. So I'm very pleased with that comparison.

Q. The *Los Angeles Times* ends with a quote good enough to be inscribed on your tombstone: "Hassler lures the reader into their lives as easily as butter melts on fresh hot bread. . . . Hassler's characters have old-fashioned values and typical human failings; they make this a novel to restore your faith in humanity" (Victoria K. Musmann, February 3, 1985).

A. Yes, that goes along with the other one which I'm going to have on my tombstone from the *New York Times*—"Hassler's a writer good enough to restore your faith in fiction."

Q. Father Alfred Deutsch, an English professor at Saint John's that taught both of us, although at different times, wrote about *A Green Journey* for *Community* (April 18, 1985), a Saint John's weekly newsletter. His approach, of course, since he was a priest, came from a completely different vantage point. The last paragraph of his essay reads:

> Hassler's greatest contribution to fiction is what has been pre-occupying him since the publication of The Love Hunter. This time comes a gentle and compassionate probing of celibate love. In the years since he has been teaching at Saint John's he has been cast into the environment of a religious community where celibacy is a vow and consequently a way of life for the Benedictine monks. Agatha McGee is his model of the celibate. What he had undertaken was probably a more difficult task than his search into married love. Younger readers may fail to empathize with Agatha because they cannot know the struggles of a pre-Vatican Catholic who winces at a Bishop who calls himself Dick and because the experience of celibacy is beyond their understanding. Yet the unencumbered prose which Hassler has used so well in his previous books might attract these too. One almost ancient celibate I know gave up some hours of sleep over his fascination with the compassionate insight Jon has portrayed in A Green Journey.

Father Alfred had been a writer, too, with *Bruised Reeds and Other Stories* and *Still Full of Sap, Still Green*, both somewhat fictional, I believe. Did

**Saint John's have any influence on you in your writing?**

A. It did when it came to *North of Hope*. I don't know about *A Green Journey*. I think that was in me before I got to Saint John's actually, even though I didn't begin it before I got there.

Q. Did *A Green Journey* **receive any honors or foreign reprints?**

A. It was printed in England by W. H. Allen and Company and distributed in Ireland, but I never saw it. I was never given a copy. I don't know what became of it.

Q. **However, the biggest non-publishing news of any of your novels occurred with** *A Green Journey* **ten years ago this month actually.**

A. Yes, in October 1990, NBC broadcast *The Love She Sought*, a movie based on *A Green Journey*, starring Angela Lansbury as Agatha and Denholm Elliott as James, and that proved to be a good movie. Except for the ending which was changed for Hollywood purposes, it stays pretty close to the book, so I was very pleased with that.

Q. **I have some correspondence from you during this time period.**

> Sauk Rapids - *5/2/90* - "If I weren't trained to expect disappointment from Hollywood, I'd say take half a Valium—NBC has decided to go ahead with *A Green Journey*, and 'She' of *Murder She Wrote* has agreed to be Agatha. (I forgot her name.) Jack Lemmon is out. They're considering Christopher Plummer. Filming possibly this summer in Dublin. All of this last night from Pat [Karlan, Jon's agent]."

> Postcard - Saint John's, Collegeville - *5/10/90* - "Up-date - Now it's Albert Finney they're supposedly seeking for James O'Hannon. Today Producer Fenady is supposedly flying to Dublin to look for locations. The director's name is supposedly Joe Sargent."

> Postcard - Saint John's - *5/22/90* - "Surprise—I have read the AGJ screenplay and I like it. I have responded to Orion with my blessings and a dozen editorial suggestions. A check for full payment has supposedly arrived in Pat's office."

Nevis - 8/10/90 - "Andrew Fenady home from Ireland and reporting all sweetness and light to Pat Karlan. The screenwriters have written me with the same sort of message. The entire project appears to have been blessed."

Postcard - Saint John's - 10/11/90 - "Watch 'The Love She Sought,' starring Lansbury, Elliott and [Robert] Prosky, on Sunday, Oct 21, at 7:00, and see if you recognize it. How bad can titles get?"

A. That's right. That was *The Love She Sought* which was a terrible title. I guess they wanted it to correspond to *Murder She Wrote*. That's why they called it that. But that wasn't as bad as the original title they had in mind which was *Last Chance for Romance*.

**Q. I had seen this rebroadcast a few years ago with *A Green Journey* as the title in the actual main titles. Did you know about this change?**

A. Yes, you or somebody told me that happened. I was never notified about it. Also, another mystery about that movie is that it's never been available just to buy or to rent as a video.

**Q. Do you remember what your feelings were during this time?**

A. That was pretty exciting actually because I had read the screenplay and I approved of it, so I was glad to hear that they were going ahead with it. They did film it that summer and it was broadcast that very fall.

**Q. Loretta Young had been interested in playing Agatha. You had given me a copy of a letter she had handwritten to the producer Andrew Fenady. "I have read the book 'Green Journey' you so kindly sent to me. I found it amusing, tender, strong, and bittersweet, a nice combination. Especially the main character. Under the right circumstances and proper casting, I'd be very interested in playing Agatha McGee—She's a girl after my own heart." Do you know what happened to this?**

A. That's the last I ever heard from her.

**Q. What did you think of the eventual casting?**

A. I was very pleased—some of those surprised me at how good they were in their roles—Robert Prosky as the Bishop, for example. He was so much older than the guy I had imagined, and yet he was so lifelike, so lively. Cynthia Nixon—she was awfully good as Janet, I thought.

**Q. Weren't you amused that she has one of the leads in the TV series *Sex and the City*? I just find that so funny that Cynthia Nixon, our dear Janet Raft, is one of the leads in that sexy mini-series.**

A. Yes, she's certainly grown up.

**Q. When did you finally watch the TV version? I know that you did not see it for some time because you didn't want Angela Lansbury to become, in your mind, Agatha McGee.**

A. That's right. I watched it in the spring of 1998 which was eight years after it was made. My wife Gretchen watched it, and she loved it so much, she prevailed upon me to watch it with her. I loved it, too. In fact, I wept in some places.

**Q. Who was your Hollywood agent for the sale?**

A. Her name was Patricia Karlan. She later became my book agent as well.

**Q. Necessarily, changes from the novel had been made, and we were mentioning some. I know that the description of a statue in the River Liffey, "a floozie in a Jacuzzi," was not written by Jon Hassler. What are the main differences? Is it mostly the ending?**

A. That was the main difference, yes, the ending has changed. Agatha came home and wrote to James right away which didn't happen in the book. Also, Randy didn't fly to Ireland in the book. He remained home, but in the movie he flew to Ireland to prove his love for Janet.

Q. Regarding the ending, one of your readers, a professor of English at the University of Michigan, reacted strongly about this:

*I thought that the program was well cast and directed, and that Agatha and the Bishop were especially good. But I was distressed indeed by the new ending which seems to me to run counter to the full thrust of your work and especially to its pressure on the reader to face the reality of limits. This seems to me important because in our culture so many forces ask us to believe that there are no limits on the human will, or on the economy, that we can have everything always. The new ending seemed to me to move your work from one that resisted the premises of the modern consumer culture to one that reinforced them. I hope that this was done over your objection; and if there are to be others in a series, I hope that you are allowed to insist on your own vision more completely.*

**Would you comment on this?**

A. Yes, he believes the ending runs counter as he says to the full thrust of my work. It's too easy an ending—it's contrived, and that's the way I thought of it, too.

Q. **But it worked for the viewer, especially those who hadn't read the novel?**

A. Yes, it did.

Q. **Another big change is James's retreating to his family pub. Did this work for you?**

A. Yes, it did. It seemed to me to fall in very naturally.

Q. **I thought so, too. You could have written that part. I would like to quote from two positive reviews in very influential publications, the *New York Times* and *Variety*. The first is from the *New York Times*, October 19, 1990, by John J. O'Connor:**

The Love She Sought *has been adapted tenderly by Ron Cowen and Daniel Lipman from Jon Hassler's novel* A Green Journey.

*Joseph Sargent has directed with his customary thoughtfulness for story and cast, while managing to convey an inviting sense of place that should cause grins of delight at the Irish Tourist Board. And the performances are just about perfect, which is what you would expect from three wily veterans on the accomplished levels of Ms. Lansbury, Mr. Elliott and Mr. Prosky. All of which adds up to a television movie of substance.*

**And now from** *Variety* **dated October 22, 1990:**

*A class act from start to finish ... Orion has provided Lansbury with a first-rate script and extraordinary supporting cast that bring out her best. ... Director Joseph Sargent is extremely generous to his actors, frequently letting the life-worn faces of Lansbury, Elliott and Prosky fill the screen. ...*

*The production seems more like the best of Britain's Film Four International than an American TV movie. One can only hope for more of this ilk from Orion TV and NBC.*

**Were you gratified to read these?**

A. Yes, certainly I was. To think that I was responsible for the story was very gratifying. Both papers loved the story.

**Q. TV critic Noel Holston in the December 30, 1990,** *Minneapolis Tribune* **summarized the TV year 1990, picking "10 of the good reasons for turning on the set," and he included** *The Love She Sought:* **"Other than the icky change of title, there was plenty to like about this spiritually faithful adaptation of Jon Hassler's bittersweet novel,** *A Green Journey.* **Angela Lansbury found a role worthy of her talent in the redoubtable Miss Agatha McGee, a Minnesota spinster schoolteacher who travels to Ireland to meet the longtime pen pal with whom she's fallen in love."**

**I understand that** *The Love She Sought* **won a prestigious award.**

A. Yes, it did—the Christopher Award out of New York City. That was given for various media things over the years that coincided with Catholic teaching, I guess. So that was good.

Q. Were you invited to attend the festivities at the Time-Life Building in New York?

A. No, I wasn't. I didn't remember when it happened, actually. But I remember getting a letter about it after the fact. Also, let's see, I was going to say that Angela Lansbury did an excellent job in that role. She seemed better than she was on her other shows. She seemed deeper. She seemed to be doing better things with herself. She looked the part better.

Q. She wasn't quite as glamorous. She may have been still a little too glamorous for Agatha, but not the usual Angela Lansbury glamour. Any concluding thoughts about *A Green Journey*?

A. Nothing, except to say that I remember what a relief it was when it was published since it had been four or five years since my last book. I was very relieved when it came out. It meant I wasn't washed up as a novelist. I've written, what, six since then.

Q. Jon, you and I will revisit Agatha and James soon. My days in the next few weeks will be filled with the pleasure of becoming reacquainted with them in *Dear James*.

A. Thank you, Joe, you're very kind. Thanks a lot.

# Grand Opening

Grand Opening was the subject of our second interview. [*The Dean's List* interview in 1997 began the series.] We had hoped to conduct the interviews in the order the novels had been published, and on the whole we succeeded, but in the year 2000 Jon had recently adapted *Grand Opening* for the stage, and the Jon Hassler Theater in Plainview, Minnesota, opened its inaugural season on June 16, 2000, with a production of it, thus providing the impetus for our interview at this time.

The Jon Hassler Theater was the brainchild of some citizens of Plainview, where Jon had spent eight years during his youth. They began by establishing the nonprofit Rural America Arts Partnership and then enlisted the Lyric Theatre of Minneapolis as a partner. The Lyric had already produced Jon's adaptation of *Simon's Night* and his original *The Staggerford Murders* as well as Sally Childs's adaptations of *Jemmy* and *Dear James*, all performed at the Hennepin Center for the Arts in Minneapolis. In 2000 the arts activists of Plainview converted an International Harvester dealership at 412 W. Broadway (on Plainview's "Main Street") into a 225-seat theater and named it after Jon. I told Jon that he had joined the ranks of Neil Simon and Helen Hayes in having a theatre named after him.

While riding with friends to Plainview for the grand opening of the Jon Hassler Theater, I remember looking out the car window, trying to picture the environs of Plum. Rolling hills and cornfields dotted the landscape. *Grand Opening* seems to yield fewer descriptions of nature and the countryside than most of Jon's novels. However, I did find a few examples. "Nine miles out of Plum the road tipped downward, beginning its descent through the densely wooded hills" (179-180). ". . . and so the snowfall wasn't blinding as

Hank made his way across the farmland and down the winding road between the bluffs" (189).

Much of *Grand Opening* takes place in the fall and winter, so the descriptions of the area fit those calendar months:

> *Three miles east of town the road took them up over a rise known as Higgins Hill, from which the view was unobstructed in all directions. Rolling fields deep in snow. Leafless trees a lifeless gray. Here beside the road was the red barn of Lester Higgins with an advertisement for spark plugs painted on its side. Horses and cows stood in a pen breathing steam. Ordinarily Catherine enjoyed the long vistas offered by high ground, but here, looking back at Plum huddled in a snowy hollow so remote that God Himself might overlook it, she shuddered. . . . (193)*

Aside from the TV antennae, the region hasn't changed much since the mid-1940's when *Grand Opening* takes place. Jon confirms this: "The rural landscape is exactly the same. The town is slightly bigger."

*Grand Opening* is the only one of Jon's novels to be set entirely in the distant past—1944-1945. Jon has not only changed the era but expanded his canvas to include more themes and characters, many of which the reader gets to know rather intimately. The Fosters are the major characters, but so many people come into contact with one Foster or another that they are almost like drops of rain dimpling a lake with circles of association spreading out across the town of Plum in every direction. Jon's concerns and subjects have grown to include not only family relationships but also religion, small town as well as national politics, prejudice, reform school, World War II, small-town businesses, change, the youth and the aging, evil, repentance, martyrdom—the list seems endless. And all of this is accomplished with growing artistic deft and confidence.

When people ask me which of Jon's novels I would recommend to read first, I say *Grand Opening*. In fact, I often give this book as a gift. I realize that *Staggerford* would be the response of some, but I believe that *Grand Opening* is a perfect introduction to Jon's fictional world. What gives this novel its heft, I believe, is its moral implications. In a subtle way Jon maps out in *Grand Opening* how each of us, regardless of sex, age, religion, class, or profession, should act towards one another. Each of us is a resident of Plum, regardless of the actual name of our town or city, and our relationships with others in our environment determine the moral well-being not only of ourselves but of our families, friends, and society as a whole.

- J. P. August 2002

**August 16, 2000**

Q. Jon, the year before *Grand Opening* was published, 1986, proved to be a watershed in your literary career.

A. Yes, in July 1986 Ballantine came out with its first paperback of one of my works—*Staggerford*. It was a turnaround for me because all of my work had been out of print by that time. And now it began to come gradually back into print. It's been in print ever since, and many of these books have gone to many printings, so that was very satisfying to have that happen. I owe this publication to Cissy Tiernan, a sales rep for Ballantine, who had been pressured by booksellers in Minnesota to get me back into print. She has since left Ballantine. I gave her one of my oil paintings as a going-away gift.

Q. You sent me a postcard from your cabin in Nevis (August 2, 1985), with a short message that said it all: "Joe: Ballantine! All four [*Staggerford*, *Simon's Night*, *The Love Hunter*, and *A Green Journey*]. -Jon" That really sums it up.

A. That's good. I was very succinct, wasn't I?

Q. Probably of all your novels, *Grand Opening* has gone through the most changes and transmutations. Was the short story, "Dodger's Return," now in the collection *Rufus at the Door & Other Stories*, the beginning, the seed, for this novel?

A. Yes, I believe it was; I wrote that short story before I wrote the novel about Dodger, and when I began to write the novel, Dodger was of great importance in the book, more important than I had foreseen. Dodger grew out of a childhood experience I had in Plainview. When we moved there I was ten years old, and his prototype befriended me. He proved to be the wrong kind of person to make an impression. He was a thief; his parents were divorced. He was an outcast, so I ended the friendship in about three days and that was the last I ever saw of him. He and his mother moved away after that, but evidently he was very important to me because he turned out to be such a big part of this boyhood novel *Grand Opening*.

Q. *Grand Opening* wasn't your working title for this novel; what were the earlier titles?

A. "Plum" and "The Book of Brendan."

Q. In an Easter card (Flag Day - no year - ca. 1985), you say: "Proceeding steadily with 'Plum' and would like to finish this draft by July 31, which will require a great deal of guts, push and inspiration. 'Up out of the trench and into the fray one last time,' I say to this book. 'Follow me, trust me, I know this time where I'm leading you.' Did I tell you that Dodger will die?" You had a great deal of difficulty with all of these different versions. Would you explain these changes and surgeries?

A. I began writing "The Book of Brendan" in 1981 after I moved to Saint John's. It concerns the boyhood of a monk, and his name was Brendan, and then that proved to be unpublishable, and so I put it away and went on to *A Green Journey*, which did prove to be publishable. And then I wrote two novels based on "The Book of Brendan." *Grand Opening* deals with his boyhood, and *North of Hope* deals with his adolescence. The beginning of that book is pretty much taken out of "The Book of Brendan," so I got two novels out of one that way.

Q. Both your editor, Harvey Ginsberg, and agent, Harriet Wasserman, vetoed "The Book of Brendan" as you had it. Did they see the same difficulties as you had?

A. I was uncertain about the book from the beginning for some reason, and Harvey said that he didn't care for it very much—he said he'd publish it if I wanted to, if I loved it enough. I said, "What does that mean?" He said he'd publish it, but he couldn't support it very much in-house because he didn't believe in it, that is, in the publishing house. So I took it up to the cabin one weekend to decide how much I loved it—I had it in a box and I read everything else besides that. I couldn't open the box that weekend, I remember. My son David was up there hunting. On Sunday I said, "David, we're going to have a funeral." We buried the book in the ground near where I had buried Ginger, our dog, the year before, so we had a little ceremony to get it off my mind so I could go ahead and write another novel. Then later, after I wrote *Grand Opening*, Harriet, my agent, said, "You should dig that up because this is a resurrection," so I decided that was a good idea, went to the tool shed, got out my shovel, and I couldn't remember if the dog was on the left or on the right, so I left it in the ground.

**Q. Good, Jon, I was hoping you would share that story, but it was a resurrection—two good novels out of one. Sandy Brown of the *Brainerd Daily Dispatch* interviewed you for the June 18, 1987, issue. Responding to her question about when you started writing *Grand Opening*, you said, "It seems like centuries ago. In 1978 I started writing my memories of my boyhood in a journal, and thought about stringing them together in a book. Then I put it aside, and wrote *The Love Hunter* (Morrow, 1981) and *A Green Journey* (Morrow, 1985). This book was the hardest one to write—there was no thread connecting the episodes. It took awhile to work it out." Are those your memories of writing this?**

A. Well, you know, the work of writing disappears after time. I don't remember how hard it was. I don't remember how hard any of my books were after I finished writing them. All that effort disappears. Just the book exists.

**Q. How many hardcover copies were printed?**

A. Gee, I don't know. I don't remember. It might have been 15,000 at the most. I guess that's about right.

**Q. Did *Grand Opening* win any awards?**

A. Oh, yes, the Society of Midland Authors, which is a group in Chicago, voted it the "Best Fiction of 1987," so that was my second award from out of Chicago. *Staggerford* had won the Friends of American Writers Award from Chicago, too.

**Q. Would you explain the dedication, "To Betsy"?**

A. Betsy was my second wife. I married Betsy in 1986. The marriage lasted less than a year, but I was writing it mostly while she was there, so it seemed to be her book.

**Q. I read that you had written the first paragraph of *Grand Opening* thirty-five times. I'll quote it for the reader:**

> As they followed the Mississippi out of the Twin Cities on U.S. 61, Brendan wondered why his parents and his grandfather seemed not to share his dread. Year after year he had listened apprehensively to his mother and father talk about moving to a small town and going into business for themselves, and now it was happening. Tomorrow he would begin the school year among strangers in a village he had never seen. The lawn mower was strapped to the roof of the car and his bike rode the front bumper. The moving van was some miles ahead. It was Labor Day. A light rain was falling.

**Could you explain in some detail the rewriting and revising involved just in this paragraph?**

A. I can't remember much of it; I do remember the part about his dread, however. Harvey Ginsberg, my editor, was always saying we want the reader to worry more. I didn't have dread in that first paragraph, so I said as they followed the Mississippi out of the Twin Cities, Brendan wondered why his parents and his grandfather seemed not to share his dread. I put that in after several revisions. I don't remember why it took me so many times to get the rest of it together, but everything's in there, I guess. Of course, as you write the first paragraph, you don't know what else is going to fall in place in the book, and you have to go back and add stuff, like beginning school in the morning, I had to add that, and the fact that it was Labor Day, and I remember going back, telling what they were carrying on the car, the bike strapped to the front bumper and the lawn mower on the roof. That was just the way it was when we left the Twin Cities in 1943 and moved to Plainview.

Q. Ross is the protagonist's name in "Dodger's Return," a short story. When and why did you decide on Brendan?

A. Because by that time I'd written "The Book of Brendan," and I decided I liked the name better than Ross since it was Irish. I have an affinity for Irish names—they seem to make me work better when I use an Irish name in a book.

Q. And then, of course, the grandfather is Irish. Willowby (W-i-l-l-o-w-b-y) is the name of the town in "Dodger's Return." Willoughby (W-i-l-l-o-u-g-h-b-y), with a little different spelling, also was the original name of the town that became Staggerford. How did you decide on Plum? And why the difference in the spelling of the two Willowby's?

A. I decided on Plum because I wanted to use the first two letters of Plainview. Plainview was a real town and Plum is a fictional town, and it seemed to me it was kind of a plum held out there for Hank and his grocery business—a promising thing. And then, it was such fertile country down there; I liked the idea of fruit standing for the town. As for the difference in spelling, it must have been a lapse of my spelling ability, I think. I can't remember any other reason for that.

Q. The titles evolved to *Grand Opening*. Would you please discuss the different meanings of the title as you see it?

A. The literal meaning is the grand opening of Hank's store, which takes place during the book, and of course the symbolic meaning has to do with Brendan and his life—his life is opening out into adulthood. He learns about his place in society and what people are like in this book, so for him it's a grand opening into his adult life.

Q. Was *Grand Opening* a grand opening also for you in your development as a novelist? What I mean is that this seems to have a broader canvas than your previous novels.

A. I guess it does, doesn't it. I don't know if I'd been able to do it if I hadn't been so familiar with the town I was writing about. It's a historical novel, too. I mean it takes place in World War II instead of contemporary times, and so that's another stretch for me.

Q. And did the story itself, in a sense, dictate the larger canvas of *Grand Opening*?

A. Yes, that's true. The family itself is four people; the town has at least sixty people and they all bear on Brendan as he grows up

Q. The hardcover book jacket of *Grand Opening* featured an evocative illustration. Please describe it and the coincidence involved regarding a painting.

A. When I was in New York about 1975, I went to the Museum of American Art, the Whitney. I saw on the wall this painting called *Early Sunday Morning* by Edward Hopper. It pictured a city street with sunlight falling along the street, nothing else. They were the sort of buildings with apartments above. It seemed to look just like Plum, so I bought the poster. I put it up in my room as I wrote the book. Then, when I finished the book, I took it down and folded it up and put it away. Then, when I got the book in the mail, Morrow had commissioned an artist to paint this very picture, the same one I'd been looking at, all the while. It's taken from the Edward Hopper idea; it was amazing, of course. The only difference is that the apartments above are taken out, but the stores look exactly the same. That's one of three mystical things that happened with this book. The other two have to do with the names of people. Wallace Flint—I named him Wallace Flint long before I knew he was going to start a fire. The Fosters—I named them the Foster family long before I knew they were going to take in Dodger as their foster child.

**Q. In reply to questions about how much of your novels is autobiographical, you often respond, "Exactly 37 percent." However, I believe that the percentage is substantially higher for *Grand Opening*. In fact, I think this may be the most autobiographical of your novels.**

A. I think you're right, Joe; I may be up to 38 percent because the family situation is the same. My father and mother owned the grocery store. Grandfather came to live with us for a time, so the family situation is 100 percent mine, and the things that happen, I make up a lot of them, but a lot of them happened to me. For instance, Dodger's encroachment into my life was part of my life, and the school board election which defeats Catherine—that actually happened to my father in Plainview when he was defeated for the school board. After that, Plainview lost its hold on him, I think, and we moved away shortly after I graduated from high school.

**Q. Brendan was twelve when he and his family moved in September 1944 to Plum. I think you said you were ten. How long did you and your family live in Plainview? The Fosters stayed almost a year.**

A. We stayed almost eight years in Plainview, 1943 to 1951; I loved the town. My dad liked it just fine because his business was good. My mother never cared for it, so that was the reason we moved away after a while.

**Q. Did your parents experience prejudice and boycotting similar to the Fosters because they were Catholic?**

A. It wasn't as clear-cut as that—there were Lutherans who shopped with us, but for the most part, the people who shopped at the grocery store did so because the merchants' theology matched their own, it seemed to me. And there was definitely a religious division in that town.

**Q. By the way, where technically is Plainview/Plum, Minnesota?**

A. It's located on Highway 42 between Wabasha and Rochester. You go down 61 on the river, you turn right into the bluffs in Kellogg, and you come to Plainview thirteen miles up into the bluffs. Or, if you go to Rochester, you go northeast from Rochester toward the river, and you come to Plainview, so it's off the beaten track.

**Q. Grandfather McMahon in *Grand Opening* is one of the richest characters in all of your work. How similar is he to your real grandfather?**

A. He is—my grandfather is the one person in my ancestry who was a real character. He was a railroad man—he told railroad stories all his life. In fact, I didn't learn until after his death that he'd lost his railroad job as early as 1914 for letting his friends ride free; he was that sort of guy. He was an expansive extrovert—he'd break into song or tell a story at the drop of a hat just as he does in the book.

**Q. How long did he live with you and your parents?**

A. He died at the age of eighty-eight in 1954 when I was a junior in college, so he'd come to live with us periodically, and other than that, he lived at the Sheridan Hotel in downtown Minneapolis. He'd come to us for six weeks at a time over the years.

**Q. I really enjoyed the closeness shown in the scene on page 281 when Brendan tells Grandfather the truth about Dodger not pilfering the money from the money bag. "Never before had he opened his heart to Grandfather in exchange for the five hundred stories Grandfather had told him. Listening to Grandfather over the years, Brendan had always been aware of the man's great age, but now, their roles reversed, the six decades between them fell away to nothing." Agatha McGee [from *Staggerford*] became close to Janet [Raft] in *A Green Journey* and also, I think, with Beverly [Bingham] in *Staggerford*. Is the mutual bonding of the old people and the younger ones one of your themes and/or concerns?**

A. It certainly is—it's one of the themes I've been aware of—most of my themes, I'm unaware of—I've always been aware of the gaps between generations and the bridges.

**Q. You wrote a really fine article, "Tell Me a Story," that was published in**

the December 10, 1996, issue of the *Saint Paul Pioneer Press*. Could you synopsize this article for the reader?

A. Oh, it has to do with my grandfather telling me stories, reading me books when I was little, and the effect that had on me. I think it prepared me for understanding old people. I remember sitting on his lap listening to [L. M. Alcott's] *Jo's Boys*, a very boring book, night after night. If there had been television, I wouldn't have done it, of course. I would have gone off and watched television. But because there was no alternative, I loved it. I was very comfortable sitting there listening to him read, and then he'd tell stories all about his life, and I think that's what turned me into a storyteller.

Q. A mutual friend, Dan Lange, said that he remembered your saying an earlier version of *Grand Opening* had the entire town showing up for Dodger's funeral. Is that correct? And if so, why the change?

A. Well, I thought I would throw a little curve at the reader there because that's when the election of the school board is supposed to happen, which Catherine's running for, and I thought I'd get her hopes up. And they'd be dashed again when she turned out to be defeated in the election. However, it didn't seem to hold, it didn't seem typical of the people in the town that they would turn out, so I changed it. I made very few people come to the funeral.

Q. Rufus is an important character in *Grand Opening*, and he also is in the title story of your recently published collection, *Rufus at the Door & Other Stories*. Tell us about Rufus. Did Plainview have a Rufus in town?

A. Yes, his name was Clarence Kronebush, and he came uptown with his mother, and every day practically, his mother left him off at our store just as she does in the story, and he'd stand there looking out the window in the door until she came and got him. So that was the basis of Rufus. We all wondered what would happen to him when his mother died. That's why I wrote the story, to find out, and as it turned out, life was easier on Rufus than I was because by the time his mother died (she lived to be very old), there was a rest home in Plainview that took him in. I'm told that he lived to a rather happy old age there.

Q. In rereading *Grand Opening*, I wanted to warn the other characters about Wallace's skullduggery. I especially worried about Dodger. It's akin to seeing a performance of *Othello*, watching Iago do his dirty work especially to Cassio and Desdemona. Wallace is a small town Iago. Had Iago crossed your mind at all when you were thinking about Wallace?

A. He certainly had. It's interesting we both thought that, but I thought that because he comes on as just plain evil so much of the time as Iago does.

Q. Is your parents' grocery store still a store in Plainview fifty some years later?

A. It's a variety store now.

Q. Plainview is beginning to claim you as its native son. Please tell us what has been happening in this regard.

A. Well, they formed a corporation called Rural America Arts Partnership, and that's a non-profit organization in which they hope to promote the arts and history in that town. They set up a historical society and a history museum which is very good. They've started a theatre called the Jon Hassler Theater, which is very good as well. It's a first-class theatre with good lighting and good sound, and that's where *Grand Opening* was performed this summer as their opening play. It seemed to work out very well—it was a sellout.

Q. This was the second stage version of *Grand Opening*. How difficult is it to translate or transfer a novel from one medium to another?

A. It's hard to do, I found. It's easier to write a play from scratch, which I did last year with the *The Staggerford Murders*. It's difficult to cut out all that beautiful prose, of course, and reduce the novel to its dialogue.

Q. Were you pleased by the Plainview production?

A. Oh, yes, I was very pleased by it.

Q. Historical and cultural references abound in this novel, i.e., Amos and Andy, radio commentator H. V. Kaltenborn, Armistice Day in 1918, the death of Franklin Delano Roosevelt. Did you need to research these periods, or did you mainly rely on your memory and imagination—and journals?

A. I don't research anything as I work. The 1918 one, of course, I hadn't been alive for that one, but I remember my mother telling me about the priest coming out on the steps of the Basilica and holding his arms out and asking people to come in and pray for thanksgiving because the war was over. And the others, I remembered the death of FDR, for example—it was a clear memory for me.

Q. And in what town were your mother and the priest?

A. That was in Minneapolis. She was coming home from the University on a streetcar. She looked and she saw he was standing there calling to people to come in and pray.

Q. Those are rich memories and rich stories. Chekhov is one of my favorite playwrights. His plays often focus on arrivals and departures, endings and beginnings. Do you see similarities between Chekhov's work and this novel?

A. Certainly there are arrivals and departures, with which this play begins and ends, and I'd like to think the richness of the characterization, too.

Q. That's a good point, and I suppose the small town yearnings also. Chekhov could be described as autumnal. The hardcover edition of *Grand Opening* contains 309 pages. The autumn section covers 121 pages, winter 85 pages, spring 81 pages, and just 10 for summer. Fall and winter occupy two-thirds of the novel. Is this in keeping with the storyline, the problems that the Fosters encounter in Plum, especially Catherine?

A. I thought it was a matter of telling the story. I mean, there was so much I had to tell in the first two parts. Then, when spring came, the culmination, it didn't take long to tell that, and then the denouement, the summer time, was only ten pages. I'm surprised it was only ten; I thought it was longer than that, but it stood for the autumn of their life in Plum.

Q. Could this also stand for the autumn in their interior lives?

A. Yes, certainly. A reader comes to a book with his or her own experience, and that's entirely fair to draw those conclusions, even if the writer didn't have that in mind, I think.

Q. And that's the power of literature then?

A. Exactly.

Q. In *Staggerford* you used a days-of-the-week schema. Here it's the seasons. Is this a helpful technique to organize your story, like an outline?

A. Yes, I seemed to need that in my early writing, something to hang my story on, some sort of time line to hang it on—that's why I did that.

Q. And also does going from autumn until summer help convey the moral awakening of Brendan? He is becoming more alive morally and spiritually.

A. I think that's surely true, although I didn't have it in mind when I wrote it.

Q. In an article last November [1999] in the *Fargo Forum*, you're quoted as saying, "I moved away from Plainview three days after high school. And my life there seemed ideal to me, so I was surprised at the darkness in *Grand Opening*." Would you amplify on that, please?

A. Well, Mary Ann Grossmann, when she reviewed this book in the *Saint Paul Pioneer Press*, said it was about the dark side of small town life, which surprised me, but I guess she's right. There's a lot of darkness in this book, including the death of Dodger. I probably idealized Plainview in my memory to the point where I subconsciously tried to react against that idealization as I wrote the book, tried to balance it with the dark side of life, too. Maybe I overdid the dark, although it makes it very dramatic.

Q. In one article in the *Twin Cities Reader* (July 29, 1987), you say, "I'm getting less funny, don't you think? . . . There are less laughs in this book. Why, I wonder?" And yet so many lines are extremely funny and unexpected. Someone asks Stan Kimball what kind of dog his wife has, and he replies, "The incontinent kind." The mayor's wife, Mrs. Brask, prattles, "What will you hang over the fireplace? The DeRoches had a Biblical picture there, Geronimo battling the Philistines or some such thing." And Grandfather tells about the man being struck by a train, being killed, and crossing two state lines; thus, "as a dead man he had traveled nearly five times as far as he had while alive." How do you think of really funny lines and situations?

A. Writing humor is hard work. It's hard where the timing and everything has to be perfect. I don't know how I think of them. They just come to me as I work, I guess. They don't come to me so much anymore, however; I don't think I'm very funny anymore.

Q. But you are in real life—you're one of the two or three funniest people I know. Is it partly that your wry sense of looking at life carries through to your working as a novelist?

A. That must be it.

Q. When you gave readings of *Grand Opening*, what sections would you choose to read aloud?

A. I always read Grandfather's part and his getting on the train and being carried out of town because he thinks he's on the right train— he's out of his mind, sort of. People are waving at him. And that's the part I read because it's amusing.

Q. Yes, people do respond well to that. Wallace Flint's frescoes, "all those bug-eyed, bruise-colored people," remind me of Nadine Oppegaard's science-club project in *Staggerford*, two dozen gigantic oil paintings of cancer of the mouth, "the purple, pink, and ochre blossoms that appeared to be growing malignantly out from the walls." Are people's artwork one way of describing or illuminating them? I don't recall any other author using this method.

A. Yes, and that's true—I use it in two other books, too. I use it in *Jemmy* with the painter, and I use it in *Rookery Blues* with Connor, the painter. He painted mothers and daughters because his family was breaking up. His wife and his daughter—he was losing them both. He was obsessed with mothers and daughters therefore.

Q. So many of your short descriptions seem just right. I suppose this is a result of rewriting many times. I'll quote a couple. "Watching them [a dozen bald boys with Dodger at the Home School for Boys] bounce on their benches, Brendan thought of the rising and falling of pistons in the DeSoto, energy pressing against confinement; compression and combustion" (143). And perhaps my favorite in the whole book occurs early on, and I think it's many other readers' favorite also (14): "his parents were linked by a love as direct and mute as a beam of light, and very few of Brendan's joys equaled that of coming between them and feeling himself pierced by that beam." I think that even your author heroes, John Cheever and Evelyn Waugh, would stop and reread that sentence, and then perhaps even read it aloud. Are there patches of your writing in *Grand Opening* that still give you pleasure?

A. It's very gratifying to hear. I know I love that sentence about my parents being linked by a love as direct and mute as a beam of light. It seems to be just right. I think the other part that I'm especially fond of is the part where Grandfather goes after the train—that seems to be a heightened kind of writing there. When Constable Heffernand goes out and kisses Mrs. Clay under the street lamp, that also seems to be a heightened kind of writing. When Grandfather's with her on the day FDR dies, that scene seemed to write itself.

**Q.** *Grand Opening* is probably the novel that most deals in history.

A. Yes, it does. It's my boyhood book and it deals with World War II, and I have everything in there from World War II except ration stamps which I forgot to put in. It's strange, too, because we dealt with them in the grocery store. But the last chapter of that book is the day the war ends, and as a friend of mine at Saint John's says, it's one of the most exciting chapters he ever read. Brendan goes around delivering groceries and sees the reactions of people as the war is ending.

**Q.** Your writing recalls the Eisenstaedt photograph of the sailor and the woman hugging. Yes, so the work, the prose, captures that. One of the themes of *Grand Opening* occurs on page 154. At Christmas Eve Midnight Mass, Brendan thinks about Rufus, wondering "Wasn't this village . . . a kind of peaceable kingdom after all?" I thought of Edward Hicks's famous painting, *The Peaceable Kingdom*, illustrating that the lion will lie down with the lamb. Is this what the Body of Christ really should be, a peaceable kingdom, both in Plum and elsewhere?

A. Yes, I think that's right. I think that's where the word "peaceable" came to me that way.

**Q.** Now that we're talking about the themes of *Grand Opening*, a couple of writers mention the loneliness, the "fearful loneliness and isolation," inherent in this novel. Comments?

A. Well, first of all there's Catherine's loneliness in a strange town. There's Wallace Flint's loneliness—Wallace Flint has never fit into this town. There's Dodger's loneliness—he's shunned by all his classmates. Those are the three major lonely cases, I guess, in this town.

**Q.** I have some examples, too: Dodger's parents, and Larry-the-Twitch Romberg, who won't be allowed with his older brothers and their friends; Mrs. Flint, who's really a recluse in the house for much of it; Paul Dimmitburg, who's more on the ball than most others; Rufus, Mrs. Ottmann, Mrs. Clay, Father O'Day, Mrs. Lansky, who lived upstairs alone next door to Dodger, and maybe even Grandfather in a way. That's quite a gallery.

A. There's certainly a lot of lonely people.

Q. And that carries the theme, too, because if we all were doing what we should be doing, they wouldn't be lonely.

A. That's right.

Q. Was it deliberate on your part to use the deaths of FDR and Dodger to illuminate each other, a correspondence between the macrocosm of society and the microcosm of the family and individual? FDR died, but "the haberdasher from Missouri" continued his policies and guided the country through the last weeks of the war and the transition to peacetime. Dodger died, but his death especially affected Brendan in his behavior. Prosperity for the United States and the Foster family was literally "just around the corner." So is there a connection between the country and the characters in Plum?

A. I don't know if I thought of it as I wrote it, but there certainly is a connection.

Q. Along with this, World War II ends in the last chapter of the book, parallel with the ending of Brendan's war within himself—he saves Rufus, whom he could not touch, from falling into the grease pit. Would you comment about the ending of World War II and perhaps Brendan's inner war?

A. The ending of World War II made the ending of the novel very dramatic. Brendan's going out delivering groceries, and everywhere he stops, he learns something, it seems, and he's growing up by the minute, and that afternoon, finally, it all comes together when he tries to save Rufus from dropping into the grease pit. He takes his hand, leads him away, and he can't get out of the idiot's grip, as it says in the last line in the book; so you see, this sort of responsibility has its hold on him for the rest of his life.

Q. The novel ends with the word "grip." Does this help to reinforce the theme and meaning?

A. It does, Joe. You're right.

Q. Paul Dimmitburg's sermon/homily at Dodger's funeral underscores the basic theme of *Grand Opening*. "Take at least one thing home from Dodger's funeral: my assurance that each time we fail to care for one another we carry out, one more time, the act of crucifixion" (290). And then on page 306: "Dodger needed Brendan's promise never again to be as unkind to anyone as he had been to Dodger, his promise to go through life more openhearted toward others and less concerned with himself." Which came first, the story or the theme?

A. For me the story always comes first. I never saw that theme until I got to it.

Q. A short answer for a long question. Steve Eide in the *Minnesota Daily* [July 6, 1987] invoked Sinclair Lewis in his critique, ending with this observation: "It's as if Lewis looked at the world cerebrally and Hassler with his heart and hopes." Yes?

A. Well, I guess I like that critique all right. I think I do have an emotional connection with my characters that Lewis didn't, so that's true.

Q. The *New York Times Book Review* continues its hot and cold relationship with you, publishing a short review in the June 7, 1987, issue, but one that is basically positive:

> *His new book features themes from his earlier ones: small-town culture and conflict and the nature of Christian charity. . . . Despite a few slow moments and stock secondary characters, this well-constructed novel effectively portrays human weakness and triumph. Without sentimentality, Mr. Hassler illustrates—in the spirit, if not the virtuosity, of Flannery O'Connor—that we often learn more about God from misfits than do-gooders or saints. While the grand opening of the title refers specifically to Hank's store, it finds an ironic parallel in Brendan's expanding sympathies and growing awareness.*

Do you agree that this summation is basically positive?

A. Yes, I like being compared to Flannery O'Connor, for example.

Q. **And that has happened more than once, hasn't it? I notice when I'm going through the reviews from your novels, her name often comes up.**

A. Yes, I didn't realize that, Joe. I didn't remember that.

Q. **I don't have many reviews of *Grand Opening*, but I'll quote from one more—Timothy Brady in the August 1987, *Minnesota Monthly*: "It is in this era of global destructiveness that Jon Hassler chooses to set his new novel, *Grand Opening*—the tale of one urban family's adjustments to the peculiar foibles of life in a small Minnesota town." Brady quotes the scene when Mr. Heffernand kisses Mrs. Clay on Christmas Eve and then really describes your writing's strengths very well:**

> *This is Hassler at his best: We see the fearful loneliness and iso-lation in the community, the basic shyness and muted emotions—but then, suddenly and joyfully, some connection is made, and the possibility of change emerges. From* Staggerford *to* A Green Jour-ney, *Hassler has made a specialty of these small yet moving epiph-anies. He's not given to overstatement. We're not rolled through an emotional wringer as we read his work. Yet there is an understated power to his writing.*

**Do you think that Brady was a sympathetic and comprehending critic?**

A. Yes, I sure do. I like the review a lot.

Q. **And, finally, Leonard Witt, then of the *Minneapolis Star and Tribune* (April 26, 1987), noted that you had said one of your goals was to write prose that will outlive you. Do you think you accomplished that with *Grand Opening*?**

A. I think I probably have. I think the book will last maybe ten years beyond my life at least. That isn't very long, of course, in the big scheme of things.

Q. **I think it will last longer than that. Thank you very much, Jon.**

# North of Hope

I don't know how many Catholic authors attempt a novel about a priest, but some certainly do. A number of these books could be classified as romance novels or superficial crowd-pleasers, but others are considered classics. I think of Graham Greene's "whiskey priest" in *The Power and the Glory* and J. F. Powers's two protagonists, Father Urban in *Morte d'Urban* and Father Joe Hackett in *Wheat That Springeth Green*. I recently reread *Monk Dawson*, published in 1969 by the English writer Piers Paul Read; the paperback carries a Greene quote: "A remarkable novel . . . profoundly moving." A relatively unknown novelist, Crawford Power, wrote a really fine *The Encounter*, which I remember with pleasure from many years ago.

Into this illustrious company I would certainly place Jon's *North of Hope*. In this work Jon expands both the canvas of his characters and the moral concerns they wrestle with, presenting some really despicable people in the process (Judge Bigelow and Tom Pearsall come readily to mind). The themes are familiar, but they come into greater focus here, becoming more extended and refined. What is goodness? What is evil? Can one change? Does one keep one's vow to God? Is one of this world or of the next—or a mixture of the two? These issues envelope not only Frank and Libby, but all of the characters that people this ambitious novel.

Frank represents the typical Hassler hero—a loner, a person who wants to do the right thing regardless of the consequences—and Jon gives us an extended look at the hero or protagonist in both childhood and adulthood, which adds to the novel's richness. Frank in some ways serves as Jon's Hamlet character. He's somewhat indecisive, but he never wavers from his priestly calling. The dying words of Frank's mother, misquoted, it is true, "I want Frank to be a priest," serve a purpose similar to the ghost of Hamlet's father. Frank, like Hamlet, spurns his "girlfriend" with disastrous results. And so on.

I once asked Jon about the parallels that I see between these two works of art. His reply: "Very true. They certainly are alike."

*North of Hope* garnered interest in Hollywood, with Minnesota-born Jessica Lange expressing interest but then deciding against it (you will find out why in our interview). Warren Stitt (who produced *The Spitfire Grill* in 1996) renewed an option on the book four times before allowing it to lapse.

When Jon finally watched the NBC-TV movie *The Love She Sought* (based on *A Green Journey*) a number of years ago, he was moved to tears. I told my Jon Hassler class (at Central Lakes College) that he would also cry if he ever did see the *North of Hope* movie, but for entirely opposite reasons. Jon informed me that the screenplay Stitt was planning to film has Tom Pearsall, Libby's husband, injecting poison into Libby's neck so that she would go back with him to Chicago. As Tom is driving across frozen Lake Sovereign, the car goes through the ice. Frank comes by, dives into the water, bringing Libby up to the surface. He then goes back for Tom and drowns. Thus, the matter is settled—they can't possibly both live and yet not have a sexual relationship.

- J. P. October 2003

**October 30, 2000**

Q. Jon, here we are in your living room in Minneapolis, ready to discuss *North of Hope*. After rereading six of your novels, I believe that *North of Hope* is your masterpiece, thus far, anyway. Ballantine published it in 1990. Your previous novel, *Grand Opening*, appeared in 1987 with a Morrow imprint. I was going to ask why you changed, but I found the answer in a letter to me dated November 22, 1989:

North of Hope *will be a Ballantine Book. Friday [Bob] Wyatt came through with the equal of Harvey's [Ginsberg] offer [at Morrow] (plus a better paperback deal) and yesterday Pat K. [Jon's agent] phoned my regrets to Harvey. Wyatt is so excited he shrieks over the phone. Contrast that with Harvey, who was grousing about the length and structure of the book right up to the end. I expected an angry phone call from Harvey, but his only response to Pat was, 'Oh.' Is it too much to hope that once again I have an editor like Judy Kern [at Atheneum] who respects my vision? I'm very relieved to be out from under Harvey's thumb, and to have the negotiations over with. There's no denying that Ballantine's hardback list is thin, but he claims that his entire sales force will be eager to sell* North of Hope *because the paperbacks have proved such steady sellers.*

**Do you have anything more to add?**

A. I disappointed Harvey because I didn't keep writing *The Love Hunter*. He loved *The Love Hunter*, and then I wrote *Grand Opening* and *A Green Journey*—he didn't care for those so much. He told me on the phone when we were negotiating *North of Hope*, "Nobody wants to read about a twelve-year-old boy and a seventy-year-old woman," which was very disappointing to me. It's the first I knew about that. I was glad to get out from under him—get over to Ballantine and Bob Wyatt.

**Q. My question was to have been the standard, was Harriet Wasserman still your agent for *North of Hope*? Then, when going through your correspondence, I was rather shocked to learn that Harriet no longer was your agent at this point in your life. I hadn't realized the end occurred at this time. In a letter dated March 21, 1989, from Sauk Rapids, you wrote:**

*The novel seems good. I've sent the opening 66 pages to Bob Wyatt, with the understanding that it's not for sale (Harvey, of course, has first look) but merely to tease him. In a week or two I'll have 600 pages Xeroxed for my agent search. I guess I'll send it to one agent at a time, beginning with Claire Smith at Harold Ober because she likes long novels and dislikes Harvey and answers her own phone.*

**I had never met Harriet, of course, but I always liked her from what you**

told me about her. What caused the break?

A. Well, she was neglectful. I'd write to her and I'd phone her, and she'd never answer my letters, she never returned my phone calls. And that made me feel very insecure out here in Minnesota. I was so far from New York. So I wrote and told her this. I said I suffocate out here when I don't get a response from you. And I said I'd have to leave her as an agent and find another one. And she never wrote back, but I did find another one.

Q. And is that Pat Karlan who then became your book agent for *North of Hope?*

A. Yes, Pat Karlan was a movie agent. She had worked with Harriet actually on *The Love Hunter*. And then I asked her if she'd be my book agent as well, and she agreed to do that. She'd never sold a book before, so mine was the first. So Patricia Karlan became a book agent and a movie agent for me.

Q. Who was your new editor at Ballantine?

A. I had the best editor I ever had then, Bob Wyatt. He was from Oklahoma originally and went to school in the East. He was very perceptive. He answered some questions about the novel that I had along the way, and by the time I came to Ballantine with my next novel, *Dear James,* he was gone. But they hired him back freelance to edit this because they knew I liked him.

Q. This may be covering it again in a different way, but what were Bob's strengths and weaknesses as compared to your previous editors, Judith Kern and Harvey Ginsberg?

A. Bob gave me a longer leash, for one thing. He let me write what I wanted to write, and then when I had a question, I'd call him up and ask him about a plot twist or something. He always had a very good answer for that. The others never got into plot very much with me, except to criticize it.

**Q. How many copies of *North of Hope* were printed in hardcover?**

A. When I went to New York, I asked that question. They said they were going to print 75,000. I think they printed 28,000 in reality. They sold about 20,000.

**Q. I think that the novel did sell rather well judging by different clippings. Dave Wood, in the *Minneapolis Star Tribune* (December 2, 1990), wrote that "Hassler spent an unprecedented 11 weeks at the top of this newspaper's bestseller list." It also appeared at the top of the "Best Sellers—What Twin Citians are reading" (*Saint Paul Pioneer Press*) for some weeks. *Seattle Times* (October 28, 1990) reported that it ranked number 5 for its best sellers in the Northwest that week. Dave Wood (*Star Tribune*, January 13, 1991) then published a ranking of Twin Cities' best-selling books for 1990 (B. Dalton and the Hungry Mind chose not to divulge their numbers); *North of Hope* firmly commanded first place with 1,490 copies; next was Dr. Seuss's *Oh, the Places You'll Go!* with 777. Harvey Mackay's *Beware the Naked Man Who Offers You His Shirt* brought up number 10 with 254 copies. Harvey Mackay will figure later in our interview. Did changing to Ballantine help cause this new visibility?**

A. I think it did. Also, it was more of a grabber as a book, I think. The reviews were good, too. The timing was good. Everything about it worked, I think.

**Q. Ballantine reprinted *North of Hope* in paperback in 1991, and that also sold well, first place for Paperback Fiction in the October 20, 1991, *Saint Paul Pioneer Press*. The U.S. of A. List, compiled from independent bookstores throughout the United States, had *North of Hope* listed number 7 for paperback (all genres). Had Ballantine also strongly advertised you in paperback?**

A. I guess they must have. I don't think it was advertising as much as distribution, which spread it all over the country, so it was available to people in airports, etc. This must have been the highlight of my popularity; according to Odegard Books St. Paul, from January to March 1988 I occupied four of the eight slots in their paperback fiction best seller list. In the first year and a half after *Staggerford* was issued in paperback, the St. Paul store sold more than seven hundred copies.

Q. And that probably is even more important than advertising. Did *North of Hope* garner any awards or foreign reprints?

A. By this time the Minnesota Book Awards had been instituted, and it was nominated in the fiction section for the Minnesota Book Award, but it didn't win. It was translated into Korean by somebody, I don't know who—I have a Korean friend who read it and said it wasn't a very good translation—that's all I know about it; I can't judge that, of course.

Q. The dedication reads "For my son Michael," the oldest of your three children. Was there any special reason for this dedication? You had dedicated *Four Miles to Pinecone* to all three of your children, "For Mike, Liz, and Dave."

A. Well, it was time to dedicate each book individually to my kids, and I started with my oldest child.

Q. The artwork for the book jacket of the hardcover edition is really striking. You had written me on April 27, 1990: "Cover art arrived today—stunning—blue & silver." Would you describe the artwork?

A. The print is so well done on the navy blue background, and then there's a small picture in the upper right-hand corner of a snowy woods with a sliver of a moon in the sky over it, and it looks very cold and wintry. Of course, the book takes place in the winter mostly—it's a very cold book where a man dies by going through the ice on the lake. Another man dies walking home on a wintry night, so it's a fitting cover.

Q. It really is an evocative cover. Your unpublished "The Book of Brendan" from the early 1980's also dealt with a childhood similar to Frank's. Is *North of Hope* an outgrowth of that?

A. Yes, it is. The first 150 pages are the teenage love story of Frank and Libby, and a lot of it had been written as "The Book of Brendan," so I used that to start this book.

Q. **Would you explain the title of** *North of Hope*? **Of course, the Hope Unit at the Berrington Hospital serves as Verna's refuge. Also, Libby says: "It's like hope doesn't reach this far north" (498).**

A. She says that while very depressed, of course, during the course of the book. I guess you've explained it, Joe; I think you've explained both meanings.

Q. **Some Hassler geography: are Linden Falls and Basswood based on actual northern Minnesota towns?**

A. I don't know where Linden Falls is exactly. It's near Red Lake, I guess. I kept seeing Red Lake when I'd see Sovereign Lake in the novel. Sovereign Lake is a huge body of water with the Basswood Indian Reservation next to it, so I would use that. And then I made up the town of Linden Falls. It's up around Bemidji, Minnesota, probably north of Bemidji somewhere. It's far north.

Q. **And Basswood?**

A. The basswood tree and the linden tree are the same, so the Basswood Reservation—Linden Falls has a sort of unifying effect, and that's all I can say about that.

Q. **Jon, is Aquinas College another name for the actual Saint John's University in Collegeville or not? Both have seminaries, of course, on their campuses.**

A. Yes, that's true. I kept seeing the Saint John's campus as I wrote the part about Frank and the seminary and playing basketball, so that's true—it's a rural campus.

Q. **Pages 91 to 94 describe Frank's visit to the St. Thomas Aquinas campus. "After supper in the refectory (sausage and fried potatoes) the** community filed into the church, where the evening sun falling through the great window behind the altar suffused everything in a rose-gold light, and where the prayers were chanted in Latin" (94). Is this your experience as an undergraduate at Saint John's in the early 1950's?

A. Yes, it is. It's the magic of that sort of chant that draws Frank into the seminary.

Q. Frank returns with Libby and Verna after some years to his old Alma Mater, St. Thomas, which has now become Berrington Vocational Institute. Instead of the church, he finds the student center. Is this modeled after Saint John's where, after the new Marcel Breuer church was built, the old church became the Great Hall, a kind of large lobby?

A. No, actually this is based on a church in Cold Spring which is a beautiful old church, and they built a brand new one next to it, which looks like a night club. I went into the old church one day—I found it contained a foosball machine, and it was a place for serving dinners.

Q. Would it be correct to infer that all of your Catholic colleges are somewhat based on Saint John's?

A. It certainly would.

Q. Both you and Frank Healy were born in 1933. Part One (pages 3-104) deals with Frank's adolescence, from the age of sixteen to roughly twenty. Is at least some of this first section based on your life and experience?

A. Yes, of course. I think I was like Frank in that I was shy of girls—I didn't have any dates. I fell in love with a girl in high school and she became my obsession, and that was about as far as it went. Unlike Frank, my mother and father were both living. But there were a lot of similarities. I used to candle eggs for my dad in the grocery store the way Frank does in the egghouse. Things like that are similar.

Q. You mention that candling eggs was part of your experience, but it's such a good passage, I would like to quote it. It's on pages 15 and 16, and you very convincingly describe Frank's work at the egghouse:

*There was something comforting, almost mesmerizing, about holding dozens and dozens of eggs, one by one, up to the funneled light to make sure they weren't bloody, fertilized, or cracked; something sensually rewarding about the vague, floating shapes of their illumined yolks and their various shades of shell—white, cream, tan, brown. He fell into periods of deep reverie at the egg table, eggs triggering his fantasies the way the rosary triggered his prayers in those years. As one by one, like oversized beads, the eggs passed through his fingers, he entered into a lengthy daydream, the same daydream over and over. . . .*

Is the intent almost mystical?

A. Yes, it is.

Q. When thinking about this vignette, I came up with the question I'm most proud of: I almost see this as being symbolic, a foreshadowing of Frank's priestly life, candling souls up to the funneled light of the Holy Spirit. Is that too farfetched?

A. Not at all, Joe, I never thought of it, but it's wonderful. I like it a lot.

Q. Frank, as is true of most of your characters, is entranced by water. On page 10 he enacts a ritual:

*. . . and they [Libby and Sylvia] saw Frank, in swimming trunks, cross his front lawn and cross the street and wade into the river. He was carrying a football. He went in slowly, up to his waist, then stopped and stood still, facing downstream, as though in a trance. He kept moving his right hand back and forth, palm down, over the surface of the water. . . . He turned and threw the ball upstream. . . . Waiting for it to float down to him, he lowered himself into the river until nothing but the top of his head was visible. Then he stood up again. He did this a number of times, dipping down and standing up.*

Then you ask as the writer: "Was he bathing? Evading mosquitoes?" What *was* he doing? Would you explain the significance of these actions?

A. He found a way to play catch with himself. He's a loner, see. So he throws the ball upstream and it floats down to him, and he throws it upstream again. As for those motions of his hands, I don't know what they mean.

Q. Frank's roommate at the Aquinas College is "a grocer's son from Milner, North Dakota." Is this, by chance, a take-off on our mutual friend, Brother Benet, whose father was a grocer from Casselton, North Dakota?

A. I'm sure that's where I got the idea for a roommate—he was your roommate, right?

Q. Yes, he was—for one year at Saint John's. I'm always glad to learn that you obviously liked movies as much as I did when young. Do you remember seeing *A Portrait of Jennie*? Its date, 1949, helps set the time period.

A. I saw it and then I saw it recently before I wrote *North of Hope*. I remember I wrote down a line from the movie which I used in the novel. I never thought Jennifer Jones was so pretty, but Frank sure does. My favorite star was Gene Tierney actually, but Jennifer Jones, she fits the pattern. And she fits the novel fine. And so does Joseph Cotton.

Q. Does the movie still hold up?

A. No, it doesn't. I watched it again recently. A fan sent me a copy of it because of *North of Hope*, so I watched it again. It doesn't hold up—it's sort of foolish, I think. The ending is so foolish.

Q. I didn't see it; probably my parents wouldn't let me go since I'm three years younger than you and would have been thirteen then. Seeing the movie made Frank cry. I checked Pauline Kael's capsule review in her *5001 Nights at the Movies,* and she confirms, in a sense, this effect on the viewer: " . . . Selznick poured on the gloppy grandeur—a Dmitri Tiomkin score based on themes from Debussy, an impressively large-scale skating scene, a hyperdramatic hurricane sequence—and though the story may not make much sense, the pyrotechnics, joined to the dumbfounding silliness, keep one watching" (466). Had you considered any other movie for this key scene at the beginning of the novel?

A. I considered *Kiss of Death*, which is my favorite movie from my youth, but that didn't seem to fit the romantic part of it, so I used this instead. I think maybe Frank goes to *Kiss of Death* later.

Q. I haven't seen this either. I'll have to get the video one of these days. Later in the novel Billy Annunciation takes Elaine to *Taxi Driver*. Is this Scorsese film an ironic counterpart to *Portrait of Jennie*? So much had radically changed not only in movies but also in society from 1949 to 1976.

A. Yes. Although I never saw *Taxi Driver*, I read enough about it to know what it was about.

Q. On page 40 you describe Frank's sense of humor: Libby'd "never before known anyone to be funny in the wry and understated way that Frank was funny. Instead of depending for laughs on jokes and insults and vulgarities the way most boys did, he invented humorous ways of looking at everyday things, and he delivered his lines so quietly you could miss them if you weren't paying attention." This accurately describes your humor, I think. Was this conscious?

A. Oh, I guess it was, yes, I think so.

Q. Frank was a football player in high school, playing quarterback. Please share some of your high school football memories.

A. High school football was the biggest thing in my life in its day, and it was one thing about high school I loved. I didn't like high school as a student much. I loved it as a football player but I didn't play quarterback. I played center and linebacker which meant I tackled a lot of people, but I made Frank quarterback since that's more or less the center of the team, and he calls the plays. He's smart.

Q. You had written a story entitled "The Backup Boyfriend." And I would like to quote an Easter card from you. We'll have to determine the year. And this is about the story.

*Harriet Wasserman says that "The Backup Boyfriend," which won me ten thou from the [Minnesota] State Arts Board, has been turned down by both the* New Yorker *and the* Atlantic *as being a bit too old fashioned, and now it's at McCalls.*

**Did this story constitute much of Chapter 9 (pages 75-82), when Frank takes Libby to the Loomis Ballroom?**

A. Yes, that's right. He is the backup boyfriend she falls back on. Her own boyfriend deserts her for a time.

Q. Was it ever published as a short story?

A. No, it never was.

Q. The graphic incident on pages 44 and 45 concerns Doc Gilpatrick's inserting his arm, up to the shoulder, into the cow's rectum. Did this really happen?

A. Yes, that's word-for-word from my life. We lived next door to a doctor in Plainview. His name was Doc Kirkpatrick. He was a veterinarian. He'd take me out on those lovely summer mornings, and we'd go and do things like that to cows.

Q. Is Father Adrian Lawrence based on a particular person or a composite?

A. Well, you know, I had my father in mind when I wrote about Adrian Lawrence. He was a friendly guy, very gentle and saintly, I think. And that's why Adrian Lawrence is one of my favorite characters I've ever written about.

Q. Is the Father Zell story (pages 71-73) true?

A. Yes, Father Zell by another name. It was a French name—it started with "L" [Father Lawrence Lautishar, a Slovenian priest]. He became Father Pierz's assistant. He came over from Europe to help him spread Catholicism throughout Minnesota and the wild areas of the north, and there were only two priests in northern Minnesota at that point. This priest was one of them and Father Pierz was the other. And the priest died just the way Father Zell did in the book, crossing Red Lake to bring communion to another family on the other side.

**Q. Was this the germ or genesis for *North of Hope*? Or did something else set off your creative impulse?**

A. Gee, I can't remember. I don't think that was it, though. It was a boyhood story, of course, that I got going on. Also I had worked with a priest and a girlfriend earlier in "The Book of Brendan," but that was different. But I guess I needed to complete that before I went on to another book, so I went back to that theme.

**Q. Would you agree with me that *The Love Hunter* and *North of Hope* are similar in many ways and unlike the "usual" Hassler novels?**

A. That's true—I've always thought of them as a pair because they deal with the dirtier side of life—drugs and things like that.

**Q. Landscape often plays a role in your writing, but in *North of Hope* it becomes a major character. Do you agree?**

A. Yes, I do. In *North of Hope* Sovereign Lake has a sovereign effect on the characters, it seems to me. It sort of separates Indians from the whites. It kills Tom, Libby's husband, and it provides fish for the Indians. And they ice-fish out there. It's what you see from Judge Bigelow's bar. Yes, I think Sovereign Lake in particular is a character in this book.

**Q. Description is always one of your strong suits. I would like to quote two that especially appeal to me: "A little blood had congealed in the hair [of Roger], and there was a rosy spot on the gray blanket where the head had lain—not the red of blood, it seemed to Libby, but the delicate pink of the wild roses that had bloomed along the reservation roads last summer" (160). Finding beauty ("delicate pink of the wild roses") in a head wound of a dead person requires great visual insight. Do you like this description?**

A. I do. And I'm surprised by it—I forgot about it.

Q. And the second is worthy of writer Flannery O'Connor: "Jackpines and bare aspens. A frozen swamp. A barn at the crest of a hill. More jackpines. There was a blood spot in the southern sky where the sun was going down" (214). Do you have any favorite descriptions in this novel that you remember?

A. There's another one when they discover that Roger is dead. When that little boy goes tramping off through the deep snow—I remember loving that one. Some of the descriptions of the ice on the lake I liked. I guess those are two that I remember.

Q. Page 145 carries an especially evocative descriptive paragraph:

> [Highway] Thirteen curved along the shoreline for a mile, then it left the lake and snaked through the forest. The trees stood deep in a blanket of snow. Birch and aspen and jack pine—white and gray and dead green. Here and there a tributary road led to a clearing where a small house stood under its cloud of chimney smoke. Most of these clearings contained, at their edges, a few snow-covered cars and pickups with flat tires or no tires at all, rusting beaters bought from used-car dealers in Linden Falls and Berrington and driven only a few miles before they died.

Are your descriptive talents, especially of nature and landscape, honed by your painter's vision?

A. Yes, painting made me look at the landscapes more closely than ever before. Also, I remember writing about the jack pines in this book. It's another passage I like where Libby's trying to paint jack pines. She finds them so depressing.

Q. This leads to Libby's unfinished painting which disturbs Frank.

> The shades of violet and pink made a pleasing harmony, but the tree line made his scalp tingle. There had obviously been a violent sort of abandon in her technique, the greens and blacks having been

*laid quickly and recklessly over one another with a palette knife and allowed to dry in wartlike bumps and razor-sharp edges. (450)*

**Is this a visual representation of Libby's mind, her way of looking at life?**

A. Yes, it is. She feels abandoned up here in the north country, and that's an example of what she's thinking at the time—how she feels.

**Q. By the way, Jon, what sections of *North of Hope* did you read at public readings?**

A. I read mostly from the youth sections—Frank and Libby. There was a part in there about Frank being raised by nuns. He was aware of sin all his life—that always made a big hit with people. Also I read about Vernon Jessen and the cow episode where the veterinarian took Frank out to look at the cow, things like that.

**Q. Let's return to Father Adrian. While in Coronary Care, he tells Frank: "I saw an angel" (300). His vision is of a nurse: "the pretty, cream-haired young woman remained, standing by the window in a shaft of sunlight" (299). She is wearing white, and the nimbus of light appears as a halo, so the reader can see why Adrian thinks this. It is amusing, but also does this show Adrian's goodness? If anyone would see an angel, it would be he.**

A. That's what I thought when I wrote it. He deserved to see angels.

**Q. And this was many years before the TV program *Touched by an Angel*. Mrs. Tatzig, along with many other Christians, is too practical and earthbound to see angels. "But it's one thing to believe in angels and another thing to actually see one. That's what separates Christians from loonies" (306). That line sounds like something from Flannery O'Connor country. So Adrian and Mrs. Tatzig are at opposite ends of the faith spectrum.**

A. That's right—Mrs. Tatzig is so brusque and practical. Adrian is so spiritual.

**Q. Father Adrian tries to pray for anyone and everyone who has died, from his own relatives to the most famous movie stars. "The list begins**

with my grandfather Lawrence, who died when I was seven, and it extends down through the years to Hubert Humphrey." This is a fine example of character description, but also the reader learns the approximate year the action is taking place, 1978 (*Taxi Driver* and Jimmy Carter's first year as president help also). Is it difficult to have character traits and dialogue serve at least two purposes in the grand scheme of the novel?

A. Well, it's a matter of technique which I get better at as I go along. It isn't so hard anymore.

Q. As Father Adrian is having his heart attack, he is reciting from the morning's liturgy: "The spirit of the Lord God is upon me, the spirit of the Lord God is upon me." Flannery O'Connor (again) believed that the last action one of her characters committed before death would determine heaven or hell for that character (I don't have the source of this in front of me, but I think that is the gist). In that case, Adrian would go directly to heaven if he had died.

A. I believe so—I believe that's right.

Q. I'll read a short passage from *North of Hope*:

> Over the sound of TV, they [Frank, Tom and Libby] heard the ice of Sovereign Lake rumble and crack. Tom's eyes grew large with fear—feigned or genuine, Frank couldn't tell. 'Why does the lake do that, Frank Healy?'
>
> 'Ice expands and contracts with the temperature. It opens up long cracks.'
>
> 'Jesus, and people drive on it.'
>
> 'They aren't wide cracks. They're only an inch or two and they freeze shut right away.' (121)

This no doubt foreshadows Tom's fear—and eventual fate?

A. Yes, he's fated to die in the lake.

Q. I believe that Libby's suicide attempt is the first and perhaps only one in all of your novels. Libby takes stock of herself while preparing for the suicide:

*She was full of energy and purpose and her heart was beating fast ... It was a long-range vision affording her a clear view of the hopeless mess her life had always been and would continue to be if she didn't take control of herself and end it.... She was unable to afford a used car. She was unable to get along with her daughter. She'd had a dolt and two perverts for husbands.... It was a relief to recognize after forty-four years of mistakes that they could all be gathered together and thought of as one overriding mistake. The mistake of having been born. (491-492)*

That *is* bleak. How does a novelist convey such a character, and how does one plumb that person's depths?

A. Now you're getting into the imagination. One tries to just imagine what people are experiencing, write it down, and sometimes it works and sometimes it doesn't.

Q. Libby really does go through an emotional wringer in *North of Hope*. At the discovery of Roger Upward's body, she sobs:

*She was crying for this little cluster of humanity awaiting the ambulance.... She was crying for the three little children thigh-deep in the snow ('Caw, caw,' they called, peering up at a crow flapping high in a tree), beautiful little children already reconciled at six and eight to becoming the next generation of this furtive, aimless band of Indians forever skulking around in the forest they'd been banished to. And most of all she was crying for herself, banished like the rest of them to this wilderness of lost hope in the forty-fourth year of her life. (163)*

Any comments then about Libby?

A. Yes, she's hopeless. She's hopeless so much in this book. And that's an example.

Q. And her crying relates directly to her comment about her painting thirty pages earlier: "I do a little oil painting. In order to get jack pine green you have to mix in a lot of black, which is made from charred animal bones" (134). This must symbolize all of the people, including herself, that she is sobbing about: the bones of the original settlers, the native Americans, and the current ones, too, people like Roger killed in this harsh climate, Libby's second and third marriages, the "skeletons in the closet," her unfulfilled love relationship with Frank, many more. Is this somewhat what you meant?

A. Yes, and it all came to me when I read what was in the tube of black paint I was using—charred animal bones, it said. So that's why I used that.

Q. And it suggests all of this then?

A. Yes, it does.

Q. And the jack pine does survive in this hostile environment, as do many of the people, even with the severe winters. What makes some of these individuals survive—drugs, liquor, God?

A. Your questions are getting so profound, Joe. Drugs, liquor and God, I guess.

Q. Libby, of course, becomes very emotional and sick upon hearing that Tom has been having sex with her daughter Verna for a number of years (390-391). How do you as a novelist, and this probably we already have covered, visualize—and then create—these traumatic incidents in Libby's life?

A. I was having coffee with my mother one time in Staples, and a friend of hers came in the restaurant and said, "How do you know all that stuff to write about in *North of Hope*?" I didn't think of the answer at the time, but it was through newspaper articles I'd read, so that helped. And I just imagined the effect on people.

Q. Would you explain a little bit more about newspaper articles?

A. Well, newspaper articles about incest, drugs, and things like that.

Q. Frank has a dream that he was walking beside a large body of water.

*In a cove he came upon a middle-aged woman sitting on a rock and looking sad. She might have been his mother. She might have been Libby. She was being comforted by a little boy who was murmuring something in her ear. He was her son, obviously, for the two of them had the same eyes and cheekbones. Soon they were joined by an older child, a daughter of twelve or thirteen, who had her mother's mouth and complexion. This girl put her arm tenderly around the woman's shoulders and sat silently beside her, listening to the little boy continue with his message of solace. (377)*

**Would you analyze, please?**

A. I don't know if I can analyze that. I know where it came from. I saw that scene in Ireland by the seaside one time. I saw a woman with her two children and they were consoling her like that. It was such a sight that I never forgot it. I put it in the book.

**Q. And yet another dream:**

*[Frank] dreamed Libby was walking with him on the grounds of the Aquinas College and Academy, which were vastly transformed by a glacier that had moved through overnight. Ravines had been cut, trees uprooted. The buildings were ruins. The sky was black. They walked to a treacherous cliff edge where they stopped and looked down and Libby pressed Frank's hand to her cheek and warned him of some terrible event to come. (284)*

**Does using dreams convey more to the reader than the character's own thoughts or speech could?**

A. Yes, I think if they're used sparingly, they work. This foreshadows the dire things that are going to happen in the story. I think if you don't spend a lot of time on a dream, you don't have too many in there, they work; otherwise, they bog the story down.

**Q. Dear Father Adrian also has dreams: "'Adrian, what if we had married?' asked the voice of Jo Stafford, resuming the dialogue he had been carrying on with her in a dream. 'What if you had had children, sons and daughters of your own flesh, do you ever wonder about that, Adrian dear?'" (492).**

Of course, this dream segues into real life when Libby mistakenly thinks it's Frank on the phone, telling Adrian "I love you and you're not to blame." You are able to capture the wistfulness, pathos, and humor all equally in this vignette. Was that the purpose?

A. Yes, it was. This is as close as Adrian Lawrence ever got to a relationship with a woman—in his old age imagining singer Jo Stafford in his dreams.

Q. A punch line occurs right during Libby's "confession": Adrian's "fantasy life, so gratifying of late, was becoming downright exciting" (493). It's like a musical riff.

A. Yes, it is—it's good.

Q. Another technique that you use in both *Simon's Night* and *North of Hope* concerns the main character transporting elderly people—Simon driving some of the Norman Home residents to pick up Mrs. Kibbikoski's leg and Frank taking the shut-ins to visit Father Adrian in the Berrington Hospital (Chapter 32, pages 316-326). I would think that you enjoy writing these scenes.

A. I do; for some reason I enjoy writing about old people particularly. I love the way they often speak at cross-purposes.

Q. Yes, having a diverse group of people talking at cross-purposes is a literary component of yours. Another example appears on pages 289-296 at the Berrington Hospital cafeteria; the cast of characters includes Frank, Vernon, Verna, Father Gene DeSmet, and Violet and C. W. Habnett. Pigs and pork bellies and the mistaken identity of Frank and making runs to St. Paul and "having the runs" all intertwine in this collage of conversation. I've asked this before, but are such scenes a challenge to create or not?

A. They're a challenge in that you have to write them over and over until you get the timing right, but they're so much fun to write that they don't seem difficult.

Q. And there's really a rhythm to them also. In a rainstorm Frank and Libby talk in Vernon's pickup at the Aquinas College campus. That brought to mind Miles Pruitt and Beverly Bingham from *Staggerford* sitting in Miles's Plymouth on a rainy Sunday afternoon. (Beverly had driven over in the Binghams' black GMC pickup.) Does the rain help symbolize that these relationships could never work out? Frank is going to be a priest, and Miles the teacher wouldn't ever marry a student.

A. I guess it does. You know that scene at the seminary between Frank and Libby; that happened to me at Saint John's in 1955 when I was a senior, and a girl from my home town who had been engaged to a friend of mine came to the campus to tell me she loved me instead of the friend. I sat with her in the car in the rain, so we hashed this out together.

Q. This may put a strain on our interview, but I remember the movie *The Bridges of Madison County*. As luck would have it, the day after I thought of this parallel, the film was shown on television, and I watched this pertinent scene. Meryl Streep (Francesca) is sitting in the pickup, her husband is at the store, and it is raining. Clint Eastwood (Robert) gets out of his pickup and walks part way, then stands, waiting for her reaction. She doesn't move. Streep's husband gets back in their pickup, and at the red stop light, Eastwood's pickup is stopped ahead of the Streep one. Streep has her hand on the door and almost gets out to join Eastwood but doesn't. It's pouring rain. Do rain, pickups, and doomed love fit together?

A. They do for him and me, I guess.

Q. The reason I thought it was tacky of me to mention this title is that you had been quoted about the novel in a *Minneapolis Star Tribune* article. Would you elaborate?

A. Yes, I didn't like the book at all. It seemed so cheap—I was never able to finish reading it. I got to page 150 and couldn't go any further. Yet it sold so many copies, I thought people were being hoodwinked. And my reaction to that book is mentioned in a novel I'm reading entitled *Welcome to my Planet* by Shannon Olson. She talks in here about my disliking that book: "Jon Hassler ... just railed against this book, and I thought, Geez, what a strong reaction, and so I read it. And it's true. I mean, the writing is very simple and plodding and clanky and uninteresting, and I thought, Hell, I could do this."

Q. As is true about your other novels, characters from previous ones appear or are mentioned. Bishop Swayles, talked about in *A Green Journey*, is discussed again. Bishop Dick Baker also from *A Green Journey* (published earlier) appears in *North of Hope*; he still wants to be called by his first name. Do these appear by chance, or do you see their role long before you come to that section?

A. They just crop up as I go along. I didn't foresee the bishop coming back in.

Q. The housekeeper Mrs. Tatzig does not acknowledge her Indian background, and this is also true of Smalleye's daughter in *Simon's Night*. Is this creative license or observation or intuition?

A. This is based on an attitude I have found prevalent in Park Rapids where some people would not admit to being Indian.

Q. You covered *Staggerford* in nine days and *Simon's* action in six days; here the story stretches for almost thirty years. Does this illustrate a growing confidence in your abilities to create and maintain a more convoluted plot?

A. Yes, it does. When I started out, I needed the time framework very much, but I don't seem to need it so much anymore.

Q. *Grand Opening* began in September and ended in August. The adult story of *North of Hope* (Parts Two through Five) begins in December, and during the harsh winter, deaths, mental illness, a suicide attempt, murder, a heart attack, and drug dealing occur. The novel finishes in April. Does this indicate that everything is more or less satisfactorily resolved, that spring is in the future for the main characters one way or another?

A. That's what I had hoped to convey by it, yes.

Q. Two of your protagonists, Simon and Frank, pray, exposing to the reader what is really in their minds and hearts. Have you had other characters do this?

A. I don't believe I have. I can't think of others who prayed.

Q. I can't either. At the bottom of page 314, Frank thinks: "Dear God, the barriers between us. The walls." That certainly was the theme for *Grand Opening*. Is that also partially the theme here?

A. It is, certainly. Things that separate people are more interesting than the things that bring them together.

Q. Are Rachel of *Love Hunter* and Libby closely related? Both are resilient, independent, attractive women. Please discuss what you see as their similarities.

A. Yes, they are both very appealing to the main character. The main character is obsessed by them—in love with them. And they are both resilient, although Libby is depressed more of the time than Rachel ever was.

Q. Are there other differences between the two?

A. Well, I hate to judge people's troubles, but I think Libby's troubles are greater than Rachel's who had a lot of trouble.

Q. You were on the faculty at Saint John's University in Collegeville with J. F. Powers. That made me think: how similar is Frank Healy to Powers's two priests from *Morte D'Urban* and *Wheat That Springeth Green*, Fathers Urban and Joe Hackett?

A. I've thought about that myself. I find Frank Healy unlike them and more appealing than they are. Where they seem to be more urbane and they're older and more cynical, Frank isn't so cynical. Frank is a better priest, I think, than those guys.

Q. Aquinas College and Academy had closed, and "Frank went into an emotional tailspin. It was a vocational crisis" (170). Is this in a sense male menopause?

A. Yes, it is. He'd been teaching all his life and suddenly had nowhere to teach. As he said after the last of his boys went home, he had no one else to play with, so he had to grow up and be a parish priest.

Q. How much of Frank is in you—or you in Frank?

A. Thirty-seven percent.

Q. I should have known. Frank identifies this crisis as "My big leak … I've sprung a very big leak, and my spirit is draining away." Then, some pages later, Frank "sensed, with a sinking heart, that he was having another homiletic blackout … His first sign of the big leak" (152-153). Did you suffer a "big leak" or male menopause in your life?

A. I never did actually. I've been optimistic all my life. I was born optimistic, I think. So I never did.

Q. A priest had written you from the Yukon in Canada after reading *North of Hope*: "These past weeks it's been a real gift to me, prodding, delighting, bringing stabs of recognition…. Today I gave my first homily worth listening to in a long time, tying together my own experience of 'the big leak,' and the search of the Wise Men." That's astonishing testimony to your artistic creation. Had you received other such letters?

A. I have actually—maybe not quite as moving as that one. The effect that these books have on people's lives is very gratifying.

Q. When you had given talks and readings to Catholic and Lutheran clergy over the past decade, did you use *North of Hope* as part of your presentation?

A. I usually did, yes, because they related to it so well.

Q. Frank's fourth homiletic blackout ended with the words "God is elusive," which sounds very sensible and true—and adds to the theme of the novel, I believe.

A. That's right. God doesn't always speak to us, you know. He's hard to find sometimes.

Q. Frank does get cured, one feels; how would you describe his cure?

A. When he discovers he's good at his parish work—of course, he has Libby to confide in always. I think they'll always be around, those two. They'll always be in each other's lives. And he has Adrian Lawrence, he has his home parish, he goes home. He heals up there.

Q. Libby knows that Frank "had a dimension she lacked, a mysterious dimension from which he drew strength, a spiritual dimension she'd never believed existed until she saw it in him" (513). *North of Hope* is a very religious and spiritual novel; is part of the theme that God makes a difference in lives?

A. Yes, He does, and Frank has the spiritual make-up, of course, to illustrate this.

Q. Since we're edging into the elusive area of theme (we said that God is elusive and themes also are elusive), I would venture that betrayal is a big part of the main theme. In high school Frank unknowingly betrays Libby by not allowing her into his home, causing her to go to Dennis Hedstrom's motel cabin and have sex. Libby betrays Frank at the Loomis dance, only using him to get Vernon jealous. Harris Highsmith betrays both Libby and Verna by having sex with Verna. Tom betrays both Libby and Verna by having sex with Verna. Tom dealing in drugs betrays his Hippocratic oath as a doctor. Judge Bigelow betrays Tom. Even Eunice Pfeiffer in a sense betrays both Frank and his mother by not saying the exact, more ambiguous words of his mother, "I hope Frank will want to be a priest," but instead "I want Frank to be a priest." Is betrayal the theme?

A. Betrayal provides the evil of this book certainly.

Q. A note from you written on January 31, 1988, states: "The play [*Simon's Night*] has been canceled. Theatre 65 was counting on a big grant from the

Jerome Foundation and didn't get it. I feel betrayed. Again." Did betrayal help fuel this novel?

A. Yes, it did.

Q. **I think readers would be fascinated to know some of your thoughts during the writing of** *North of Hope*, **so I've gleaned some snippets from your correspondence to me.**

Nevis - 9/2/88 - "You're right, Verna will move into the rectory for a few days."

Saint John's, Collegeville - 9/28/88 - "6th consecutive day of working 5 hrs on NOH without writing anything new. A bad time – better count me out of 'Don Giovanni' – I'm feeling too pressed."

Sauk Rapids - 10/18/88 - "Diligently writing away. Got unstuck, thank God. Poor Frank, he's got so many people depending on him. He's 42. If he were 52 (as I am now) he'd shorten his list by 14. It's inspiring to have a calendar as empty as mine."

Sauk Rapids - 11/9/88 - "NOH, growing and growing, is curtailing my trips to the city along with almost everything else in my life. I still meet my classes and see my mother on schedule, but that's about all."

Saint John's - 2/2/89 - "I may be back on track with the novel. I see now that I'm definitely at work on the ending—but such a vast, complex ending. Did I tell you I talked to Claire Smith at the Harold Ober Agy? She has another writer like me whom she's working to release from Harvey's [Ginsberg] bondage. (Also she loves *long* novels.)"

Saint John's - 5/19/89 - "Bob Wyatt called to say he likes the first 60 pp. of NOH & wants to read the rest. I'll use him as my second opinion."

Sauk Rapids - 12/26/89 - Feast of Stephen - Christmas card - "The river is frozen from bank to bank. First time in my 5 years here. Will my fiction stop flowing?"

New York - 3/31/90 - "Ran the gamut at Ballantine, listening to praise of my book from about 20 staff. Galleys soon, maybe 3 weeks. . . . I was photographed in a warehouse by a tall blond from Germany. She'd shot Calvin Trillin the day before."

Blue Cloud Abbey, Marvin [SD] - 4/7/90 - "From Broadway to Blue Cloud - to read from 'North of Hope' to 30 Lutherans and to share a bathroom with a Trappist nun who seems never to urinate. Oh, life is so random."

Saint John's - 9/12/90 - "Sorry to be absent when you call. I'm so pleased that you like the book. Your opinion means even more to me than anybody else's. Powers likes it too, at least as far as he's read. / / Spent the weekend at UMBA [Upper Midwest Booksellers' Association] in Mpls, was one of 4 speakers - Noah Adams (mildly amusing), Carol Bly (concise & serious), Kaye Gibbons (sensationally funny)–and autographed 150 copies of NOH which Ballantine gave away to booksellers. / / Seattle, La Jolla, San Fran & Chicago have been added to my itinerary. Oh yes, and Brainerd (Little Prof.) Nov. 23. / / I'm sending your editorial note to Bob Wyatt. / / Still no author's copies."

**Your letters and postcards are true treasure troves. Do you have any comments on these excerpts from ten or so years ago?**

A. They remind me of how much work that novel was to write—I'd forgotten that, you see, because I forget about the troubles as the novels are published, but it was very hard to write, and there were times where I'd gotten lost in it and had to go back and start over, so I'm very pleased to read these. Also, I'm reminded of that photographer in New York who took my picture—her name was Sigrid Estrada—she lived in a loft where her bed was hanging from the rafters, and her camera was on a tripod, and I had had three hours of sleep the night before. I looked terrible. I remember opening my eyes wide—she snapped the shutter and that was it. So that explains why I look like a deer struck by headlights in the picture on *North of Hope*. Ah, let's see what else. I was also between agents on this book, and I remember writing to Claire Smith at the Harold Ober Agency trying to get her interested in my work. She got interested and then Bob Wyatt bought the book, so I didn't need an agent. And then some years later, Michael, my son, in trying to publish a piece of fiction, sent it to Claire Smith, and she wrote back a very nasty letter asking him how he could possibly want her when I had rejected her. So I guess she was still mad at me for that. I remember UMBA, the Upper Midwest Booksellers' Association—that's where I told the story of the plumber who came to my cabin to clean out my plugged toilet, and he was spattered with shit—he paused and looked up and said to me, "I hear you write books." I said, "Yes, I do." He said, "Boy, I'd sure hate to make a living that way." That made a big hit with the people—I remember that.

**Q. You had mentioned that you were being sent on an autographing tour by Ballantine for *North of Hope*. Please share some of your experiences.**

A. That was my first book tour. When I first started to write, I couldn't make a book tour if I wanted one, and, of course, I didn't want one. I didn't want to go out on this one either, but, of course, I went out. And I went to Washington, D.C., went to Washington state, went to San Diego, Milwaukee, and Chicago. Chicago's never given me much of a turn-out. I remember flying from Washington, D.C., to Washington state one time next to a young man who had earphones, and I heard this rock music all the way for four hours across the nation—this tinny rock music coming from his earphones. And I remember driving from Seattle with a driver up to Bremerton. It was at least a two-hour drive—I gave a reading and drove two hours back to Seattle in the evening and it was very tiring. I was in San Diego—I met your brother. Yes, La Jolla, that was great. That's a nice book store in La Jolla; it's called Kincaid's.

**Q. Mary Ann Grossman of the *St. Paul Pioneer Press*, May 20, 1990, wrote that "speaking of ABA's [American Booksellers' Association] convention, Jon Hassler is one of four authors being honored by Ballantine—Del Rey—Fawcett—Ivy at a reception in anticipation of his new novel, *North of Hope*. . . . The ABA reception is clearly Ballantine's acknowledgement that Jon Hassler is a big-name author." Then, in the June 10, 1990, issue, she reported: "Jon Hassler and three other Ballantine authors were**

honored at a reception at the Desert Inn's Country Club building, surely one of the most beautiful spots on the Vegas Strip. The shy Hassler, who'd never been to an ABA convention, stayed about four inches from a friendly wall and never did get near the center of the room. The publicists had to keep bringing people over to the wall to meet him." What do you remember about this reception?

A. I remember how crowded it was. I wasn't aware that I was being shy or out of the way, but I remember being sort of pushed around by a lot of people. I remember I lined up my first readings at the Hungry Mind. David Unowski, the owner of the Hungry Mind (now Ruminator Books), said he put a cafe into his bookstore, and he had a contest for the cafe's name—the winner, Table of Contents, was announced that night. I remember a man who wrote *Quinqunx* was there, too, because Ballantine published that lengthy book; he was an Englishman who was even less at home than I was.

Q. I believe that you have a story about Harvey Mackay, who also attended this convention. What book was he touting? Please share that story.

A. He might have been touting *Swim with the Sharks*. It was a book on how to get ahead in life using mostly unethical principles. He was on the plane flying out to Las Vegas in an orange sweatsuit, I remember, going up and down the aisle talking to people. I didn't know who he was. Then, when I got off the plane—I was one of the last ones off—my driver said to me on the way to the car, "I've got another rider here. He wanted to go ahead without you, but I said no, we'd wait for you." So I got in the car—it was Harvey Mackay. We drove into Las Vegas from the airport. He was telling me how to write novels because he had a secretary who was trying to be a novelist, and he had been telling her how to go about it. So then he suddenly looked outside and said to the driver, "Don't go this way. This is not a scenic way. Go another way to the hotel." The driver just gave him a dirty look in the mirror and kept on going. We got to the hotel. Harvey got out his bag, and he said, "Wait here, driver. You can drive me over to the convention center after I check in." The driver said, "No, I have other fares I have to pick up." So he went inside, and as the driver was getting my bag out of the trunk, he said, "Do you want me to drive you over to the convention center? I'll wait for you." So that showed you how far Harvey Mackay's methods got him.

**Q. That's a great story. Somewhat surprisingly, *North of Hope* received two particularly nasty reviews along with some extravagantly positive ones. Let's do the two negative ones first. Of course, one is Carolyn See in the October 1, 1990, *Los Angeles Times*. She postulates:**

> *The main character in this book is the weather.* North of Hope *is a long novel with long winters, and it's most often 20 degrees below zero.* . . .
>
> *Yes, the winters are long and terribly hard. Frank grows up (if indeed he ever 'grows up'). That's one of the arguments, one of the themes of this novel.* . . .
>
> *What is it with Frank? The housekeeper has told him that his mother's dying wish was for him to be a priest. (The reader who believes that must think that nobody in this story is going to fall through that thin ice.)* . . .
>
> North of Hope *is a conundrum. There's no conflict, in the way the reader has come to expect, because lust, as such, comes way, way down on this priest's list of priorities—further down than making green Jell-O or folding up brown paper bags. Women don't even make it onto his list of ordinary daydreams.* . . .
>
> *Frank goes on and on to Libby about his chastity. Is Catholicism different in Minnesota than it is in Southern California? Is chastity still so prized up there* North of Hope? . . . .
>
> *If you asked any of the characters in this novel about these matters, they'd be far too busy getting in and out of their thick winter clothes, knocking back rum drinks and checking their thermometers to see if it's going to hit 20 below again tonight.* . . .
>
> *You can't ask a book to be what it's not, but I wish I had a clearer idea of what the author thinks of his very chilly hero.*

**What are your comments about See's review?**

A. I don't believe it—I believe there is a conflict in the story. I believe they do other things besides getting in and out of their winter coats. I think there's more going on in the novel than she sees. She obviously has this bad feeling about priests or something. Anyway, in the *Washington Post* about my next book, *Dear James*, she praised it a lot, so she changed her mind about me between novels.

**Q. The next one probably is more damaging, written by an Ojibway, Jim Northrup, Jr.** (*Duluth News-Tribune,* **December 9, 1990**):

> *It is clear that Hassler doesn't know doodley-squat about Ojibways. His stereotypical portraits of Indians are shallow. The covert racism displayed in this book is no different than that displayed every spring on the boat landings of northern Wisconsin. . . .*
>
> *Even the Indians' dogs catch hell in this story. They are 'nervous little mongrels with dull coats and hungry eyes.' A character wonders if it's true that Indians eat dogs. . . .*
>
> *Hassler gave one of his minor Indian characters a job at the Basswood Museum, a 'cement block teepee.' Hassler knows as much about construction as he does about Indians. How would one build a round teepee out of square cement blocks? . . . .*
>
> *I can't get over how the Indians are portrayed in this novel. Maybe Hassler should be sentenced to spend some time on a real reservation.*
>
> *Maybe he should also try to build a cement block teepee while he's there.*
>
> North of Hope *is hopeless. Hopefully, Hassler won't try to write about Indians again.*

**Do you have any response ten years later, or should we move on?**

A. I want to respond to the cement blocks—also to my independence as a writer. He said I shouldn't write about Indians again. I'll write about them whenever I please. It's a white man's view of the Indian—I'm not an Indian. The cement block teepee was intended to be funny; they made it themselves. And I think he's wrong on every count; he quotes people such as Mrs. Tatzig who doesn't like Indians and says that's my attitude toward Indians. You see, he's just hung up on the subject of Indian identity.

Q. On a positive note, after those two sour ones, Father Andrew M. Greeley, sociologist and novelist, discovered your work. He wrote the following to Clare Ferraro at Ballantine Books on June 25, 1990: "*North of Hope* is one of the most exciting books I've read in a long, long time. A parable of grace and redemption, it is unquestionably the best book about the Catholic priesthood since Graham Greene's *The Power and the Glory* and Jon Hassler is certainly one of the very best Catholic novelists since Graham Greene." Greeley also wrote a lead article in the November 17, 1990, issue of *America*, "The Catholic Novels of Jon Hassler." I'll quote a little from this article:

*Minnesota author Jon Hassler's new novel* North of Hope *is a Catholic classic in the making, a remarkable story about the revitalization of a battered priest that ought to be read by every priest in the country. The 57-year-old Hassler, whose work has received extraordinarily favorable reviews in the secular press, including praise for* North of Hope *from the* New York Times, *is one of the leading lights of contemporary Catholic fiction. . . .*

*I could not put the book down. . . .*

*The struggle is not merely internal.* North of Hope *is also a fascinating mystery story, a compelling suspense novel and a poignant love story. It has all the makings of that rare book that can be both a literary success and a popular best seller. . . .*

*The mystery of why this fine writer seems unknown beyond the book review columns and the precincts of Saint John's became more puzzling.*

*I persuaded his publisher to send me the other Hassler novels and devoured them in a weekend. While* North of Hope *is his masterpiece, the others are all brilliant and challenging stories . . .*

*One cannot capture the work of a gifted writer in a few short paragraphs that summarize his six novels. All that one can do is to hint that the writer is a superb storyteller, as well as a man of deep and powerful hope and enormous literary talent.*

Comment?

A. Father Greeley probably introduced my novels to a Catholic readership because, after that, articles about my work began to appear in Catholic periodicals.

**Q. Both the daily (for the first time) and the Sunday** *New York Times* **car-ried reviews of** *North of Hope.* **Christopher Lehmann-Haupt in the Octo-ber 1, 1990, Monday issue opened with "Frank Healy falls in love with beautiful Libby Girard in the opening chapter of Jon Hassler's irresistible new novel,** *North of Hope"* **and ended with "Like Jon Hassler as an artist, Frank Healy may lack the power to make the earth move. But while they're both around, they make it seem a little better to live on." Novelist Richard Russo, author of** *Nobody's Fool,* **had some reservations about the novel, but not the novelist, in his review in the Sunday** *New York Times Book Review* **dated October 21, 1990:**

> *In fact, Mr. Hassler is one of those writers who make storytelling look so easy that the severe guardians of contemporary literature may be suspicious.*
>
> *Part of Jon Hassler's brilliance has always been his ability to achieve the depth of real literature through such sure-handed, no gimmicks, honest language that the result appears effortless. So perhaps it will not be surprising if* North of Hope, *his brooding, meditative new novel, is the one that makes him the household name he deserves to be. It's his longest and, in some respects, his most ambitious novel, but it's also a book that, for all its virtues, reveals its author's struggles. For once Mr. Hassler hasn't managed his customary illusion of effortlessness. . . .*
>
> *Throughout most of the book, Mr. Hassler seems to follow Frank and Libby out of affection and duty; his minor characters he follows with joy and, we suspect, blessed relief. For this reason,* North of Hope *is unlikely to replace the flawless* Grand Opening *as Jon Hassler's masterpiece. But Mr. Hassler is a writer so good that he suffers only by comparison to his own best work.*

**Do you have any comment on either review?**

A. Well, they're both very positive, and the important thing is they're in such an important place. It's the *New York Times* that makes or breaks a book. And the first one, of course, is better than the second, and the second is good enough.

**Q. The** *New York Times Book Review,* **November 24, 1991, included** *North* *of Hope* paperback in "New & Noteworthy": "A priest bringing Roman Catholicism to a forlorn Indian reservation in northern Minnesota has a surprise meeting with the one woman who has ever been able to compete with his love for God. Last year our reviewer, Richard Russo, called this Jon Hassler's 'most ambitious novel.'" The reviews in the *New York Times* then do affect the sales of your fiction.

A. Yes, they do. The two negative reviews of *Staggerford* and of my most recent book, *The Dean's List*, diminished the sales.

Q. *USA Today* for its only time mentioned a Hassler novel in its January 2, 1991, issue. Bruce Allen, in an article entitled "Neglected American fiction that deserves a nod," wrote: "Excellent new novels from writers in mid-career include ... *North of Hope* (Ballantine, $19.95), the perpetually underrated Jon Hassler's warm, involving story of a middle-aged priest's compromised efforts to live in the real world he finds he cannot, after all, reject." Were you surprised—and pleased—by this mention?

A. Surprised and pleased both, yes.

Q. And then *USA Today* has forgotten about you for the next ten years. I'd like to quote from one last review, a really lovely piece written by William Jayne for the *Washington, D.C. Times* (October 22, 1990):

> *The winter of 1977-78 was a bleak season.*
>
> *Remember? Hubert Humphrey died in January. Storms and frigid temperatures battered the northern tier of the country, and transplanted Southerner Jimmy Carter was discovering a malaise in the American people.*
>
> *Against this temporal backdrop, Jon Hassler places the characters of* North of Hope *in the bleakness of northern Minnesota, where Indians die untimely deaths and it's 18 degrees below zero at noon.*
>
> *Yet Mr. Hassler shows the reader that love is still possible, faith exists, and no matter how far north people travel spiritually, hope goes with them.*
>
> *This is Mr. Hassler's sixth novel and, like the others, is placed in the locales where he has lived. Parallels with writers such as*

*Flannery O'Connor and even William Faulkner are tempting but not illuminating. . . .*

*Yet the novel does not conjure up the literary aspects of its geographic place as much as it explores and maps the bleak, spiritual north of our time. . . .*

*This is a true 'adult' novel. No panaceas for angst emerge. Remedies for psychic ills are shadowy and poorly understood by characters too real to change overnight.*

*Yet, in the short space between Advent of 1977 and Easter of 1978,* North of Hope *brings us through the bleak winter of the spirit and out again to a new spring. As springs have always been, it is hopeful, if imperfect.*

**My, that is such a perceptive and well-written review; I kept wanting to quote even more. What did you think? Any comments?**

A. I loved the review, particularly because it's well-written. How far north people travel spiritually—hope goes with them, he says, and he says the novel explores and maps the bleak spiritual north of our time. And he says remedies for psychic ills are shadowy and poorly understood by characters too real to change overnight. Those are all very good descriptions of the book, it seems to me.

**Q. I almost thought maybe Mr. Jayne should be doing these interviews, he's so perceptive; that is probably one of the finest reviews you've received for any of your novels.**

A. That's true.

**Q. I understand a Minnesota actress had shown interest in a possible movie of *North of Hope* some years ago.**

A. Jessica Lange, yes. She did—she inquired about it, but never picked it up for an option.

**Q. Why?**

A. The love wasn't consummated. See, that's the thing about this novel. I remember when I got to that point in the book, I called up

Bob Wyatt, and I said, "Can you write a love story without the lovers going to bed?" And he said, bless him, "I don't know." So he gave me freedom to explore that.

Q. But *North of Hope* is still alive as a possible movie.

A. Yes, it is. A man named Warren Stitt—he's had an option since 1996—I don't know if he's going to do anything with it or not. He's still trying to raise money to go into production. [The option was not renewed.]

Q. And he produced one movie previously, *The Spitfire Grill.*

A. Yes, he did. It was a pretty good movie.

Q. Anything else to add about *North of Hope* or this time period from your life?

A. I don't know. It was a book that took me three years to write; it seemed well worth the time, and it seems well worth all the difficulties I had getting it out.

Q. A fitting coda to *North of Hope*, Jon. Thank you.

# Dear James

Jon did not follow up *A Green Journey* immediately with a sequel; in fact, eight years elapsed, and two novels (*Grand Opening* and *North of Hope*) appeared before Ballantine published *Dear James* in 1993 in hardcover. A number of quotes from Jon's letters and cards to me during this gestation period with *Dear James* are included in our interview, but since then, I have unearthed two more:

> Nevis - 4/29/91 - "This comes to you from the cabin, where almost immediately I am able to delve into a deeper level of concentration than in Sauk Rapids, which is to say I have 209 pages of this draft ready for Bob Wyatt (and Pat Karlan) [Jon's editor and agent] to see, and I'm perhaps 20 pages beyond that. Getting to know James again is the hard part."

> Saint John's - 12/29/91 - "Relieved of my filial duties at Christmas, I've spent a week in Mpls revising my ms. & being fed & watered. (But not fed too much because my cholesterol was recently checked - 297 & climbing.) . . .

> I almost came north for the BCC [Brainerd Community College] open house, but my novel wouldn't let me. The last chapter keeps spawning other last chapters. A good enough book, I think, despite being long & rather slow."

Jon's correspondence indicates that *Dear James* was not an easy book to write. But Jon's creativity and writing skills had developed in the interval after the publication of *A Green Journey*, and *Grand Opening*, *North of Hope*, and *Dear James* exhibit greater scope and more complex moral themes than *A Green Journey*. In teaching Jon Hassler to college students of all ages I often observe that the added richness of these later works generate greater excitement. Perhaps this is because Jon is more willing to take chances with his characters, introducing out-and-out "villains" such as Wallace Flint in *Grand Opening*, Judge Bigelow and Dr. Tom Pearsall in *North of Hope*, and Imogene Kite in *Dear James*, for example.

In *Dear James* Jon also extends the scope of his story far beyond the small-town world of central Minnesota to include Vietnam, Rome, and northern Ireland. His characters meet up with distress, violence, and evil, and they come to terms with these things in one way or another, making subtle decisions that touch the reader more subtly than I can adequately suggest here.

Jon's talent as a moral writer has elicited praise far and wide, and I'd like to reproduce one such comment here, from Professor Anthony Low, Department of English, at New York University. His February 21, 1995, letter contains this observation:

> I'm on sabbatical and should be doing my work instead of reading novels and writing letters. But it's not often that I feel such an urge to thank a writer for his work. You have Flannery O'Connor's gift for treating the things of the spirit without falseness or sentimentality, to immerse them in real life, and to do it in a way that even those who don't understand what you are up to are bound to appreciate.

These reflections certainly fit *Dear James*.

J. P. September 2002

November 30, 2000

Q. Jon, whenever I start preparing an interview with you I suddenly worry that I won't have any sensible or cogent questions to ask and that the interview won't turn out very well. How magnified that must be for you in creating fiction. I'm dealing with facts basically, or at least non-fiction, and the absence of a safety net is daunting enough, but that's minute compared to what you have gone through in the past twenty-some years in creating fiction. Any thoughts?

A. Well, that's interesting, Joe. It's true that I start out my books without any sort of assurance they're going to work, and then as I work through them, they do. Most of them have turned out okay. One or two have failed along the way—"The Book of Brendan," of course, in the early '80s, but otherwise, they've been working out, so I've been lucky that way.

Q. Ballantine published *Dear James* in hardcover in 1993, three years after *North of Hope*. Did you have any tentative titles before deciding on *Dear James*?

A. That was one of those titles that was with me from the start. When I first conceived the book in the late '80s, I thought of *Dear James* as the title.

Q. I'm not surprised—it's certainly an appropriate title. This novel is, in a sense, a sequel to *A Green Journey*. Can readers read *Dear James* and appreciate it as much without having read *A Green Journey* first?

A. Yes, I believe they can, since I put in the essentials from *A Green Journey*. The reader is clued in on what happened before.

Q. How many copies were printed in hardback?

A. I have no idea how many copies were printed. It sold something under 20,000, maybe 14 or 15,000 in hardback. That's all I know.

**Q. Who was your agent for this novel?**

A. For this novel my agent was Patricia Karlan. She was from the West Coast, she had been my movie agent before, and she sold *North of Hope* to Bob Wyatt at Ballantine. She sold this one to Clare Ferraro [editor-in-chief] at Ballantine.

**Q. And your editor at Ballantine?**

A. My editor, Bob Wyatt, who had edited *North of Hope*, had left Ballantine by this time, but they hired him back as a free-lancer to edit this book with me, and I was very happy about that because I liked him a lot. He was a very good editor.

**Q. Did he suggest many changes?**

A. The only change I can remember that was major had to do with the ending of the book. You see, I originally ended the book in Ireland with Agatha walking along the beach with that little boy. He read it and said, "This is a Staggerford novel. This has to end in Staggerford. That's where it began." So then I put in the part about the library tea which seemed to fit just fine.

**Q. And you were pleased about the way it did end then?**

A. Yes, I was.

**Q. Any more comments about your working relationship with him?**

A. Well, he was so good because he enjoyed my work a lot, of course. That's important to a writer. And then he had good suggestions. He had me re-do the ending of *North of Hope*. I don't remember how I changed it, but he had me do that. And he was an enthusiastic editor. I haven't had another editor like him since. I didn't have one before him that was as good as he was either.

**Q. Sally Childs adapted *Dear James* for the Lyric Theatre in Minneapolis, which ran from September 5 until October 5, 1997. Please discuss what**

changes you remember. I know she pared the cast down to five characters.

A. Yes, I have to say that was a very good adaptation, too. I think it's the best of my plays, and I didn't write it. She cut out a lot, of course, the part about Ireland—other things in it, but it's a good play. I don't remember what changes were made, Joe, do you?

Q. Not too many that I can remember, but I think it was more between James and Agatha. Noel Holston in the September 10, 1997, *Star Tribune* opines: "But *Dear James* is frequently amusing and occasionally hilarious [this is about the stage production]—more comical, perhaps, than Hassler ever intended. Dry-witted dialogue from his novel, which Childs has excerpted mostly verbatim, often gains a wicked crackle on stage." Any comments on this or anything more about Sally's adaptation?

A. I remember reading an early draft of the play in which she had made up a lot of dialogue. I advised her to use more of my dialogue since I'd worked so hard on it that I perfected it. I knew it was pretty good. So she went back and she put in my dialogue instead of hers. This seemed to work very well.

Q. Any movie nibbles for *Dear James*? Of course, one would think that the producer Andrew Fenady and NBC-TV, who put on the television movie of *A Green Journey* starring Angela Lansbury and Denholm Elliott, would have been interested.

A. Andrew Fenady, the producer, went to Angela Lansbury with it, and she said no, she couldn't do it because Denholm Elliott, who portrayed James, had died. She couldn't imagine doing it with anybody else. So that's too bad.

Q. That's lovely—bad for *Dear James*, but that illustrates Lansbury's humanity. Any foreign reprints or book awards for *Dear James*?

A. Nothing, nothing.

Q. Please explain the dedication "For Gretchen."

A. Gretchen's my wife, and it was the first book that came out after we met, actually, so I dedicated it to her.

Q. I was going to ask how you thought of the idea for *Dear James*, but then you answered that question in the *Dear James* theatre program at the Lyric Theatre—September/October 1997. I would like to quote this in its entirety:

*Dear James* was born in Rome on Epiphany Sunday, 1986. I was admiring Michelangelo's Pietà in St. Peter's Basilica when I suddenly imagined Agatha McGee and James O'Hannon standing beside me. I recorded the moment in my journal:

*The Pietà is marvelous beyond my expectations. Mary is so young, Jesus so dead. Does Agatha see the youth, and James the death? Is James mortally ill?*

We were a group of seven adults and ten college students who had flown to Italy for January Term, and from this point on I saw the sites of antiquity and the renaissance with a kind of triple vision. Besides my own reaction, I kept imagining how Agatha and James were seeing things. And now, reviewing my journal from eleven years ago, I see how my entries reflect these two imaginary companions of mine. James's devotion to his Church, for instance:

*As glorious as its monuments is the Church's ability to draw its faithful from all walks of life. I saw at St. Peter's, together, the same segments of the population I had earlier seen in various parts of Rome: women in furs and leather skirts and patterned hose, bejeweled and tanned and escorted by dark men in plain, rich overcoats; scar-faced women with worn shoes and tattered tote bags; little old widows with the shakes; nuns, priests and other spinsterish celibates, both male and female; old men with hearing aids; teens in jeans; tourists with cameras, maps and new walking shoes—all in a stream flowing uphill across the piazza and to the bronze doors of St. Peter's.*

And Agatha's acerbic views:

*Italian is a fat-sounding language. The Italian face is jowly, large-eyed, heavy-browed. The Italian character is overexpressive, underreflective. Not my people!*

*Rome in the rain – glum as Dublin.*

*Rome in the sun – the color of an overripe apricot.*

*Our hotel is clean and in good repair, but it lets in no daylight.*

*This is the worst cold I've had in years. I'm dripping mucus in all the holy places.*

*Each* ristorante, *no matter how small, is staffed by the entire cast of* Guys and Dolls. *At least the guys.*

*I wish Assisi had a Sunday paper I could read.*

**Any comments?**

A. Well, this passage from the playbill takes me back to that trip to Italy which was wonderful. I went with Bob Spaeth, the dean at Saint John's, and the students, and these are things I put in my journal about it. I remember my cousin who is Italian came to the play, and he read this comment, "The Italian character is overexpressive, underreflective. Not my people!" He challenged me on that. He said, "What's the matter with Italians?" So I said that was Agatha's opinion, not mine.

**Q. And this was Bob Spaeth's Galileo trip to Italy?**

A. Yes, Bob Spaeth was very interested in Galileo because Galileo would challenge the Church. Bob was always challenging the Church, too. So he followed Galileo around Europe. Wherever he went he looked for a statue or some memento of Galileo.

**Q. Were the students in Agatha's group similar to the students you traveled with from Saint John's?**

A. Yes, they were. You know I wrote more about the students than I did about Italy. That's the way it is when I go somewhere with my journal. I write more about the people I'm with than what I see. I look at the people around me instead of what I should be seeing.

Anyway, there were a lot of students, and I exaggerated some of them, made some of them dumber than they were.

**Q. No Diet-Coke then?**

A. Well, that was true, yes. We got to Assisi after nine days in Rome. It was so peaceful and wonderful. We sat down to dinner the first night. This girl from St. Thomas [in St. Paul] said to me, "I just love Assisi. They have Diet-Coke."

**Q. To continue with the autobiographical threads, Agatha and the group arrive at the Da Vinci Airport in Rome to learn that terrorists had killed a number of people (154-157). Please explain where you got this idea.**

A. This happened three weeks before we left the United States. In fact, we were thinking of canceling the trip because of that, but we went anyway. And so I put in what I read about it in the paper. Also, the guards with their guard dogs were all on duty at the airport when we got there. So I didn't have to make that up.

**Q. On your January 1986 trip, you enjoyed Assisi as much as Agatha. In a postcard from Assisi, dated January 11, 1986, you exclaim:**

> *With Assisi it's love at first sight. Such views! Attended Mass in this church—in the crypt where Francis's stone coffin sits above the altar. Then I went to Clare's church and (Horrors!) saw her on display in a coffin of glass.*
>
> *Vatican museums yesterday. Besides the antiquities, a surprising and wonderful collection of modern art—Pope Paul VI on wheels, for example. Two days here, then Florence.*

**At this point did you realize that Agatha would also relish Assisi?**

A. Yes, I did. I felt that she was with me all the way on this trip after I discovered her at the Pietà in Rome.

**Q. In a postcard from Rome dated January 8, 1986, you shared:**

> *Saw the Pope here Sunday noon, and returned today for his*

*weekly audience held in a huge, new auditorium. He spoke to us*
*in Ital.Ger. Sp. Pol. Fr. & English. Then a troupe of acrobats came*
*out & performed for him—and us.*

*Up to Castel Gondolpho yesterday then back down under-*
*ground to the catacombs.*

*Well-planned tour, compatible group. I'll be ready to leave*
*Rome —it's such a city! Eager for Assisi.*

Thus, the segment from pages 307-312 is based mostly on your own observation.

A. Yes, we went to an audience in the audience hall, so we sat there just as Agatha and James do. Also, when Pope John Paul II came down the middle aisle, he would take people's faces in his hands—I was so struck by that. That's why I had him do it to James. Then, of course, it's a miracle that he knows what James is about. He can discern his choice to go home to Ireland and work for peace, and how he knew that, that's a miracle. That's the only miracle I've ever put in my books, I think.

Q. That's exactly what I was going to quote—the Pope who "took James's face in his hands, turned it to the left and spoke briefly into his ear. Then he bent forward and touched his forehead to James's forehead, his hands still cupping James's face like a precious vessel" (309). That's a very graphic and powerful image, and you had observed that at least in general.

A. Yes, he had done that to several people up and down the aisles, mostly old people.

Q. He really is charismatic.

A. Yes, he is.

Q. And you had been in the modern audience hall.

A. Yes, it's the modern audience hall with sculpture behind the Pope— looks like seaweed, actually, pretty homely, I thought, but the Pope himself was very vigorous in those days. His voice was wonderful. They had a carnival going on for him. Somebody on a trumpet played

"O Mein Papa" in his ear. All those things that happened in the book happened that day.

Q. **Have you visited Lourdes? James's account sounds realistic and authentic (172-173).**

A. I've never been there—that's one of the few places I've written about where I haven't been.

Q. **On page 95, Agatha compares the handwriting of letters from James written two years apart and notices a wobble in the more recent one. Was James's handwriting based on your own, or was this incident too early for your micrography?**

A. It was too early for my condition.

Q. **So you were prescient again?**

A. Yes, I was.

Q. **Is Father Virgil from St. Andrew's (207) a tribute to the Saint John's Father Virgil that we both knew?**

A. Yes, of course.

Q. **Father DeSmet from *North of Hope* is wearing shorts and a T-shirt with FIGHTING IRISH stenciled on the front (429). Facetiously, did this mention of Notre Dame help you be granted a Doctor of Letters from Notre Dame three years later?**

A. I hope not. I don't think it had anything to do with it, Joe. I forgot Father DeSmet was in this book, too. That's interesting.

Q. **Notre Dame's citation is really fine. I'll quote this in its entirety:**

At the 151st Commencement
The May Exercises
The University of Notre Dame
confers the degree of

Doctor of Letters, *honoris causa*, on a Minnesota storyteller whose novels plumb the placid depths of small towns, quiet loves, and muted yearnings, searching them for avenues of grace. Living, working, teaching and dreaming in Midwestern towns occasionally overlooked by mapmakers, he guides his readers into similarly neglected regions of the human soul. A realist in matters spiritual, he aims his narratives at the place where human folly encounters divine mystery, and so becomes an artist of the sacramental. On Jon Francis Hassler, Collegeville, Minnesota.

**Why do you think you were selected for this singular honor, Jon?**

A. Well, Father Malloy, the president of Notre Dame, had been using my books in class, and I think it was his idea that I get an honorary doctorate. When I met him, I told him that he was in a book because when Father Frank Healy leaves the Academy for the last time, he's playing basketball with his students. I had remembered reading that when Father Malloy was elected president of Notre Dame, he'd been playing basketball with his students and had to interrupt his game to go to the meeting, so I put that in *North of Hope*. I told him he was in a book—he was pleased to hear that.

**Q. And then in the year of *Dear James*, you received an honorary doctoral degree from Assumption College (Worcester, MA) on May 22, 1993. Did you attend?**

A. I did—I went to that, too. That was an easy one to get since I didn't have to speak. I didn't have to speak at Notre Dame, either. I remember sitting on the stage at Assumption College, and as my time drew near, I said to the woman next to me—she was a fat English teacher—I said, "Let's see, what should I say. Should I say thank you or should I give a little speech?" She said to me, "Say nothing." So that was what I did.

**Q. Any memories from the Notre Dame ceremony?**

A. Yes, that was a great weekend because Gretchen and I went down there, and they treated us royally for two days, and they had a big

Mass in the fieldhouse, which was very inspiring, and then the next day, the Commencement, and that was all very flattering, actually.

Q. Maybe I should have waited to discuss honorary degrees in one of your college novel interviews, but Worcester and 1993 and Father DeSmet's Fighting Irish T-shirt seem to indicate this is the proper place for including these. Any other honorary degrees?

A. I've had two others. One I had at the University of North Dakota, 1997 perhaps. Then in the spring of '99, I went to St. Norbert's College in De Pere, Wisconsin, which is next to Green Bay, and I got one there, too, so I have four now.

Q. Was North Dakota partially because you earned your Master's degree there?

A. Yes, it was.

Q. Friends sometimes ask if I've ever been depicted in one of your novels, and I always say, "No," which I believe is true. However, one bit of dialogue of Professor Finn's does sound like me. He calls to his travel group, "People, people," which I've often said to both students and members of our school's travel trips. Am I the source?

A. Yes, you are. You were in another novel which didn't get published, too. I remember I had a hugging professor there by the name of Josiah Tulp. That was his name—Josiah Tulp.

Q. What novel was that?

A. That was "The Book of Brendan," I believe.

Q. I never knew that.

A. Yes, he didn't survive—he'll come back, though.

Q. Congressman Kleinschmidt thinks of the Rookery State faculty as "a mixture of radicals, eggheads, and foreigners who consistently voted for his opponent" (43). Is this faculty based on any particular college or university faculty that you have been associated with?

A. When I first began writing about Rookery State in *Simon's Night*, I based it on North Dakota University, where I had done my graduate work, which had a very tough English Department.

Q. Very early on, page 5, you subtly make your point about Agatha's letters to James: "If I could talk to Lillian, Agatha mused, there'd be no need to write these readerless letters to Ireland." Immediately, the reader is brought up short by the word "readerless." Are many revisions and rewrites involved in distilling the essence of the thought to a few words? Your style often is so economical.

A. Yes, that comes from revision, of course. And I try for understatement wherever I can. That's an example because later on when she finishes the letter, she tears it up, throws it away. She hasn't been sending these letters she's been writing.

Q. The TV movie of *A Green Journey* ends with Agatha mailing a letter to James. Of course, the novel did not end that way, and the reader for *Dear James* knows right away that in the intervening years no communication has been broached between the two. I suppose in a way you tip your hand with the title *Dear James*; one assumes that the relationship will start up again.

A. Yes, of course. It was too good a relationship to let go. I had to develop it further.

Q. Agatha hosts a Thanksgiving dinner in *Dear James*, which covers, I think, pages 13-60 at least. This is probably the centerpiece of Part 1. What did you hope to accomplish in this section?

A. First of all, I hoped to show Agatha's disappointment with her current life. She's surrounded by friends, but they don't fulfill her, and she finds fulfillment with James. Also, I wanted to portray these people—I got carried away with people like Sylvester Juba who's such a boor, his daughter Sister Judith, Father Finn, and Congressman

Kleinschmidt. French is there, too. So I have a lot of fun with these people around the table.

Q. And did you accomplish then what you had hoped to?

A. Oh yes, I think I did. Agatha breaks down and cries before the meal is over, and Sylvester insults her. Sister Judith makes some awful remarks about theological concepts. And French talks about Vietnam and Father Finn delivers a letter from James.

Q. So each reveals something basically about himself or herself. Tell a little about the Thanksgiving dinner chapters.

A. That was the longest Thanksgiving dinner in history. It goes on for about fifty pages and yet it seems like a good dinner. It seems interesting enough to me. Writer Bill Holm wrote me a note about that one last year. He finally got around to reading *Dear James*. He wrote to me about how much he enjoyed Thanksgiving dinner with Agatha, so he liked it, too.

Q. You define Agatha's depression, her state of mind, effectively during the Thanksgiving dinner. Her estrangement from James causes her momentarily to converse with him; he is more real to her than her actual dinner guests. "'Don't laugh,' would be Agatha's response, a statement directed at James in her imagination but now uttered aloud in her dining room, and attracting—since no one was laughing—a curious glance from each of her guests" (25). Rather than present her condition in capital letters, you let the reader know indirectly without overly intruding into Agatha's personal life. Do you usually respect your characters, or have you sometimes been more merciless in depicting them?

A. Well, gee, that's a big question, Joe. I've written about, let's see, almost six hundred characters in my life. I can't say, but that's another example of understatement which I love to use with people.

Q. I might be getting amnesia (I sound like your first editor Judith Kern, who said she had had a stroke. You learned that was her sense of humor after you sent her a get well card), but was French in any of your previous novels? He seems like an old friend, but was his only previous appearance in the story, "Staggerford's Indian"?

A. Yes, I believe that's where he first appeared. Yes, sure.

Q. It just seemed like I knew him much more than just from the one story. That's really good. Where did French come from in your experience?

A. I don't remember. All I know is I love writing about the down-and-out people such as the Raft Family in *A Green Journey*. And Jemmy in *Jemmy*. And I had this Vietnam vet who is shell-shocked, and he just grew for me. I remember "Staggerford's Indian"—that's the one about the Christmas movie—and I put that in as a chapter of this book to introduce him to this story.

Q. French is psychologically maimed from his experience in Vietnam. "It was the same old dream about war—babies and young women dead in a village—that French had been dreaming for ten years or more" (8). Does his mental state, in a sense, parallel and comment on Agatha's?

A. Yes, of course, but his is more serious. He borders on the psychotic occasionally whereas Agatha's merely depressed. But they're both in need of companionship, and later on, of course, they find it in each other.

Q. You successfully use flashbacks both to describe French's state of mind and to present his disturbing Vietnam experiences. Were these flashbacks difficult to write?

A. No, for some reason, they came along just fine.

Q. Did you do any research or studying about post-trauma shock syndrome in regard to French's condition? I know that Imogene knows all about it, but how did Jon Hassler find out?

A. I found out the way I find out about most things in my books—I read it in the newspaper.

Q. Agatha's assertion, "A statement is either true or false, Frederick," regarding French's false claims to having looked for work, causes him to reassert his moral integrity—at a financial cost to himself. He doesn't lie to the employment officer about having looked for work (as everyone else does). He also becomes a moral beacon for the boys who stole candy from the Morgan Hotel. He is trying to choose a more noble path. In a way, Agatha has to change her stance, too, regarding James. Again, the situation of each reflects and illuminates the other. Any comments?

A. Well, that's interesting. I think French, of course, is influenced by Agatha since she's so straight and he tries to shape up for her sake, I think. And then Agatha changes in her regard to James because she says at one point, "How can a woman be in love with a priest?" And then she finds out in Assisi it's possible.

Q. James tells a story about a priest in Belfast and a man going to confession. "A man came into the box and knelt down and said, 'Bless me, Father, for I have sinned, I have shot a British soldier,' and the priest said to him, 'Get on to the mortal sins'" (167). Had you heard that story?

A. Yes, I heard that from our friend Brother Benet at Blue Cloud Abbey in Marvin, South Dakota. He told me that story, which happened in Ireland.

Q. I should have known. The whole intricate set of tales about Con Stitch and his murder and Liam O'Malley and the sniper Tommy Feehan—fact or fiction or a mixture?

A. Well, let's see now. The one about Con Stitch I read in a *New York Times Sunday Magazine*—a story very similar to that. As for Tommy Feehan, I made that up entirely.

Q. I was struck, when devising this section of questions, how a partial—or maybe total—theme of *Dear James* is the violence people inflict on each other with bombs, guns, grenades. We are given graphic images of French's Vietnam experiences, James's anecdotes about killings, and the terrorists' attack at the Rome airport. Were these deliberately incorporated to convey this moral theme?

A. Well, of course, they were all in there for the reason of pointing out the way humanity seemed to be going—the way it shouldn't go, it seemed to me.

Q. And these mirror the personal attacks by Imogene and the townspeople against Agatha.

A. Yes, Agatha discovers her own sort of violence when she gets home—discovers what Imogene has done to her reputation.

Q. This theme harkens back to *Grand Opening*—how we should treat one another. Twelve-year-old Brendan realizes that "Dodger needed Brendan's promise never again to be as unkind to anyone as he had been to Dodger, his promise to go through life more openhearted toward others and less concerned with himself. *Atonement* was the term the nuns of St. Bonnie's had been fond of using in cases like this. They said it was never too late to begin making amends" (306, *Grand Opening*). Plum is the microcosm in which this happens. *Dear James*, it seems to me, contains both the microcosm, the small world of Staggerford, and the macrocosm, the whole world, i.e., Vietnam, Italy, Ireland. Each comments on the other—the malicious small-town gossip and the worldwide senseless violence. Does it help to convey the theme and meaning of this novel by using both the small-town canvas and the world's canvas?

A. Yes, of course, it does. I remember thinking that as I wrote that Staggerford was the microcosm of the world.

Q. Well, that's good to know. In a sense, Agatha and French represent this connection between the two. Agatha is hurt by the small-town people, chiefly Imogene, and French is injured by the military conflict in southeast Asia, the world canvas.

A. Yes, right, they're both injured.

Q. But Agatha is able to forgive James for his deception of not telling her that he is a priest, and she and James enter into a deeper spiritual communion, spreading peace in Ireland. Similarly, French tries to do the right thing (not lying at the employment office, withholding candy from the thieves), and he is rewarded with the news that he is Agatha's relative and that he will live in her home when the Morgan Hotel is torn down. Each tries to change for the better, and each gets rewarded in the process. Is that a somewhat accurate reading?

A. That's right—they're rewarded for doing good. Agatha, at the end, too, forgives Imogene which is a very good thing for her to do. The thing readers comment most about the book is the ending—when she forgives Imogene.

Q. And she votes for her to be the librarian. I was going to wait until later in the interview to discuss the themes, but Agatha and French propel me to ask them now. "By what flaw in God's plan (Agatha asked herself) were most people in need of more love than they were getting?" (190). And Agatha makes quite a list, which ends up including nearly everyone in the novel. Do you agree?

A. Yes, of course, I agree. I think my novels have always dealt with lonely people.

Q. On page 353, at St. Isidore's Church in Staggerford: "And now there she [Agatha] sat with a rare look of contentment on her face, her smile beaming up at James in the pulpit. Never in his life had Father Finn witnessed so clearly the transforming power of love." Obviously, this is a statement of your theme.

A. Yes, James has finally come to Staggerford, and Agatha's happy to have him. She's just happy, just content with life there, for the moment at least.

Q. Agatha, in a conversation with Congressman Kleinschmidt, says: "Murder is killing someone," and a few lines later, "Murder is taking a life" (375). Agatha's reputation has been "murdered" by Imogene; her reputation has been taken away. Is this partly what you meant?

A. Yes, it is, sure.

Q. Agatha often has pithy observations, and I would like to quote two. These could be called Agatha's Aphorisms: "She'd never known a book lover to grow up to cause trouble" (408). And another, "You measured distances by taking your bearings from things close at hand" (417). Are such thoughts and statements part of her character, of who she is?

A. Certainly they grew out of who she is, yes.

Q. On page 289, we find Agatha thinking:

*So why, now, did everything seem suddenly reversed, her assumptions overthrown, her desires upside down? By what trick of fate or hellish magic had James, by not living there, made Staggerford now seem off limits? For his invitation to Ireland had made her not want to go home.*

Is this an epiphany or premonition of Agatha's about what is going on in Staggerford, her reputation being ruined?

A. Yes, she says that Staggerford seems off limits now. She doesn't know it at the time, but she'll discover that it's off limits to her.

Q. Each of your novels is like a puzzle, with various shapes and pieces fitting together to complete the picture. One Hassler trademark is your use of dreams.

A. Yes, I often have people dream in my novels. At first I described the entire dream. I discovered that wasn't a good idea. It's much more effective if you summarize a dream.

Q. Works of art, especially paintings, always figure prominently in your writings, Jon. Of course, having Agatha and James in Italy would be natural—and expected—for this to occur. They encounter Cimabue and Giotto in Assisi:

*She [Agatha] loved whatever her eye fell upon in Assisi. The domed and towered churches so numerous . . . the floor of the valley spread out below the town in a crazy-quilt pattern of greens and ambers and winter browns—all of this appealed at once to*

*Agatha's eye for beauty, and fed, somehow, her hunger for spiritual transcendence. She felt nourished and consoled. . . .*

*She revealed this to James shortly after noon in the Basilica of St. Francis. . . . They had stood a long time studying Cimabue's portrait of Francis—his tonsure and fringe of red hair, his little mouth and long nose and big ears, his eyes looking worn out by the privations of the abstemious life he'd chosen to live—and they'd agreed that a handsome Francis would not have been nearly so inspiring. Then, climbing the stairs and coming out into the tall and airy upper church, filled as it was with a hazy noonday light that lent the frescoes a kind of soft, ethereal beauty, Agatha had blurted, 'I can't stand to think of leaving here, James.'*

*'Exquisite, isn't it?'*

*By following Giotto's two dozen illustrations from the life of the Saint—Francis gives away his mantle, Francis preaches to the birds—they found themselves at the arched doorway leading outside. (255-256)*

**When you were at Assisi (and I believe that you, like Agatha and James, stayed on when the group left for another town), did you make copious notes in your journal to capture this flavor of the Basilica?**

A. Yes, the group left to go to Padua, and I couldn't stand to leave, so I stayed an extra day.

**Q. At St. Peter's, Agatha and James stand, looking at the restored Pietà of Michelangelo. Here, as in Dublin, Agatha and James learn from each other in appreciating a work of art. Agatha "was immediately drawn to the Virgin's face, so pure and innocent, so young, so beautiful. Meanwhile, James, standing beside her, was transfixed by the Savior's inert face, drained of life" (217). Such reactions help explain your characters. Do you have reproductions of the artworks in front of you as you write?**

A. No, I don't, I wrote that from memory, but that's what I thought when I stood there looking at it in Rome—I remember Agatha thinking how young the virgin looked. I remember James thinking how dead Christ looked.

Q. And it's very effective, too. And that leads me to a few examples now of your descriptive talents: "On her [Imogene's] right the Badbattle was dark and light in irregular masses like the hide of a Holstein—black in the swift places where it hadn't yet frozen, white with snow-covered ice" (133). "Agatha bent over the [audio] tape and studied it for a moment before nudging it delicately with her forefinger. It might have been a large crustacean that had crawled up on her end table and died" (327). And if one knows Belleek is Irish china, this is very effective: Agatha "walked across the hard-packed sand to the edge of the water, tiny seashells crunching underfoot like broken Belleek" (408). Do you still like these?

A. Yes, I'm very fond of those. Let's see—a lot of people don't know what Belleek is—it's a very thin type of china. Bob Wyatt, my editor, didn't know what it was even. It's made in Ireland. We went to the Belleek factory, so it seemed like it would be just right for seashells crunching underfoot like broken Belleek—seemed to fit her time in Ireland.

Q. Do you have some favorite descriptions that you remember from *Dear James*?

A. Well, I remember the dialogue of Trish and Darrin as they're riding on the bus—I love that. Maybe I could read it to you—it's very short. It's on page 301. Father James O'Hannon is riding on the bus. Behind him he hears Trish ask Darrin:

> *'Should we go see the Pope tomorrow, Darrin?'*
> *'What for?'*
> *'The old folks are going. Doctor Finn says his brother can get us tickets if we want to go along.'*
> *'Who'd want to?'*
> *'I don't know—I thought it might be cool. I guess he wears this neat white outfit.'*
> *'I seen enough Popes.'*
> *'You have not, you haven't seen any.'*
> *'I seen their statues.'*

*'I guess this one talks ten languages.'*

*'You mean he's alive?'*

*'Of course he's alive—what did you think?'*

*'I thought you couldn't be a Pope until you were dead and a miracle happened.'*

*'That's a saint, you dumb shit. Come on, Darrin, go with me. He'll bless us.'*

*Was there a teenager anywhere in Ireland, James wondered, who didn't know the difference between Popes and saints? How foreign America must be. How pagan. How mysterious.*

**Q. Was this actual dialogue that you remembered from your group?**

A. Nobody was quite as dumb as this Darrin and Trish in my group.

**Q. Well, that's encouraging to know.**

A. This is a similar conversation from that same chapter on page 303.

*'What are you guys doing?' asked Trish.*

*Lisa said, 'We're working on our papers.'*

*'When do we eat?' asked Darrin.*

*Agatha replied, 'I believe we're on our own for dinner tonight.'*

*'What's your paper on?' Trish asked Lisa.*

*'Scientific measuring devices.'*

*'Interesting,' said Trish, without interest.*

*'Mine's on male-dominated systems,' said Paula.*

*Trish yawned.*

*'What are you guys doing tomorrow?' asked Darrin.*

*'We're going shopping,' said Paula, speaking for herself and Betty Lou.*

*'I'm going to the Vatican Museums,' said Lisa.*

*Trish said, 'We might be going to the Vatican, too. Right, Darrin?'*

*'Yeah, we might go scope out the Pope.'*

I love "scope out the Pope" so much I had to put it in.

**Q. This is one of the worst examples of the American abroad, right?**

A. I knew where I got that "scope out." I was listening to the radio one time in St. Cloud. They were interviewing a high school kid from Royalton about a new high school course they were teaching on forestry. And the interviewer asked the kid what he did in that course. He said, "We go out and scope out the woods."

**Q. By the way, are there passages that you prefer to read at public readings? I suppose what you had just read might be a couple.**

A. Yes, of course, and then there's a description of Assisi from the hilltop which I always liked a lot, too.

**Q. Another highlight that I always enjoy immensely is having your characters speak at cross-purposes or juxtaposing their conversations. Contrast is the essence of humor, and you mix the sacred and the profane, and high tone and low tone. Three examples in *Dear James* stand out; the first is about eggs:**

> Lillian said, 'If they'll serve sausage patties and baste my eggs, you can count me in.'
> 'I hate eggs,' blurted Sylvester. 'Especially deviled eggs.' [And that is what Agatha had served at this dinner.]
> 'Speaking of eggs,' said his daughter, 'it's a lot easier to think about Creation if you imagine it as God laying an egg.' (39)

Another effective example takes place in Rome where you juxtaposed the tour guide (Signora Razioni) with Lillian and her two new American friends (201-202):

> The larger woman continued, 'Another thing our hotel doesn't have is variety on its menu—everything's so salty. Are you one to watch your sodium intake, Mrs. Kite?'
> 'I should, but I don't. When my daughter was living at home, she used to keep after me about sodium, but now that she's gone, I keep forgetting.'
> Agatha divided her attention between this discussion and the

*words of Signora Razioni, who was preparing the group for its entrance into the Colosseum. 'You will see the excavations where the underground rooms are revealed. In these rooms the wild beasts and the gladiators wait until the time for their performance.'*

*'Sodium is hell on blood pressure,' the larger woman told Lillian. 'Annabelle's husband died of a stroke.'*

And on and on—priceless. The last concerns Bishop Dick Baker's phone call to the Jubas, and father and daughter get on different phones. The three-way conversation perhaps owes something to the Marx Brothers. Where do you get the ideas for this type of humor? Did any writers or TV or movie comics influence you?

A. I guess I don't know. I remember doing it first in *Simon's Night* with the old people in the old folks' home. It worked so well I've tried to do it ever since, although it strikes me I'm not doing it in this book I'm writing now [*The Staggerford Flood*]. I should be doing it. I guess I'll try to do it tomorrow.

Q. I'll look forward to that. Agatha launches into a paean to small town life, i.e., Staggerford, when she is having lunch with James in Rome. "But 'we' was more than that. By we, Agatha meant all of Staggerford, everyone in town, the cohesive whole of the place. . . . Staggerford was the community of souls whose values Agatha, more than anyone of her generation, had helped to sustain. Staggerford was her entire life . . ." (231-232). Of course, unbenownst to her, Staggerford will be rejecting her because of Imogene's campaign against her. What small town were you thinking of when you composed this *Our Town* theme?

A. I was thinking of the two important towns in my past, both in Minnesota of course; one is Plainview, the other Park Rapids. Plainview is where I lived as a boy, and Park Rapids is where I taught for six years, and I got to know Park Rapids better than any other town I've lived in.

Q. Do you miss this communal feeling, this being part of "we," by living in Minneapolis?

A. Yes, I do. I think it's not possible in the city quite so much, although we do have a circle of friends here. It's different from knowing the whole town; however, it isn't a serious lack.

Q. On the second-to-last page of *Dear James* (437), Agatha is fêted at a library tea:

> *She looked deeply into the eyes of each well-wisher, and there she read fondness and goodwill. She saw how much she meant to them, and she felt how much they meant to her. Last winter she had witnessed, at the Vatican, the two-way current of love running between the Holy Father and his admirers, and that's what she was feeling now, that same powerful surge connecting heart with heart.*

Have you felt this way at any gathering in your honor?

A. Yes, I have. I've felt it a number of times such as last spring when I was given the Flanagan Prize in St. Paul [for Excellence and Achievement in the Literature and Culture of the Midwest]. Also, last spring, I received the Minnesotan of the Year Award from Bemidji State University in Minnesota. I've had a number of occasions where I've felt this current of love running between my readers and myself. It's a wonderful feeling.

Q. After I finished rereading *Dear James*, I felt a kind of letdown. I suppose one wants to know what happens next—does Agatha return to Ireland to see James in September? Will James be safe in his ministry? What will happen to James's brother Matt and the pub? Do you think that all of your novels end with such an open-endedness?

A. I think more and more of my recent ones do. Certainly *North of Hope* does. And this one. Also *Rookery Blues*. I think we wonder about all of these characters later on. I rather like to write that way because it seems to me the novel then lives on beyond the last page.

Q. And now for one of my favorite questions—a cursory look at your correspondence during the writing of *Dear James*. Who knew that you would be writing these cards and letters for posterity (and that I would be saving them)? I'll have you comment on these excerpts after you read them.

Nevis - 6/26/90 - "Toiling away at novel nine, the tenuous thread still holding. Ballantine (P. Karlan tells me) wants to make a deal now on my next book."

Saint John's, Collegeville - 1/8/91 - "Having fun with novel nine."

Nevis - 6/4/91 - "Bob Wyatt very fond of the first 208 pages."

Nevis - 6/27/91 - "Now that I've brought James out of the shadows, he threatens to outshine Agatha."

Nevis - 8/27/91 - "The novel grows. My first book with a female villain (Imogene Kite). Agatha is just now home from Italy and discovering the damage Imogene has done to her reputation. . . The Ballantine contract has been signed."

Ireland - 10/12/91 - postcard of Dunleer, Ireland - "It's to Pat's I go for my newspaper & postcards (about 4 miles from my house) but it's 8 miles farther - Drogheda - to a good meal & a good cup of coffee. After 4 days of rather frenzied touring, I've settled into working on the novel–an Italian scene. Ulster depresses, the sea refreshes."

Sauk Rapids - 4/15/92 - sent to me at Chester House Service Apartments in London - "Bob Wyatt says he'll be spending Easter with Agatha. We've been editing for a month and now enter into a closer reading. Date of publication uncertain. I wrote a completely new ending—extending the length by 25 pages. I like the content, but the writing strikes me as pedestrian."

Nevis - 6/11/92 - "Called Clare Ferraro [editor-in-chief at Ballantine] for reassurance. She can't find Bob Wyatt, or my 300 pages. What's going on?"

Saint John's - 7/31/92 - "Here's Chapter One of DJ, a handout for my fans who can't wait."

Nevis - 9/7/92 - "But now I'm at the cabin for a week of writing. Amazing the way this novel moves forward with the smallest of nudges from its author."

Nevis - enclosure of letter from Bob Wyatt to you with your 9/7/92 letter - "I had such a good time working on 'Dear James' in all three go-rounds. I regret that I'll not be on future go-rounds, but the most fun is always in the early work.

Incidentally, bound galleys contain the same text as the galleys sent for proofreading. Just because they are bound does not make the text sacrosanct. Of course, by the time this book is set in type, the technology could have changed again. I tremble to think how it has changed since I bought this computer."

**Any thoughts or comments on re-reading these letters from ten years ago?**

A. Yes, the major thing it brings to mind is how much I enjoyed Bob Wyatt as my editor. I think that's the major thing I liked about those letters I wrote.

**Q. The letter dated August 10, 1990, from Nevis states, "The bottom may have fallen out of my novel-in-progress." I assume that this means you had a difficult time in writing *Dear James*.**

A. I don't remember, but these letters prove that I did since the book stopped and started, judging by the letters. And I guess that happens all the time, but after the novel is finished, I don't remember the bad things. Everything seems to have gone fine.

**Q. Would you tell about the Irish cottage you stayed at in 1991 and during other visits also?**

A. This is a cottage—it's a house north of Drogheda which is north of Dublin. It belongs to a man named Don Roos, a Hollywood screenwriter who has a new movie out called *Bounce*. And he read *A Green Journey*. He liked it so much that he offered me his house in Ireland whenever I wanted to use it. He only uses it a couple weeks out of the year, so Gretchen and I went over there and stayed in it; then I stayed in it again in '91. It's a lovely little town—a very small village—only had seven or eight houses and a pub—that's all it is. But it's close to the ocean.

**Q. He had this bequeathed to him by a relative?**

A. Yes, by his aunt. When his aunt died, she gave it to him. By coincidence Don Roos and my agent Pat Karlan produced a movie together called *The Opposite of Sex*. She was his agent, too.

**Q. Have you been there since '91?**

A. Let's see. We went again in '94. I was there three times.

**Q. Do you know what happened to your editor Bob Wyatt?**

A. Well, I got a hold of him by email a year ago. He said that he wasn't editing anymore, he was traveling. He wanted to get as much traveling in as he could before he went blind. So something must be happening to his eyes.

**Q. I did discover another letter from this time period, dated November 17, 1992, from you to Clare Ferraro at Ballantine. I'll quote from the two-page letter.**

> ...Thanks for the jacket copy. I have to say I think it's overwritten. It seems to tell the reader too much about the book, without really arousing much curiosity. But then this is a perennial gripe of mine. I've never considered the jacket flap a good place to convey a novel's complexity. Aren't potential readers caught with large, bold hooks? Or with the opening passage of the novel in easy-to-read print? When I pick a book off the shelf, I'm always put off by close-set lines of flap copy, and by learning facts I'd rather discover as I read the book.
>
> ... I'll do a limited tour with *Dear James*. I'll go out two separate times, once for four nights and the other for three, with at least three days at home in between. My teaching duties will end on May 15. What I dread nearly as much as the tour are the Twin Cities autographings. Can you imagine meeting and chatting your way through a line of nearly 200 people? I did that several times with *North of Hope* and came away feeling as if I'd done permanent harm to myself. I hate to be such a complainer, but if you're not

*a true introvert, you can't know what a crisis it is to meet even a single stranger, to say nothing of 190 of them standing in a row to pick your brain. How would it be if I visited the stores via the back door, signed stock, and fled?*

*... Clare, I hope you realize, contrary to the negative tone of this letter, how much I love what you and your colleagues are doing for Agatha and James and their friends. Without you, I would not be writing the next novel with such high spirits.*

**Any comments or clarifications?**

A. Well, I'm like a lot of writers. I find book tours very draining. Also, the part about the jacket copy is true. I think the less said on the jacket copy, the better.

**Q. In the *South Dakota Review* (Spring 1994), C. W. Truesdale discussed quite comprehensively all seven of your novels through *Dear James*, "On the Novels of Jon Hassler." He finds *Dear James* "infinitely more dramatic and complex" than *A Green Journey* (66). He makes an interesting point:**

> *And in both novels, the focus of the action shifts between Stag-gerford and wherever Agatha is traveling at the moment. As in much travel-writing, these journeys are at once literal and at the same time metaphysical, since they are journeys of self-discovery and self-exploration in a foreign context. They have something, too, in common with the myths of the Hero's Journey. (67)*

**Do you agree?**

A. Yes, of course, Agatha learns a lot about herself while she's traveling. That's very true—it's a journey of self-discovery and self-exploration.

**Q. One critic, Matthew Hawn, in the *San Francisco Chronicle* (May 22, 1993), posited an interesting drawback (in his eyes) of this novel:**

> *Another area where Hassler runs into trouble is the development of his non Catholic characters. Almost without exception, they are represented as shallow and without a modicum of faith or*

*chance of redemption outside of Catholicism. One such example is professor Albert Finn, the leader of the Italian tour, described as a frustrated one-time candidate for the priesthood who has lost his faith. . . .This might be Catholic doctrine, but in this novel it tends to leave the characters flat and clichéd.*

**How would you respond?**

A. Well, I guess I thought Professor Albert Finn was as well drawn as most of the other characters. I don't agree that the Protestants are flat, although there aren't very many Protestants in this novel. I think they are as round as my other secondary characters.

Q. John H. Hafner in *America* (September 25, 1993) compared you with one of your favorite writers:

*Jon Hassler's seventh novel,* Dear James, *is a wonderful book. Set primarily in Hassler's now-famous imaginary town of Staggerford, Minn., its plot also includes memorable scenes in Rome, Assisi and Ireland.* Dear James *has a cast of characters that includes most of the townspeople of Staggerford, and Hassler does for his Catholic, upper-Midwest world what John Cheever did for his WASP New England one, though Hassler seems to have more affection for his characters than Cheever had for his. . . .*

**Any comments about this?**

A. Yes, I was very pleased to be equated with Cheever. It's true, I think, that I like my characters better than Cheever does.

Q. John F. Desmond in an article, "Catholicism in Contemporary American Fiction" (*America*, May 14, 1994), writes about five Catholic authors including you. I believe that he sums up your themes of *Dear James* very well.

*The northern landscape itself—cold, stark, barren, yet always rejuvenated—is a metaphor for the spiritual landscape of Hassler's vision, whose informing spirit is hope. His is a fiction of second chances, of possible recoveries, though not without cost to the ego-centric self. . . .*

> *A pilgrimage trip to Rome and Assisi becomes the spiritual turning point for both Agatha and Father O'Hannon. Their mutual love and the power of grace gives each a new sense of purpose and communal commitment. . . . Here, as in all Hassler's novels, a love that transcends romantic affection quietly affirms the hope that demands—and energizes—unselfish commitment to others. (8)*

**That's very perceptive—I should make copies of this article when I teach your novels this spring semester.**

A. Yes, that's very good, I think. It's very true what Father O'Hannon and Agatha go through in Ireland leads them to a sense of purpose and communal commitment. Father O'Hannon goes back to Ireland and works for peace. Agatha goes back home and forgives Imogene. And she feels united to her community once again. So that's an interesting outcome. "Love that transcends romantic affection quietly affirms the hope that demands unselfish commitment to others"—that's a good way to put it.

**Q. As is becoming apparent, many critics concluded their *Dear James* reviews in a grand, positive manner, and I offer another—Philip Zaleski writing in *First Things* (September 1994):**

> *In local communities, Hassler suggests, ancient truths abide: words retain their power to save or ruin lives, good and evil can yet be distinguished, people remain accountable for their acts, and sin, penance, and absolution are still valid coin of the realm.*
>
> *Remarkably—this is where Hassler parts company with almost all other American novelists—religion is the means whereby these small-town transformations take place. In* Dear James, *the catalyst is not only the teachings of the Church but its sacred places as well.*
>
> *Agatha and James heal their breach in the Vatican. . . . They deepen their accord in Assisi, another small town whose essence Hassler captures as well as any writer before him. . . .*
>
> *One feels a great moral force surging through this novel, a sense that lives do indeed matter, that God oversees the comedy—and that fiction is the right means to get this message across. . . . It*

*brings to mind a passage from John Gardner's* On Moral Fiction, *an important, vilified, and now forgotten book of the 1970s. 'The traditional view,' Gardner writes, 'is that art is moral: it seeks to improve life, not to debase it. It seeks to hold off, at least for a while, the twilight of the gods and us.'*

*Gardner's definition of traditional art describes perfectly Hassler's novels: creations as admirable for their benevolence as for their architecture. Here is an author who embraces every character his imagination conjures up, whether heroine, fool, heretic, or shrew. . . .Agatha, James, and nearly all of Hassler's figures suffer chastisement or worse for their failures, and nearly all are championed in this splendid work, testimony to God's tender mercies.*

I didn't expect to quote so much, but Zaleski really does capture your whole oeuvre. I had forgotten—and maybe I didn't know—what an impact *Dear James* had on reviewers.

A. I didn't remember either until you brought these up. But I've always had a very high opinion of *Dear James* myself.

Q. Another sympathetic critic/reader, Joseph Hynes, wrote a really fine analysis of your novels for *Commonweal* (November 3, 1995). Two years earlier, also for *Commonweal* (July 16,1993), Hynes reviewed *Dear James.* Resisting the temptation to quote more, I'll just quote the final paragraph of his review:

*In Hassler's novels, loneliness is prominent. It is not purged but is transformed and disciplined by ironic wit and by love, charity. Hassler's development in scope and depth in this regard is clear in his last three novels—*Grand Opening *(1987),* North of Hope *(1990), and this new book. Moving both omnisciently and epistolarily from November to July, from Staggerford to Ireland to Italy, and developing a substantial subplot concerning French Lopat and Imogene Kite, he retains his sharp-eyed ability to laugh at silliness in or outside of the church, even as he transcends the topical to give us the sacred-secular picture from long range. Hassler manifests the rare ability to write fiction both popular and important.*

A. Yes, this, too, is very flattering.

Q. Our "friend," Carolyn See, who panned *North of Hope* in the *Los Angeles Times,* made a 180 degree turn-around in her review of *Dear James* (*Los Angeles Times,* June 28, 1993):

> *Something very nice must have happened to Jon Hassler. He's cheered up. For years he has been writing about the little Minnesota town of Staggerford . . . and there hasn't been—in my memory—one cardigan sweater that didn't smell funny, one nose that hasn't been runny, one day that didn't have too much humidity in the summer and way too much snow in the winter.*
>
> *Hassler's characters, too, ranged from sad to bad to moronic and back again. You got the feeling the author didn't like them very much. . . .*
>
> *Hassler has fun in this novel. His demented sex fiend is wonderful, his Vietnam vet is desperately funny beyond his sorrow and the papal audience—where a swing band plays show tunes—is a set piece any writer would be proud of.*
>
> *All this brings up the vexing question: Maybe the author wasn't all that depressed in his previous novels. Maybe I was. This gives me the chance to go back and read them all again to find out.*

**Well. What do you say?**

A. It certainly is self-revealing about her, isn't it? Where she says at the end that she is the depressed one, not I. I think she was. I've been told that I've been funny in all my novels. She didn't see it, evidently.

Q. I seem to use the *New York Times Book Review* as a kind of bellwether since its reviewers have veered widely from one extreme to another in regard to your novels. *Dear James* elicited a short review in the June 27, 1993, issue by a Bill Kent:

> *Those who miss the regional novels of the 1930's and 40's, when the great subject of American fiction was, in William Faulkner's words, the human heart in conflict with itself, will adore Dear James, the latest installment of Jon Hassler's extended epic about*

*the fictional northern Minnesota hamlet of Staggerford. Mr. Has-sler . . . delivers a gentle examination of the fragile but enduring strengths of small-town life through characters so exquisitely ren-dered that even a first-time visitor to Staggerford will come to love them as old friends. . . . After just a little bit too much coming and going as he checks in on subplots, Mr. Hassler finally brings the novel back home to Staggerford, deftly linking its many conflicts to the redeeming power of grace.*

This review is a keeper, isn't it?

A. Yes, it is. This pinpoints the final scene of the novel. That's the library tea where Agatha forgives Imogene for her betrayal.

Q. Around this time you met a very special fan of your writings. I'll quote your May 21, 1993, postcard postmarked Worcester, MA: "A private visit with Hillary Clinton this morning—Would you believe it? Two of us—Dave D. [Minnesota Senator David Durenberger] & I—on the couch in her office. A very impressive woman with vision, a moral sense & a pretty new hairdo." Please share about this—and how the now Senator-elect from New York learned of your books.

A. I was on a book tour with *Dear James* and stopped in Washington, D.C., for a reading, and Senator David Durenberger was there. And he said that Hillary Clinton liked my books. He wondered if I'd like to go over and meet her. I said, "Sure." So the next morning we went over in his car to the White House, and I'll never forget the marine standing at the door—he saluted us as we went in. It's gratifying to be saluted by a marine. I thought we should take all marines out of warfare and put them all in places where they'd greet us every day as we'd go in to work. Anyway, we went into Hillary's office after waiting outside for a few minutes, and we had a half hour with her discussing my books. She knew all the plots. She knew the major characters' names—it was very flattering. She was very impressive, I thought, as a person. And I thought I'd like to see her as president some day. And I remember thinking that as I sat there talking to her. It was a very pleasant experience.

**Q. And now that she's a Senator-elect, that might be closer to reality. And then you saw her another time?**

A. Yes, two years later we went back to Washington, this time with *Rookery Blues*, and there I was given an Alumni Award from Saint John's actually because there were a number of people there from Saint John's. And my wife Gretchen and I, Gretchen's sister Carol, and her husband Al were all invited to the White House to meet Hillary. So we went over again. I gave her a *Rookery Blues* T-shirt. I gave her one for Bill, too. I remember Gretchen was outraged because I called him Bill [President Clinton was not present]. But, anyway, we gave her two T-shirts—she was on her way to a party, but she stopped in to see us in one of the rooms of the White House.

**Q. What did she write on the photograph of the two of you that she sent?**

A. She said, "Dear Jon, Thanks for introducing me to *Staggerford*. Hillary Clinton."

**Q. This interviewing experience for me has been extremely rewarding and fulfilling; it will be reassuring if—or, we hope, when—we see some or all of these interviews in print.**

A. That's the ideal, Joe. It's been a pleasure for me, of course. And your questions have been so much more intelligent than my answers. But I enjoyed it anyway.

**Q. Thank you, Jon.**

# Rookery Blues

Going through my file on *Rookery Blues*, Jon's eighth "adult" novel, I am finding so many unusual quotes, reviews, and publicity, a veritable treasure-trove. For example, *The Kirkus Reviews* (May 1, 1995), not always a fan, proclaimed that "Hassler displays once again why he's the novel's answer to Garrison Keillor." This isn't the first time that Keillor is mentioned in a Hassler review, although the aim and purpose and style of their writing are not at all the same; they share a Minnesota setting, and each conveys humor in his own unique way, but the dissimilarities would be easier to pick out.

A reviewer in the August 28-September 4, 1996, issue of *Christian Century* began his review with this erroneous sentence: "The bad news out of Minnesota is that Jon Hassler is writing his last novel. Hassler has made public his battle with Parkinson's disease and his intention to make a forthcoming novel, his 11th, the final one." This may have emanated from a *Star Tribune* [Minneapolis] (December 31, 1995) article telling about Jon's illness which carried the headline "Author faces his own ending." However, since that quote, Jon has written *The Staggerford Flood*, *Good People*, two novellas—*The Staggerford Murders* and *The Life and Death of Nancy Clancy's Nephew*, and *The New Woman*. Lucky for us, the readers, this dire statement has not proven true.

For the first and only time that I know of, *The New Yorker* (September 25, 1995) mentioned Jon. A list of "Recommended Reading" included *Rookery Blues*:

> *Rookery is the name of a northern Minnesota state college where five faculty members get together to play the blues as well as endure*

them. The group—a beautiful singer, a tormented artist, a woebegone novelist, and two English teachers—includes a love triangle, and political strains arise as the members take different sides in a strike. Set in 1969, it feels like 1959—in large part because of its old-fashioned, four-square, apolitical humanism.

I asked Jon what he thought about the "it feels like 1959" reference; his answer: "It's too exacting to me. I don't see the difference between 1959 and 1969."

Because of Jon's audio recording of *Rookery Blues*, *In/Audio* interviewed him in the April 1996 issue (with Jon on the cover). Jon had this to say about the recording's origin:

*I approached my publisher a number of years ago for audio books because I saw this market out there. I saw these readers who would rather listen than read. I enjoy audio books because unlike reading, you savor every phrase and word, it seems to me. So I went to my publisher, Ballantine, and asked my editor if she would ask around for some company that was interested. She asked Random House, which has a big operation, and they weren't interested. She asked Penguin and Dove and neither were they. So I thought, 'Why not do it on our own?' And we did. . . . It's more or less a cottage industry I've got going here instead of the big time.*

In the same year that *Rookery Blues* appeared, 1995, Jon had an essay printed in *America* (September 30), with the title "How Can I Find God?" I don't think most people have had a chance to read it, so I'll quote some of it here. It shows Jon's thinking at the time of *Rookery Blues*:

*I'm no authority, but I suspect that one finds God while looking for something else, much the way a novelist will find that his writing style has coalesced between the lines of his novel while he was absorbed in his plot and characters and scarcely conscious of where he put his commas.*

*Fifty-five years ago I recall Sister Constance saying that because playing came naturally to children, we served God by playing. What a liberating thing for us to hear! As third graders, we'd been*

206

*struggling so hard to memorize the catechism, pray five times a day and refrain from eating or drinking before Communion that we were led to believe that being good was like picking your way through a minefield. And then to be told that playing was not only fun but pleasing to God—whew.*

*This truth was brought home to me 30 years later, when I began seriously to write novels. At first, I was rather alarmed to discover that the deeper I went into my fiction, the less devoted I became to the rituals of Catholicism. But now after 10 novels, I've stopped being alarmed. Instead, I'm convinced that my writing springs from the same underground current that used to feed my prayer life. I pray much less often, yet I feel involved in a useful mission. I didn't see it coming, I didn't ask for it, but, judging by what I hear from my readers, I seem to have been ordained to scatter my stories among people who enjoy them, value them and actually seem to need them.*

We touch on Jon being known as a "Catholic author" in this interview, but *Rookery Blues* doesn't fit into that category.

*Rookery Blues* remains the only one of Jon's novel with arguably five protagonists. I'm sure that Jon had to stretch his talent to pull off such a difficult feat. The reviews show that his efforts proved successful. Although some readers may have found such a technique confusing, I believe that *Rookery Blues* is a strong novel in Jon's canon of books. I also still believe that *Rookery Blues* would make a worthwhile play or movie; the canvas is vast, and the cinematic potential is almost limitless. The good news—a stage play version is being fashioned from the novel with the prospect of having it performed at the Jon Hassler Theater in Plainview, Minnesota. That would be a worthy stage for this ambitious project.

- J. P. August 2004

October 8, 2001

Q. Jon, this is a pleasant change of pace, interviewing you in your office at Saint John's University in Collegeville, Minnesota. Like your earlier works *A Green Journey* and *Dear James*, your two most recently published novels, *Rookery Blues* and *The Dean's List*, are closely related. Had you known, when you were composing *Rookery Blues*, that these characters and settings would necessitate another novel set in academia?

A. I didn't know it at the time. I got the idea from my editor Clare Ferraro who said that Leland Edwards is the most Hassler-like character in the book. That got me thinking about him, and I went on and wrote the novel about him.

Q. I hadn't known that about Clare. Ballantine published *Rookery Blues* in 1995. Who were your editor and agent then?

A. My agent was Patricia Karlan from Los Angeles. My editor was Clare Ferraro—she was at Ballantine at the time. She's since gone on to become president at Viking.

Q. *Rookery Blues* is dedicated to your daughter Elizabeth. Was there a special reason, or was it her turn for a book dedication?

A. That's right—it was her turn. I dedicated *North of Hope* to Michael and *Underground Christmas* to David. It was Elizabeth's turn.

Q. Do you know how many copies were printed?

A. Forty thousand.

Q. How many sold?

A. I really don't know—I think maybe half of those were sold.

Q. I believe that this is your only novel that produced an audio recording.

A. That's true. I made a recording myself of this book. I did *Stagger-ford* earlier, actually, which hasn't been made available, but I read this book on tape and it was manufactured locally, and it's available only on my website, I think. Jon Hassler's Writing Room on the web.

**Q. What parts of this book did you think read aloud especially well?**

A. Oh, the parts where Victor comes in are very interesting. He's such a blowhard and he's so irreverent. And when he kicks the dog, everybody laughs at that part. We had to do it twice when I recorded it because the people in the recording studio were laughing so hard when he kicks the dog at the chairman's house.

**Q. You have written stage adaptations of *Simon's Night*, *Grand Opening*, and *Four Miles to Pinecone*, and Sally Childs [artistic director of the Hassler Theater in Plainview] has adapted *Dear James* and *Jemmy*. Are there any plans for a stage production of *Rookery Blues*? The music would certainly lend itself to being performed in a play.**

A. It's funny you should ask because Sally Childs decided that she'd like to do a jazz performance of *Rookery Blues* with a quintet playing. And then there'd be a reading between pieces from the novel. It sounds like a good idea—she'd like to do it in the Jon Hassler Theater as an experiment.

**Q. Be sure to let me know when—I want to attend that. I'm glad that she thought of that, too. [Sally Childs's adaptation of *Rookery Blues* was performed September 23 – October 22, 2006, at the Jon Hassler Theater in Plainview.] I know that you originally thought of a different title for this novel. What was the working title, and why did you change it?**

A. *The Icejam Quintet*. Well, it's about this quintet of jazz musicians called the Icejam Quintet. I changed it to *Rookery Blues* since I wanted the name of the town in the title. I wanted something musical in the title, too. While driving home from Southdale [in Minneapolis] one night, I remember I brought the subject up. I kept saying "Rookery," and my wife said "Blues," and that was it.

Q. And what is the double meaning? Of course, Rookery is the town. Blues is the music. Is there more meaning to it?

A. Well, all these five people are unhappy in this little college town way up north, in northern Minnesota, so I guess they all have the blues, too.

Q. Is "Icejam" symbolic of the northern Minnesota winters where Rookery is located?

A. Yes, of course. I thought perhaps I'd call it the Logjam Quintet at first, but then I thought of how icy it is in Bemidji, which is the prototype for Rookery.

Q. Jon, did your love and appreciation of jazz help plant the seed for this novel? You write very knowingly about the music practiced and performed by the quintet.

A. Yes, it did; I like jazz a lot. I had learned to like it when I moved to Saint John's, and a friend got me interested in jazz and I only became an aficionado recently. When I began to write about it, I read some jazz reviewers to learn how they wrote about it. I learned from that. I said in the *Minnesota Monthly* one time that I was going to write a novel about music. Somebody wrote me and said, "Don't write about jazz because you'll screw it up," and so I did it with trepidation, but I think I succeeded.

Q. And that's funny because my next question is about the jazz references. *The Salt Lake Tribune* interview (August 20, 1995) includes this fact: "Hassler, who plays the piano, read several books of jazz criticism to research the book's musical subject. 'I pretend to know more than I do. I'm not much of a pianist,' he says with characteristic modesty. 'So far, nobody's called me on it.'" Would you amplify on what you read to help with the jazz references?

A. Well, I don't remember what I read.

Q. One critic, Roger Sheffer in *The Corresponder* (Winter 1996), picked up on your use of art and now music in your novels:

> *While the political machinations are amusing, the best parts of the novel are the art and music, the descriptions of Connor's paintings and his feelings towards them, the details of harmony and discord within the quintet. Hassler knows the language of painting and the language of music, and when he lingers over these, the novel soars. And he can afford to linger, because the plot structure of this novel is as tight as a classical symphony, every measure part of an inevitable flow toward a satisfying conclusion.*

And that leads to the chapter titles (or, as you call them here, Part 1, Part 2, etc.); you have chosen jazz classics, as you mentioned, primarily from the 1940s—"These Foolish Things," "I'll Get By," "Mood Indigo," "Don't Blame Me," and "My Blue Heaven." I'm sure that these are some of your favorite songs, but obviously there must be a deeper reason for selecting them. Does the song comment directly or indirectly on what then happens?

A. Yes, it does. "I'll Get By" is about a breakup of a romance. "Mood Indigo," of course, is a blues type of song. "Don't Blame Me"—that happens when they lose their jobs. And "My Blue Heaven"—that happens at the end when they all gather again to play for a wedding. So I guess they do fit the parts, although I chose them before I knew that, but I did distribute them according to what part they fit best.

Q. Also, each part contains an italicized flashback about one of the quintet's childhood experiences with music. Leland's flashback occurs in Part I, "These Foolish Things." Does that song illuminate or comment on Leland? And is the same true for the four other members of the Icejam Quintet and their song headings?

A. I guess I put that in because it was the first song he played on the piano for the group. I don't remember if it corresponded with his life at all. It was the first song he played.

Q. You have created many memorable secondary characters, but is this the first time that you have five protagonists?

A. Yes, it is, and it's the last time, too. I've had readers tell me they've had a very hard time starting this book because they thought Neil was the main character in the first part, and they had trouble adjusting to so many main characters, so I guess it's the last time I'll use it.

**Q. But it worked well, I thought.**

A. I thought it did, too.

**Q. Would you say that one is more of a protagonist than the others?**

A. Well, I guess not, because Leland who became a protagonist in *The Dean's List* is not the leader here. I think they all have equal parts, including Peggy, who's the leader of the band.

**Q. Is it correct to assume that Leland is more like you than the others in the quintet? I notice you mention Clare Ferraro's comment about a Hassler-like character.**

A. He's more typical of my characters which must mean he's more like me. And when I got into his mind, and as I wrote *The Dean's List* in the first person, I felt very much at home in his mind, so he must be a lot like me.

**Q. On page 390 you wrote about Leland:**

> She [Peggy] laughed. 'What do you mean? Of course you can.' Still he didn't look at her, afraid she'd see his anguish, afraid he'd have to admit his devastation over the breakup of the quintet, which was bound to happen now that Dean Zastrow was bent on massacre. He couldn't talk about it. He hadn't known the words for heartbreak when he was fourteen and his father died, and he didn't know them now. He couldn't tell her how much of his life he'd spent dreaming of just this sort of musical friendship, and how far, thanks to Peggy, the real thing exceeded the dream. Maybe other people could talk about matters like that; he couldn't.

**Is this also about you? It certainly fits Miles and probably Simon and Father Frank; is this really the quintessential Hassler protagonist?**

A. I'm sure it is—sounds like me, all right. Somebody who hasn't the vocabulary for those emotional moments.

**Q. How did you pick the names of the Quintet members, Peggy Benoit, Leland Edwards, Victor Dash, Neil Novotony, and Connor?**

A. I remember how I picked Victor Dash—because he appeared in "The Book of Brendan," a novel I wrote in the early '80s which was never published. He was a brash guy, and I thought Dash fit his character. And then I remember choosing Leland Edwards because of Leland Stanford—it sounded so academic—he's such an academic guy, and then Connor, because he has an Irish name. I always have an Irishman in my books. And then Peggy, I don't remember why I chose Peggy, or Neil. But Neil Novotony, I chose a different name so people could keep them straight, so they weren't similar to one another.

**Q. By the way, what *is* Connor's first name?**

A. His first name is Sonny, the name he's ashamed of.

**Q. In a *San Diego Union Tribune* interview (August 17, 1995), one learns a little more about the genesis of the Icejam Quintet:**

> *For example, he [Hassler] said, the blues quintet at the center of* Rookery Blues *is loosely based on experiences from his early years teaching college. 'When I was teaching in northern Minnesota a number of years ago, I felt very insecure in my first year, and a number of us formed a small club—all newcomers, all in the same boat,' he said. 'We would reward failure and reject success and try to turn it all upside down and cheer ourselves up.'*
>
> *Unlike the fivesome in* Rookery Blues, *Hassler's academic group was not a musical one.*

**Would you tell more about this and how this gave you the idea for the Icejam Quintet?**

A. Well, it was like a support group—it's what got us through our early years teaching in Bemidji, and I thought I should write a novel about that. And I had the characters be musical because I wanted to write about music. We weren't musical at all—all we did was get together and drink beer. But I think the effect is the same. We called ourselves the Scholars.

Q. Do the Scholars still meet after all these years? You taught at Bemidji State from 1965 to 1968.

A. We didn't meet for many years, and then the last two summers we got together twice at my cabin. They all came down from Bemidji, and we had a great time visiting again.

Q. Victor, Leland, and Connor went ice fishing on a blustery cold winter day, and Connor, drunk, became sick and passed out. Carrying him, the other two put him under an outside window of his home, placing his share of the fish—five frozen fish—on his chest and stomach. Was this a Scholars' escapade?

A. That came before the Scholars—that came in Fosston in 1958. A number of the faculty went fishing on Red Lake. One of us got drunk—we placed him under his window—we placed the fish next to him and went home. Poor guy got pneumonia and wasn't in school for a week.

Q. So I was right—it was actual. Did any activities or gatherings of the Scholars provide incidents for this novel?

A. I remember Neil Novotony's basement apartment; it belonged to John O'Boyle who was one of the Scholars, and it was a messy little basement he had there in Bemidji. I guess that's all I can remember offhand. Except the makeup of the campus and the campus strike, of course. The campus strike comes from Brainerd where you and I were on strike, Joe.

Q. We're going to get to that later. Do you remember if it was more difficult writing this novel than some of your other ones, or was it easier? It seems maybe more difficult with the five protagonists.

A. I think it was, although all my novels seem easy in retrospect. I remember *North of Hope* was my hardest. This probably was the second hardest one.

Q. *Rookery Blues* perhaps boasts your biggest cast of characters yet. Did you ever get lost while writing this intricately plotted and peopled novel?

A. I never did. Of course, it was on my mind day and night, so I didn't lose track of any of it.

Q. Did you have a chart in front of you when writing this novel that would detail each character's background, friends, relations, places of employment? This is a very complex plot.

A. I didn't have—all I had was a resumé of each of them—where they went to college, what their degrees were in, and things like that. I had that on the wall, but I didn't have anything else.

Q. What sections gave you especial pleasure when you were creating or what went really smoothly?

A. I think the drinking part and ice fishing part came very smoothly. Also the striking part, I remember, when they went out on strike. Victor Dash was in charge of the strikers. I remember how much I enjoyed writing that.

Q. What sections proved more troublesome or challenging to write?

A. The last part where they break up and they get back together again. Connor disappears for a while—they're afraid he's died. He turns up, too. I remember I worked over that.

Q. Hindsight is a useless quality to possess in regard to a finished artistic creation, but may I ask if you were writing *Rookery Blues* today, what might you change?

A. I can't think of anything I'd change in that book.

Q. That's good to know. *Staggerford* featured a high school setting; Simon Shea was a retired professor at Rookery State, but I believe that this is your first novel about academic life at a college.

A. That's right—it's one of two. It was followed by *The Dean's List* which is also about Rookery State. It's about my college teaching life, whereas *Staggerford* was about my high school teaching life.

Q. You had taught at both Brainerd Community College and Bemidji State University in Minnesota; which provided more inspiration and details for *Rookery Blues*? I think we've already touched on that.

A. Well, the setting was Bemidji, but the strike was in Brainerd, so I guess I'd say they were about equal that way.

Q. And the strike, of course, becomes more topical with two State of Minnesota employee unions out on strike now. You and I were colleagues during the Minnesota Community College strike in March 1979. And I see one of our strike posters in front of me here at your Saint John's office—"Community Colleges, MEA/NEA on strike," so that really is fitting for our *Rookery Blues* interview. What personal memories do you have of that time of the strike?

A. I remember how cold it was in March when we were picketing in the snow on the beautiful campus out in the country—nobody saw us picketing among the pine trees. I remember Evelyn Matthies, our art teacher, coming out with coffee and rolls for us.

Q. And I was just going to mention "among the pine trees," Jon. In the same *San Diego Union Tribune* interview, the reporter wrote:

> At another college [Brainerd Community College] later in his career, he [Hassler] participated in a faculty strike, although it wasn't nearly as visible as the one in Rookery Blues.
> 'We picketed among the pine trees and nobody saw us,' he said.

I guess that is true.

A. You remember that yourself, don't you?

Q. We didn't stop anyone from going in either. We just had one teacher who was a scab, right? What were our grievances—do you remember? The strike vote on our campus was overwhelming in favor, I believe.

A. Yes, mine was the only vote against it, I think. It was for wages which the legislature denied us—no, the legislature gave it to us—the Board denied us. So we went on strike to get the money we thought we had coming. I figured that the courts would rule in our favor anyway, so there was no need to strike. So we struck, we got the money, then the court ruled against us. We got the money anyway.

**Q. So it was a very complex time. What situations or details did you use from that experience in *Rookery Blues*?**

A. I used to get the call from the Telephone Tree. Every evening about 5:00 the phone would ring and this guy would say, "It's the Telephone Tree—we stopped an 18-wheeler at Willmar today," and that was supposed to be happy news, you see, so that was very funny.

**Q. Were there other things that you remember using?**

A. Well, I used walking around in the snow a lot. People would bring coffee and things for the strikers.

**Q. On page 343 one reads: "While several of them [strikers] moved back and forth along the street, others stood warming themselves at a smoky fire they'd built in a big oil drum in the parking lot." Our strike was in March, the Alliance's during the winter. Do you remember our oil drum or large garbage can?**

A. I do. It was Harry Heglund [librarian at Brainerd Community College] who started that fire. This is what he used to do in the mines, so he brought a lot of wood, and we put it in an oil drum and lit it on fire, and we stood around warming our hands.

**Q. And didn't we also roast frankfurters?**

A. I guess we did, come to think of it.

**Q. Is Victor Dash modeled on a specific individual or a composite?**

A. He's a composite of teachers we've known in our lives.

Q. Without mentioning names, did someone at Brainerd Community College coin Victor's immortal line, "We are only shitting in our own hats"?

A. Yes, that was something I heard regularly at the faculty meetings in Brainerd from one instructor.

Q. On pages 123-126 you present a telephone conversation between the polar opposites in the Rookery State strike. On one end, Victor Dash. And on the other, Dr. Warren W. Waldorf, Chancellor of the Minnesota State College System, described by you on page 123:

> *If he were lucky, he'd be retired and living with Mrs. Waldorf in their condo in Florida well before any of his campuses were over-run with the faculty unrest and student militancy creeping into the Midwest from the East and West coasts. Although he'd been pre-dicting difficult years ahead in higher education, he hadn't foreseen anything quite so outrageous as a faculty strike.*

Is this based on someone actual, or is this creative license?

A. I entirely made him up. I imagined a man in the State Department who would be against the strike, and he came forth.

Q. I was glad to learn that Professor Simon Shea of *Simon's Night* joined the strike, "overseeing the assembling of picket signs in the Dashes' garage . . . took great delight in being named (and insisted on being addressed as) Chief of Construction" (301). Were you surprised that he did join the strike?

A. I was sort of surprised, but I thought, good for him. It showed his heart was in the right place.

Q. And although Larry Quinn wasn't feeling well (and we know why from *The Love Hunter*), his wife Rachel brought a large thermos of coffee and a box of Danish pastry for the strikers (310). This continues your practice of having characters from your other novels turn up once again.

A. Yes, it happened very slightly in this novel.

Q. How much of the "politics" of the State of Minnesota and Rookery State was based on the State's dealings with our Community College Association?

A. Well, I guess the money part—that certainly was true of our relationship with the State of Minnesota—we weren't getting the money we had coming, so that's why we struck.

Q. Three busloads of Rookery students descended on the capitol steps in support of the Rookery faculty. When finally Governor Gunderson appeared, he curtly said, "Find yourselves another college to go to," and went back inside (357). That certainly reminds one of our current governor, Jesse Ventura.

A. It sure does, but it wasn't. A previous governor said that—he surprised all of us. But he told the people to go to another college.

Q. I didn't realize that was accurate. I thought that was creative. Nursing students at Rookery were concerned about not having classes. I believe we had Brainerd Community College students who lobbied at the capitol in our favor, too.

A. Yes, that's right—we had the nursing program. They were afraid of not getting their degree in time for their exams.

Q. On page 385 we read what the Rookery State strikers were returning to:

> They were free once more to wallow in the small, murky pond of academe, free to take up the familiar old obscurities of their lecture notes and scholarly articles, free to indulge in the safe little jealousies and triumphs inherent in promotions and committee appointments. By the time they reached the door, somebody was telling Connor that they'd gone along with the Alliance only to humor Victor, and they'd gone on strike only for the fun and adventure of it and never really expected to succeed.

Is this Connor's cynicism, or is some of it Jon Hassler's?

A. Well, it seems to me it's mine more than Connor's because I always believed that was true. Only in academe you don't have great consequences to your acts, so you make up these little wars and things, and the backbiting and things that happen so much on college campuses.

Q. Brainerd trivia: What is the origin of the Kriss and Dale Publishers of Philadelphia which advertised a new textbook for Freshman English?

A. Kris and Dale were two singers at Brainerd Community College when I first went there in 1968. They were named "Krisendale."

Q. I know the basis of the T. Woodman Press, but I'll let you explain. Why did you like this name?

A. I don't know. Tom Woodman is a friend of yours. I'd never met him—he was from England, right? And I just thought it would be a good name for a press, so that's why I called it the T. Woodman Press.

Q. Where did the inspiration for Lolly Edwards come from?

A. She came from *Frills and Fancies* which was a radio show in Brainerd at the time run by a woman whose husband owned the station; she shared recipes and gossip, and it was a very silly show. I remember that I started out by making fun of Lolly Edwards, and then I got to love her.

Q. I think Neil Novotony is the first author to appear in one of your novels. He is opposite of you in that he writes romance novels and does poorly in the classroom. Was it fun to create such a fictional counterpart?

A. That was great fun, especially that time in the classroom when the blackboard broke down and the students broke out laughing, and the time he points out the eight weaknesses in poor poems. He calls on a girl to read her poems, and she's in tears. She said, "You've just described my poem." This sort of thing destroys his class time after time.

Q. The incident with Victor Dash and the Oberholtzers' dog Boots is a comic masterpiece, similar to the Lady Wellington episode in *A Green Journey* (the cat, Bishop Baker, and James). Mrs. Oberholtzer tells Victor Dash of all people, "Just give his balls a kick" (382). How did you think of this?

A. That came from an episode that happened in Scotland. Brother Benet told me that story at Blue Cloud Abbey [Marvin, SD]. He knew of a priest who went to visit the lady of the manor house, and the lady's dog kept bothering the priest. She said, "Just give his balls a kick," so he kicked the dog in the balls. And then he saw two badly chewed tennis balls under his chair.

Q. It's no wonder that the producers cracked up when you were recording *Rookery Blues*. Your last two novels, *Rookery Blues* and *The Dean's List*, don't have any mention of Catholicism in them, unlike your previous ones. Were you trying to broaden your appeal, in a sense, wanting to break out of the "Catholic author" category?

A. No, I just didn't feel that anything came out about the Church. I wasn't trying anything. It was like *The Love Hunter*—there isn't anything Catholic in that either.

Q. Except it's Christian, though. To continue with this question, Joseph Hynes in his article, "Midwestern Loneliness—The novels of Jon Hassler" (*Commonweal*, August 3, 1995), states:

> *All of Hassler's books enmesh their protagonists in the questions, 'Who am I?', 'Where am I?', 'Where am I going?', and 'What does it mean to be lonely?' And ironic wit and charity keep loneliness in its place in a world shown to be a vale of both tears and laughter. Of these eight novels only* The Love Hunter *and* Rookery Blues *decline a distinction between being 'in' the world and being 'of' the world. The two regard this world as the fullness of reality.*

I think we both believe that *The Love Hunter* has a deeper spiritual quality than Hynes is willing to accept. However, what is your answer in regard to the more secular *Rookery Blues*?

A. Well, this is something I didn't foresee when I wrote the book. Being in the world or being out of the world, or being of the world—I don't understand it.

Q. Do you think that there may not be any spiritual dimension in this one?

A. Well, I don't think that's true. I think all of them have these spiritual longings—all those five people exhibit them in their own ways.

Q. Maybe just not as forthright or apparent.

A. Not explicitly religious.

Q. You often have a field day with satire, and *Rookery Blues* is no exception. What did you target in this novel?

A. Well, the college faculties, of course. "Which students should be spared an 'F' as being too demeaning, which colleague should be denied tenure as too ennobling, how big a budget for hockey sticks." Those are the three big questions at Rookery State. I guess that's my main point of satire.

Q. What about Dean Zastrow?

A. Yes, of course, he fits in that. He's dean of the college, the dumbest man I ever wrote about.

Q. And how about the motto? I don't know if Zastrow proposed it, but he certainly lives by it—"Paul Bunyan's Alma Mater."

A. Yes, he believes Paul Bunyan was a graduate of Rookery State. And some teacher suggests at the faculty meeting that he bring Paul Bunyan back as commencement speaker. And he says, "No, because celebrities are too expensive."

Q. Is this a little farfetched or not? I know of your "love" for some college administrators.

A. It's a little farfetched, I guess, but then I think for satire to work it has to be a little broader than life.

Q. That's true. In fact, does the brush of satire touch all of the Quintet members? Victor Dash is as gung-ho in union work as Coach Gibbon from *Staggerford* was in sports. Leland tries a balancing act in whatever situation he finds himself so that he offends no one. Thinking he possesses writing talent exhibits Neil's delusions. Peggy serves as the *femme fatale* (and in her own eyes, too). And Connor is the romantic, alcoholic artist.

A. Yes, there's some satire there—I don't see much satire about Leland and Connor, however. But the others I do.

Q. Roger Miller in the August 1995 issue of *Book Pages* observed: "Of his [Hassler's] major characters, the only ones he doesn't satirize are Peggy and Connor." I read this review just after typing my previous question. Do you satirize Peggy and Connor? I say yes, at least up to a point.

A. Not for Connor.

Q. Why not for Connor?

A. Because he's so pitiful—he has such an unhappy life. It seems to me he's beyond satire.

Q. And Leland, too, because he's a good man?

A. Because he's so earnest and he's trying so hard.

Q. In a *Fargo Forum* interview (July 9, 1995), you said: "I tried to be funny. But I don't hit anybody in the face with it. Sometimes it works and sometimes it doesn't. Some of my books are pretty serious, but I hope all of them have at least a little bit of lightness." We probably already have touched on some of the parts in *Rookery Blues* that amused you, such as Victor and Boots, and probably Zastrow, but I'll ask you anyway. What parts do you think are funny in this novel besides these?

A. I thought the drunken scene on the ice was funny, but my wife doesn't. I guess it depends on if you've had experience with drunks or not. I thought that was pretty funny.

Q. You always anchor your novels in what is happening in America and often the world at that particular time. Ed Block, Jr., in the *Milwaukee Journal Sentinel* (August 6, 1995), mentions this fact:

> As in many of Hassler's previous novels, historical details provide realistic texture. The novel begins with Russian astronauts in space and Golda Meir made premier of Israel. Later it's Super Bowl III. At novel's end, two of the main characters lie in bed listening to the first moon landing.

Do you do any research? You wrote *Rookery Blues* roughly in 1993 and 1994, I think, and yet it takes place in 1969.

A. I think I looked up when Golda Meir was made premier—I think that's the only thing I looked up. I don't care for research.

Q. How *did* you prepare to write a novel about the late 1960s in America with the Vietnam War, drugs, student unrest? It would seem to need such a large canvas because of the many shadings and causes and effects—and background knowledge, but it's partly your time period in life.

A. Yes, it was when I was teaching at Bemidji State, and I remember all those things, especially the Vietnam War, things like that; they were all fresh in my mind.

Q. Connor's latest paintings feature mothers and daughters. Did you intend this to be somewhat ironic or symbolic since Connor has so little to do with his dysfunctional family—his wife Marcy and his daughter Laura?

A. Yes, I thought that was probably because he was upset about the disparity between his wife and his daughter—and himself. I thought he'd probably be concentrating on wives and daughters trying to make up for that.

**Q. How did you immerse yourself in Connor, especially in regard to his artistic temperament and his actual painting?**

A. Well, I remember my own painting days, so that's how I did it. I just imagined what he'd be thinking and doing.

**Q. In Connor's flashback, the bandleader Acheson made Sonny Connor laugh by telling him stories of small towns where he and his band had played, including the tale "about the herd of cows that broke out of their pasture and followed a farmer to the dance in Dorset" (316). Dorset is a small hamlet of perhaps eighteen people near your former cabin in Nevis. Was this a kind of affectionate tribute to Dorset, home of at least four restaurants?**

A. I guess I got that idea from the cows that broke out of a pasture and came over to see the movie at the drive-in theater I used to manage at Park Rapids.

**Q. We really haven't tackled the theme yet. What do you see as the main theme of *Rookery Blues*?**

A. It goes back to what I said earlier about this group—getting together to help each other through these bad times in college teaching, and the consolation of having friends.

**Q. Roger Miller in *Book Pages* (August 1995) probably summarizes the theme not only of *Rookery Blues* but of all your novels:**

> *Well, you can't have everything. Jon Hassler has delivered himself of a new novel, Rookery Blues (Ballantine, $23), but it's not set in the fictional town of Staggerford, and it doesn't star Agatha McGee, the equally fictional but wholly lifelike 70-year-old spinster school-teacher who lighted up three of his seven previous novels.*
>
> *But then, if Hassler's earlier novels have taught us anything, it is that having everything isn't good for you and is not what you really want anyway. Rather, what you should want is what you need. And we all—at any rate, all of us Hassler fans, growing in number—want and need a new Hassler novel, with or without*

*Agatha, every couple of years. So, where's the problem?*

*None with* Rookery Blues, *certainly. With each novel Hassler goes from strength to strength, and that strength is his underlying theme of the importance of love. Not sex, or romance, or lust— though all of them are in his books to a greater or lesser degree— but love, and how we need it.*

*The question is, like that rude one about sex, are we gettin' any? Most of his characters aren't, or not enough, and mostly, though not always, it's their own fault. And so it goes in* Rookery Blues.

**Comments?**

A. Yes, I believe that amounts to what I just said about the group being a consolation among themselves.

Q. You said as much in *The Salt Lake Tribune* interview (August 20, 1995): "I enjoy writing love stories which have an impediment to the love. I want to test this love to see how strong it is." Is this still true?

A. Yes, it is. I don't think there's much of a story in a love that doesn't have an impediment, so that's why it's there.

Q. Also, in that same interview, the writer, Brandon Griggs, notes: "Reviewers have noticed several themes running throughout Hassler's work. One is redemption: His characters suffer ordeals, only to emerge victorious by the books' final chapters. 'I do speak to a need people have to hear this sort of thing,' says Hassler, a self-described optimist. 'Maybe I'm just trying to cheer myself up.'" Any thoughts after six years?

A. Yes, I believe that's true—I believe there is resurrection in all of my books or, as he says, "redemption." I think it's true of all of my work.

Q. I've been telling my students that in my current Jon Hassler class. I really believe that, and they're seeing it also. At the beginning of our interview, I asked you about a possible stage adaptation of *Rookery Blues*. Now I'll ask about any movie interest. With the relationships of the Quintet members, I would think it would make a very fine film with the relationships and the need each has for the others. *The Big Chill* dealt with multiple protagonists.

A. Yes, *The Big Chill* is a good example of this sort of story. I haven't had any bites on this one, however. It doesn't seem to interest anybody.

Q. That's too bad. *Rookery Blues* was nominated for a Minnesota Book Award in the classification of "Novels and Short Stories." Other nominees in that category included Jonis Agee, Lorna Landvik, and David Treuer. Do you remember who won?

A. I think David Treuer won that year.

Q. The year 1995—and the award was presented in 1996—must have been a vintage year for Minnesota writing; others nominated in various categories were Mark Vinz, Thom Tammaro, Deborah Keenan, Paul Gruchow, Susan Allen Toth, and Will Weaver. Did you attend the ceremony on April 13, 1996?

A. No, I didn't go to that one. I'd been nominated several times and I never won, except I was given an award there last year, a $100 award—a lifetime honor—for my lifetime literature. That's the only thing I won there.

Q. And that's the only time you attended then?

A. Yes, I send [poet] Carol Connolly as my representative. She is all ready with a speech in case I win. She's never yet had to use it.

Q. *Publishers Weekly* (August 21, 1995) reported that *Rookery Blues* numbered among the top twenty-five in fiction hardcover along with David Lodge's *Therapy* ("New Fiction Hot Sellers"). That must have been encouraging, or you may not even have known that since Ballantine hadn't sent you many statements.

A. That's true—I didn't know that.

Q. For the week ending September 3, 1995, *Rookery Blues* topped the

Hardcover Fiction Bestsellers in the *Star Tribune* [Minneapolis], ahead of Pat Conroy, Patricia Cornwall, Anne Rice, James Redfield, John Grisham, and Stephen King!

A. That's pretty good, isn't it?

Q. It's great—you'll have to have that listing maybe blown up and put on your office wall. Please tell the importance of positive reviews in *Publishers Weekly* and *Kirkus Reviews*.

A. They come before the book comes out, so librarians and booksellers look at those—they decide what books to buy, so they're very important to have.

Q. Did *Kirkus* not always like your novels? Their review ended with a rave: "Hassler displays once again why he's the novel's answer to Garrison Keillor. This may not be *Lucky Jim*, but it's worthy to be mentioned in the same breath" (May 1, 1995).

A. Yes, they went out of their way that time. They used to dislike me a lot. It was *Kirkus Reviews* that said many years earlier I was a low-octane writer.

Q. And I think I found one more, maybe *Dear James*, that they really liked also. So they're coming around. Always receptive to your work, I believe, *Publishers Weekly* (May 22, 1995) came through once again: "Hassler has produced an uproariously funny, wonderfully satisfying sendup of academic tomfoolery."

A. Yes, that's very gratifying to hear.

Q. Dave Goldsmith of Northern Michigan University opened his *Rookery Blues* review in the *Star Tribune* [Minneapolis] (July 30, 1995) thus:

> Can a dead novelist take over the mind and pen (or word processor) of a living writer? No, you will say, but after reading Jon Hassler's new novel you might change your mind. The spirit of Sinclair Lewis inhabits every page of Rookery Blues.
> Happily, Hassler is a better writer than Lewis, even if he hasn't

*won a Nobel Prize, and he has more sympathy for his characters. While Lewis was usually content to ridicule anyone except his idealistic heroes, Hassler is more humane, if no less acute.*

*The author, writer-in-residence at Saint John's University in Collegeville, Minn., is best known for his serious, rather old-fashioned novels, mostly about a Minnesota town he calls Staggerford.* Rookery Blues, *however, is academic satire, and it's a hoot.*

**This isn't the first time that you've been compared to Sinclair Lewis and usually to your advantage. Do you see any similarities between you and Lewis besides the Minnesota small-town setting?**

A. It's our subject matter—we get our subject matter from the same source. Other than that, we aren't alike at all, except I do write satire, and he wrote satire, too. He wrote a different sort of satire. It's harmful, I think.

**Q. The *New York Times Book Review*, as we've seen in these interviews, flip-flops in its assessment of your novels. Most have been very positive, sometimes in long reviews, other times in just a few paragraphs. Its reviewer this time, Bruce Allen (October 1, 1995), notes:**

*Jon Hassler's seven previous novels . . . have surveyed the small-town culture of the northern Midwest with a beguiling blend of mockery and affection. He's Sinclair Lewis without an attitude problem. . . . Plotting isn't Mr. Hassler's strength, and the story occasionally dips into the tepid waters of soap opera. But his easily digestible colloquial prose has grown more flexible over the years, and his patient depiction of life in all its splendor and misery at 'this campus at the edge of nowhere' makes* Rookery Blues *one of his finest and funniest novels.*

**First, what about his comment about your plotting?**

A. Well, he's right. Plotting is what I worry about most and I work hardest at. Probably the hard work shows through occasionally. I think that's true.

**Q. Any other thoughts about this review as quoted?**

A. I think it's very good. Overall, I like it a lot.

Q. Joseph Hynes reviewed all of your novels through *Rookery Blues* for *Commonweal* (November 3, 1995). He concludes this comprehensive look with these two sentences:

> ... I want to sound the concluding note that a dominant mystery about Jon Hassler is how he can be one of the funniest serious writers alive. This fact doubtless accounts for his popularity as he goes about the serious business of grappling with our abiding loneliness.

Is that a fair statement?

A. Sure, it is. I often try to make my novels serious and yet try to make them funny at the same time, so he captured that in that comment.

Q. And is abiding loneliness one of your main themes?

A. I guess it is without my knowing it; it's turned out to be. Most of my protagonists are lonely people.

Q. That's a good point then. I think Professor Hynes ties all this together. And I thought you should have the last word for this interview. In the *Fargo Forum* [ND], dated July 9, 1995, your interview ends with this quote:

> But more than that, Hassler says he would like to be remembered the way he remembers his father, the small-town grocer. 'Just as a good man, a good person,' he says. 'In my case, as a good writer and a good teacher. You take the hand you're dealt in life and do the best you can with it. I hope that's what I've accomplished.'

Any additions?

A. No, I think that says it all, Joe.

Q. You'll have to create some more novels so that we can continue with these interviews. Thanks so much, Jon.

A. You're welcome. It's a real pleasure.

# The Dean's List

Jon's ninth novel, *The Dean's List* (1997), somewhat surprisingly turned out to be our first interview. Jon and I had been discussing the idea of my conducting interviews with him about his adult novels. In fact, just today I found Jon's letter attached to a published interview with a well-known Minnesota author. The letter, dated September 21, 1997, states:

> I'm enclosing the article ... as an example of what you and I might do ... I mean, couldn't we produce at least eleven such interviews—one per novel? We'll have to zero in on a smaller topic than the novel as a whole. Who are the real-life people behind the characters in Staggerford? Taking Agatha's route through Italy. Simon's route through Ireland. Etc. What do you think, Joe?

We started with *The Dean's List* because at that time the book was about to appear in paperback. You may notice that this interview, conducted in December 1997, contains shorter questions and longer answers than any of the other interviews. Some months ago Jon and I had a hearty laugh when we reread and edited it. I'm afraid that my questions became more verbose while Jon's answers grew more concise as the interviews progressed.

*The Dean's List* is a companion piece, a kind of sequel, to *Rookery Blues,* the novel Jon published in 1995. However, twenty-five years have elapsed between the two stories. It may be true, as Jon maintains, that one could read *The Dean's List* without having read *Rookery Blues,* but for me the experience is enriched by seeing what happened to the Icejam Quintet and the assorted other characters we were introduced to in the earlier novel. This is Jon's fourth novel having Rookery, Minnesota, as its locale—the others being *Simon's*

*Night* (in flashbacks), *The Love Hunter,* and *Rookery Blues.* In the second book poetry replaces music as the medium for communion, but in both books art of some sort serves to unify and heal.

*The Dean's List* allows Jon to resurrect some of the poetry he wrote in the 1960s for a collection entitled *The Red Oak.* In a *Bookpage* interview (July 1997), Jon shared these thoughts:

> *Poetry has never meant so much to me in my life as it has recently. For some reason, I keep going back to poems I memorized as a kid. A lot of them are Frost poems; I just love them. My head was full of poems about the time I started writing this book, so I brought the poet in. Then I decided to use poems I wrote when I took myself seriously as a poet, 30 years ago when I was teaching up at Bemidji State. . . . I decided Richard Falcon wrote a long time ago and he might have written poems like these, so I put my poems in the book.*

Music and poetry reflect, too, the contrast and connection of the private and the public self. In *Rookery Blues,* for example, Georgina and Peggy have a falling-out, yet Peggy and the other members of the quintet play at Georgina's wedding dance. Similarly, in *The Dean's List,* the stresses of Richard Falcon's private life, including Parkinson's and the mental anguish of escape, debilitate him, yet the poetry reading—the public occasion—affirms, sustains, and transforms him. In both books art ennobles both the artist and the audience.

Falcon's reading at Rookery State is one of my favorite set pieces of Jon's, and this excerpt, I think, proves the power of art, the power of poetry:

> *'And now, finally to wrap this up, if you'll please join me on a few jingles.' What? He's [Falcon] quitting already? I [Leland] look at my watch expecting to see that it's about twenty to three. It's twenty after. He's been up there for over an hour.*
>
> *'Reflection on the Water' is first, followed by two or three other poems for children, and as we recite them a strange and stirring thing happens. All five thousand of us rise spontaneously to our feet, as though for Our National Anthem or the Lord's Prayer. Our voices gradually drop away, and we stand there in silent tribute to the little*

man at the lectern, committing to memory his scratchy monotone as he comes to the end of 'Contrast.'

An oak leaf in flutter,
A bluejay in flight.

He closes his book. Nobody claps. More stirring than applause is the utter silence of these adoring readers. Not a cough, not a murmur, not the scrape of a foot. It's a silence so complete that you can actually hear the rustle of his loose pages as he gathers them up and the shuffle of his shoes as he turns away from the microphone. I step forward to guide him down the two steps, and as our fingers touch, the spell is broken by the sudden flash of our images on the scoreboard, and the arena breaks out in a thunderous ovation. (288-289)

In this novel, as in many of his previous ones, Jon once again touches the reader's soul.

- J. P. August 2002

December 26, 1997

Q. I'm excited to start our series of interviews—this is our first one, Jon. *The Dean's List* is your ninth adult novel, but it's your first, I believe, written in first person. You usually start writing first person in your other novels for fifty or so pages and then you change to third person. Why did you continue to use first person narration for this novel?

A. I think Leland's voice matched mine so well that I had a hard time differentiating between us, and I got to page 50, where I normally quit using first person, and I just kept going. I think Leland and I are so much alike, we share so many opinions and so forth; it just fit to use first person. I carried it through to the end of the book and it never became difficult. Now, as I read the book, I find that I like first person a lot, and I intend to use it more as time goes by. You see, I used to get so trapped into one character's sensibility that I stopped and changed to third person, but here I didn't mind being trapped in Leland's head because he seemed to be looking at so many different things.

**Q. You've answered my second question. Friends can see you, the author, in such characters as Miles in *Staggerford*, Simon in *Simon's Night*, and now Leland in *The Dean's List*. How much of you is in this novel?**

A. Well, there certainly is a lot of me in Leland's attitude toward life and in his years spent caring for his mother, which I did. The unhappy breakup of his first marriage, his divorce and some of his campus activities, I think, his dealing with students. Although I was never brought up on sexual harassment charges, one of my friends at Saint John's was. So I had a lot to go on there from my own life; however, I think every novel has me in its main character. I think Miles is Leland at a different age; I think Miles is Simon as an old man, also Frank Healy [*North of Hope*]. All the people along the way, even Agatha McGee, I think is myself more than anybody else. I'm in all my main characters, certainly.

**Q. There's one place in *The Dean's List* where Leland said, "I guess I've always been too innocent for my own good." Is that Jon Hassler speaking?**

A. Well, perhaps it was at some point in my life. I think I've always been a late starter, a late bloomer. The best example is my writing. I didn't publish my first novel until I was forty-four. I think I spent a good bit of my life being innocent, and maybe my adolescence lasted longer than most people's, and, yes, I didn't have any trouble putting that thought into Leland's head; therefore, I must not have any trouble thinking of it in my own regard.

**Q. Another autobiographical bit—Leland's office at Rookery State has a view of the river. I know how much you like water. This also is autobiographical, I would assume.**

A. Well, you know, I picture Bemidji State when I think of Rookery, and Bemidji isn't on the river, but it's on the lake, and it's always been important to me to be able to look out a window. It was my one complaint about Brainerd Community College the last few years I was there—I had a windowless office, and I would find myself standing out in the hallway in front of a big wall of windows. I'd be out there unconsciously. I'd pick up my book and I'd move out there and I'd stand there and read, and I'd realize where I was, and I'd go back to work in my office. I'm always drawn to windows and landscapes and air and light, so I guess that's certainly autobiographical. You know Leland's mother would like him to move because the president's office is in front of the building. But, of course, he won't move because he loves the river so much, this being the Badbattle River, and of course it ties my novels together, all of my adult books except *Grand Opening*.

**Q. Also, your parents had a cabin in northern Minnesota on Belle Taine Lake. Is this the setting for the cabin at Owl Creek?**

A. Yes, it is, it certainly is. I would go up there and rake. Some of my happiest memories are of that cabin and the raking I did in the spring and the fall. I loved that job of raking that big yard. Raking everything down on the lakeshore and then setting it afire and watching it burn far into the night.

**Q. Leland, the narrator, surreptitiously makes lists in his notebook whenever he's bored at meetings or public functions—hence the book's title. How did this idea, Leland making lists, germinate?**

A. That's the most calculated thing in the book, you see, because I wanted to call it *The Dean's List*. I wanted it to have two meanings. I wanted it to have the ordinary meaning and then I thought he should be involved in lists somewhere, so I was almost through with the novel when I thought of this, so I went back and had him make these lists just so the title would have a second meaning.

**Q. I was moved by the dedication of this book.**

A. This is to Bob Spaeth who was the Dean at Saint John's. The dedication reads "In memory of my Dean, Robert L. Spaeth, 1935-1994." He's a man who came to Brainerd when he heard that I had a Guggenheim Fellowship and asked me if I'd like to come to Saint John's for a year, which I did, because I wanted to get out of Brainerd. My family was breaking up, I sold my house. The timing was perfect. In fact, that whole deal about leaving Brainerd and going to Saint John's seems providential to me now as I look back. He came and invited me to Saint John's where I had gone to college, a place I loved, and I went down there for a year, and while I was there I realized I couldn't go back again, so I got a part-time job there and I spent the last seventeen years of my teaching career, until this past spring, teaching two courses, Creative Writing and Minnesota Authors.

I don't know of anyone who's missed more than Bob. To this day people still say "I miss Bob Spaeth." I think it had to do with his wit and his universal interest in all things. He was the best dean of a college because he was interested in all subject matter. For instance, in college he had been a great student of the humanities and yet he majored in physics, and then he went on to study chemistry in graduate school, and then he became a historian and a political scientist and taught at St. John's at Annapolis, which is a Great Books school, and you have to be well versed in all fields to teach there. So everybody at Saint John's kept getting in their mailboxes clippings that Bob cut out of papers he thought were interesting on all different subjects. For that reason he made a wonderful dean.

Q. That's very good to hear. Bob and I had been at Saint John's for at least one or two years of our time in the 1950s. Characters from an earlier novel, *Rookery Blues*, make their appearances in *The Dean's List*, such as Peggy, Lolly, L. P. Connor, Neil Novotny, and, of course, Leland as your main character. How did the idea of a sequel, if that's what we can call it, come about?

A. Well, I don't write many sequels, and yet, when I finished *Rookery Blues*, I knew I had to do another book about college teaching because there are more silly things going on around Saint John's—particularly, I thought, when they gave the Pax Christi Award to Amy Grant. So I thought I'd work that in. I mean, they can give it to whomever they want; of course, it's their business, but up to that point they'd been giving it to bishops and theologians, people important in the church, and then they gave it to Amy Grant because she sang Christian rock. There was a big ceremony there, the orchestra played, the Abbot gave her this award, and I thought that was kind of silly, so that accounts for my episode with Addison Steele who is sort of a British type of Madonna who they narrowly avoid having at Rookery State as a spokesperson of the scholarship fund. Then I thought about the athletic department and how Bob Spaeth used to despise athletics. It was the one great prejudice he had about college as a dean. And so I have this athletic director and this hockey coach selling out to the beer company, and wouldn't you know, a month ago at the University of Minnesota there was so much fuss made about their selling out to the Grain Belt Beer people that they backed out of the contract that they had with that company, so it's like art coming to life.

**Q. Athletics often seem to wither under your satirical eye, and of course Coach Gibbons in *Staggerford* is a classic example, but hockey coach Hokanson isn't far behind. Yet you did play high school athletics, and you reach first for the sports section of the Sunday paper. Can you explain this seeming dichotomy?**

A. That's true, Joe. You know me too well. I guess they're such an easy target, the athletes, you know, because it's all physical, and there isn't much mental activity going on there, so they make easy targets. All I have to do is put myself in Bob Spaeth's place. You know, at St. Cloud State, for example, they opened up this great big hockey center, the best one in the Midwest, and on the very Sunday that was dedicated, Bob had this anti-hockey editorial in the St. Cloud paper which infuriated most of St. Cloud. I remember a fellow from St. Cloud State sent him a hockey puck in the mail. I just took that up as a cause to see if I could get a few laughs out of it. I just love athletics. Football was the reason I made it through high school. I liked football better than anything else in high school, and so it served me just fine. But I have fun with athletics because sometimes they do get out of hand, and as Coach Hokanson says, he wishes that the hockey program could exist without this encumbrance of a university.

**Q. Of course, your readers have a great deal of fun reading these exploits, too. Does one need to read *Rookery Blues* first in order to appreciate *The Dean's List*?**

A. I don't think so because the story is completely different and it starts at a different point in history, and although these people existed in *Rookery Blues*, they existed twenty-five years earlier, and so I think the story line is complete in this book. I think maybe you might have filled out the characters a little more by reading *Rookery Blues*, but you could read it after as well as before.

Q. Most, if not all, of your novels have been written in the past tense. In *The Dean's List* you write in the present tense. Is this easier to do than the past tense?

A. It isn't easier but it seems more immediate as I read it. I guess it's part of the same process as using the first person instead of the third. It was an attempt to be more immediate, and I think that it seems more immediate. Some writers look down on this as a gimmick. I don't know, it just went fine with me. Also, you know in this book there are several flashbacks, and this allowed me to differentiate between the present and the past a little easier, too, by putting the flashbacks in the past tense and the present action in the present tense.

Q. Was this a conscious decision, or did it just happen when you were writing?

A. This was a conscious decision. I began it by deciding I'd try it and see how it worked.

Q. Critics speak of John Cheever Country and John Updike Country. Of course, enough evidence points to a Jon Hassler Country. What is Hassler Country from your point of view and how does *The Dean's List* fit into it?

A. Hassler Country is Minnesota, small town Minnesota. I see pine trees on the horizon. I see marginal farms, hardscrabble people living on these marginal farms. I see a town in which maybe the biggest employer is the school. There are a couple of important churches in this town. I can see the setting. When I think of my novels, the people in my novels, I keep going back to Park Rapids where I taught for six years. That was my last high school job. That became the setting for

*Staggerford*. Although the story didn't come from Staggerford, the setting did. And I see the houses of that town, and then when I think of Rookery I think of Bemidji. I keep imagining most of my settings in those two places, Bemidji and Park Rapids.

**Q. Would there be anything spiritually or metaphorically that would typify Hassler Country?**

A. Well, that's a subject I have trouble talking about because I don't understand my themes entirely. I think of the geography, I think of the concrete. I have trouble with the abstract.

**Q. Some years ago you told me that you were thinking of writing a missing person novel. In fact, you even talked to the Brainerd police chief, a former student of yours, about it. With Richard Falcon's disappearance, is *The Dean's List* your missing person novel?**

A. Yes, it is. The interesting thing is I thought I would write it from the viewpoint of the people who missed him. Now I'm writing it from his own viewpoint. He's run away and I guess I needed to do that. I don't know why. I remember the idea first struck me when I was in Los Angeles in 1983 and I turned on the television, and it told about the president of a community college in Maryland who had disappeared. He had been gone for three or four months. Nobody knew where he was and I was just intrigued by that. I thought that would make an interesting plot. Later, he published a book about how he'd run away and how he made it work. He changed his driver's license, passport, and all that. So, it haunted me, and as I say, I don't know why except it seemed like a good plot for a novel. And then, when I had Richard Falcon come to Rookery State and run away from New England, I guess I took care of that. I don't expect to be writing anymore about it.

**Q. It certainly adds to your plot. You said at a recent reading that Richard Falcon's poetry was really your poetry written some years ago. In fact, *The Dean's List* ends with an appendix entitled "The Rookery Chapbook" containing ten poems by Falcon. How did you happen to think of resurrecting your poems for this novel?**

A. Well, I had a poet in the novel, of course. He comes to Leland's college and Leland connects with him and respects him so much and he becomes a father figure to Leland. The poet has a reading—so where do I get the poetry? I have to make it up or I have to use some old stuff I used to write. You see, in 1966, when I lived in Bemidji, I took myself seriously as a poet for about two years, and that means I thought lines of poetry morning, noon and night. Walking home from college I'd turn phrases over in my mind. Lying in bed at night I'd lose sleep thinking of things to rhyme. Then I finished twelve or fifteen poems, and I self-published a chapbook called *The Red Oak*.

**Q. I remember that well.**

A. And that's full of poems. I read them now. I never could master the modern idiom. I could never not rhyme, I could never not write. A line is strict rhythm, you see, so I was writing poetry you could dance a polka to while the rest of the world went on and wrote free verse. Therefore, mine was unpublishable. And so I finally got it between hard covers here with *The Dean's List*. It isn't bad, some of it. I gleaned the better part of *The Red Oak*. What I like, particularly in this book, is Richard Falcon's autobiographical poem which he's working on, which I wrote as I was writing the book. I think some of those lines are pretty good.

**Q. Is Falcon based on an actual poet or one that you knew?**

A. He's based on Robert Frost, actually, which accounts for his testy personality among other things. Frost is an endearing poet and I like his work a lot. I guess he was very hard to get along with, so here comes Richard Falcon with his poetry everybody loves and it's hard for people to get along with him at first.

**Q. I noticed that the "Chapbook," printed in the appendix, contains three sketches which I'm sure I recognize as yours. I don't think any credit is given to you. Is that deliberate?**

A. Yes. I put some very small initials on one of them and that's the extent of it. It's such a small part of the book I didn't want credit for it. In my memoirs, I might put a number of drawings from my sketchbooks.

**Q. So this is like the beginning of it. That's good. Does painting have an impact on your writing? I know you've been painting a number of years in watercolors, I believe, and oils. I was wondering, has that had any impact on or a correlation with your writing?**

A. Well, it seems to be such a different pursuit. I know that painting relaxes me and writing doesn't relax me. I think it's because you use your hands in painting and you don't in writing—except for on a typewriter. When you form something with your hands, it's relaxing. To do it entirely in your brain is kind of stressful. However, I notice differences more than similarities. In my paintings there are no people. There are lonesome landscapes. In my novels there are sixty-five characters at least in each novel, so my books teem with human life and my landscapes don't. It's like looking at landscapes is a way to rest your eyes. I rest my brain from my novels by painting. I've just now begun watercolors after many years of doing oils, and I'm finding it fascinating and difficult both. I did twelve watercolors in Italy, and the twelfth one turned out not to be so bad actually. So that's good. I'm glad it wasn't the first one.

**Q. Falcon's reading at Rookery State is one of the highlights of this novel, and an actual event, I understand, inspired you to include this. Would you tell about that?**

A. Well, it was an event I didn't attend. I was too young. I was at Saint John's University as a student back in the 50s. I was looking through the morning *Minneapolis Tribune*, and there I saw a reference to a reading at the University of Minnesota by T. S. Eliot. It showed a picture of students sitting way up under the girders of the roof. There were 18,000 people at this reading, and it had to be moved out of Northrop Auditorium into Williams Arena. It seemed incredible to me then and it still seems incredible, but it gave me courage to try this. I decided to let Leland try to fill the hockey arena—it seats 5,000—with poetry lovers for Richard Falcon's reading. He advertises throughout the Midwest, and sure enough, early Sunday morning they begin to come on campus with their cars from Madison, from Sioux Falls, from Fargo, from Grand Forks, from all over the place. Before he's done he gets about 4,500 people into that arena to listen to the poet. It's quite moving, and I never would have had the idea had it not actually happened in the 50s with T. S. Eliot. Imagine 18,000 people listening to a poet, Joe.

Q. Probably every English teacher's dream and something to strive for.

A. It is, yes.

Q. I always found that whenever we had poets at Brainerd Community College we would be so happy how many had turned out. Robert Bly came in 1968 and we filled our Chalberg Theater, and we were so gratified and pleased.

A. Yes, I know. To this day it's wonderful to see people turn out for literary things like that. It means that literature matters. As I said in an interview, literature is more important in our lives than gasoline.

Q. Richard Falcon, of course, is a writer and a poet. You just talked about his public reading. You are a writer and you give readings. I attended a recent reading of yours, and although it lasted for about an hour, many in the audience thought it seemed more like five to ten minutes. This is exactly Leland's perception after Falcon's reading. Did you draw on your own experiences for this scene?

A. Yes, I did. I know the satisfaction of having that big audience, you know. It becomes perfectly quiet as you read. It's a wonderful thing. It means that they like your language. It means they like the sound of it and are captivated by it. So I had him do that, I gave that satisfaction to Richard Falcon.

Q. Some of your characters are based on actual people, or at least some factual facet triggered your imagination. Would you like to tell the origin about one of your memorable characters, Lolly, Leland's mother in *The Dean's List*?

A. Lolly comes from Brainerd. In about 1975 I was teaching there with you at the Community College. We began the mini-course in the novel, which meant that people would come to class three evenings a week to talk about a particular novel and then they earn their credits. I taught the first one, and it was *Crime and Punishment*; the president said to me, "You should go on *Frills and Fancies*." *Frills and Fancies* was a radio show run by June Persons of KVBR Radio. It was gossip and recipes, that sort of thing. So I went downtown, I went up to the studio, and I was introduced on the air by June Persons, who said, "And now tell us about this course you're going to teach," and I went on at some length describing *Crime and Punishment*, the ax murder, all this stuff that didn't fit *Frills and Fancies*, and when I finished, she said to me on the air, "Well, I certainly hope the course is more interesting than you sound," and that was the end of that. Well, I resented that and I thought it was funny, too, so when I began to write about Lolly, I had her in mind, but the more I wrote about Lolly, the more I loved her, and so there isn't much resentment in my book about Lolly. The only similarity is that she's a talk show host; it's become so popular. Lolly's been at it since 1948, so she was probably the first of the talk show hosts.

**Q. Lolly is endearing. I think readers enjoy her even with her faults, perhaps *because* of her faults. As we mentioned before, Leland seems more of you than many of your other characters. What others in *The Dean's List* are based on observation or some personal experience?**

A. Well, let's see now. I like the secretary a lot, Viola Trisco. She's based on a secretary we had in Brainerd who was sort of a rough and ready type in Suite A. She was only there for a short time. But she'd sit up there talking to these students about things like wrestling matches, and she had an appetite for that side of life, you know, the wrestling match and the lottery and subjects like that. It seemed so far removed from what we were teaching. I sure enjoyed talking to her about those things. Another important character in this novel is Angelo Corelli. I don't know where he comes from, but he certainly is an enthusiastic young teacher.

**Q. He didn't come from a real life prototype?**

A. I don't think so. He's important because you see Leland is fifty-eight and getting jaded. There are several burn-outs in this story, so I had to have somebody who stood for the enthusiastic teacher and that's what Angelo does. I like him a lot. I don't know where he came from. Mrs. Zastrow, we've all known Mrs. Zastrow on faculties. She's the mystery woman. We hardly ever see her, but when we do, we can't believe how she looks. She's so made up and she says nothing except she stands there drinking, and I think she only says about one or two words in this whole novel. Some young upstart comes and asks her how she likes Sylvester Stallone, and she looks at him and says, "What a hunk." And that's all she says. Somebody was telling me at a party the other day how much she enjoyed that line and quoted that line to me, "What a hunk."

**Q. So that says quite a bit, three words.**

A. Yes, right.

**Q. What about the people in the high-rise?**

A. The Sylvan Senior Hi-Rise is taken from the high-rise in Staples where my mother spent the last years of her life, and I drove up there every Friday afternoon for peach delight and coffee as Leland does, and so a lot of those people are taken from real life, to answer your question about where the characters come from.

**Q. I noticed that you really have an affinity for older people, for senior citizens, and they're always endearingly and amusingly delineated. You weren't even forty when you wrote *Staggerford* and *Simon's Night*, and I was wondering where your knowledge of these older retired people came from.**

A. I think this comes from knowing my grandfather when I was little and growing up and he lived with us. He was seventy when I was ten and we were quite the buddies, and I've written also about this relationship and how it bridged gaps between generations for me. I remember my high school friends being sort of tongue-tied when they came up against adults and I've never been that way. I think it was because I knew my grandfather so well. I bridged all the lesser gaps as well. Anyway, old folks have always appealed to me because they get into senility and begin talking at cross-purposes with people, or you get people who get so frank in their old age and you can have lines like the one the New Woman utters to Kahlstrom's wife, "What do philosophers eat anyway?" Things like that. Yes, they're fun. I've enjoyed writing about them all my life; I'll write about them more.

Q. Many of your novels have a schema, a set plan. *Staggerford* takes place on nine consecutive days. *The Dean's List* begins with the fall term and ends in June. Does using a schema help to plot the action and develop the theme?

A. Yes, it's very important to me to have an idea of where I'm going. I knew when I started *Staggerford* I intended to cover the entire school year. Then I had all that loose time in there I didn't know what to do with, so I reduced it to a month and it really improved, so I thought, well, if it made that much difference I'll try a week, and I reduced everything to a week and it gave it such power; it's like compression in a gasoline engine. I compressed the time and the book seemed to take on power. I learned something there and I've used it ever since, although some books have taken place over a longer period of time such as *North of Hope*. I think I use time to my advantage that way—by compressing it.

Q. Some people believe that you have an animus against college administrators just as you may have against athletics. President O. F. Zastrow is an extreme case in point, of course. He is called a dolt and a dope, and he believes that Albert Einstein is still alive and that Paul Bunyan is an alumnus of Rookery State. How would you defend yourself against this charge?

A. I'd put Leland Edwards up against everybody who makes that charge because Leland is now dean and we love him.

Q. That's an excellent assessment of his reputation. I know that John Cheever and Evelyn Waugh figure prominently among your favorite authors and you admire them especially for their writing style. Is there anything you can share with us in regard to your style in *The Dean's List*?

A. Well, I'm really proud of *The Dean's List*. I think it's one of my best books. I think my dialogue is the best I've written. I also think I have a number of surprises in the book.

I've come to believe there are two kinds of surprises in books. There's a surprise in the plot. Everybody loves a surprise. You have to surprise people now and then in a novel. And then there's a surprise of phrasing. I was thinking of a young man's novel I was reading for him the other day. He's a would-be novelist. And he has somebody pick up a sex book, and it described sexual positions and, as he says, "all the sexual positions known to man." You come to "known to man" and you get—it isn't quite a cliché and yet it sounds a little bit rusty. Any time that occurs for me, then I would put in a surprise because he goes on to describe these positions with animals even, so I would have just said, "every sexual position known to man, woman, and dogs" or something like that just to surprise the reader, and I'm going to tell him that. I think there is surprise in phrasing as well as surprise in plot. I think it's important to keep both those in mind as you write. Don't let anything seem threadbare.

Q. I notice that whenever I hear you reading, the incidents are even funnier, the verbal wordplays even more clever. Do you think your books should be heard as well as read?

A. I think so; I think all good novels should be read aloud. All language is meant to be read aloud, it seems to me, although nobody does it much anymore with novels, and if not read aloud I think they should be read a second time. I think good novels deserve to be read a second time so that you can savor those places that you skimmed over the first time through. So that's why I'm going back and reading my favorite books again. Right now I'm in the middle of *The Children of Dynmouth* by William Trevor. I'm also reading Carol Shields the second time. Her *Secret Ceremonies* is a wonderful book in which she has given me a line for an epigraph for my memoir actually. The line is this: "We are children all our lives, obedient to echoes."

Q. That's evocative.

A. I think so.

Q. It's true, the plot is part of the reason for reading a novel the first time, and then the second time is for everything else about it, the subtleties and the way it's put together.

A. Yes.

Q. But to continue with style, I noticed that the Exam Week chapter in *The Dean's List* ends with "'Is it cold out?' she asks," and the next chapter, Open House, begins with "It's so cold that some of our guests..." Do you work hard at such felicities of style and transition?

A. No, I didn't know that was there. I didn't realize I did that.

Q. Well, it was very pleasing. Do you sometimes work at effects like that?

A. Oh yes. I'm conscious of them often. I wasn't for that one. That's pretty good.

Q. Yes, I liked it very much, too. And your humor, as the reader would already know, rests much on style and observation, of course. How would you describe your humor in *The Dean's List*?

A. A lot of it has to do with dialogue, with being in front of dumb people, and I think the best part of the book for humor probably is that Christmas party at Lolly's house where I mix these two groups. Mixture, you know, always give you a pretty good potential for humor. I have the college faculty and I have the people from the old folks' home, and when they begin to talk at cross-purposes, that's funny.

Q. In this novel, the world of academe collides with the world of advertising, the world of business, the world of high-rise senior citizens, even Minnesota's higher education structure. Could you elaborate on that? How does academe fare in all of this? Who is victorious or is it just a draw?

A. It seems to me a stand-off mostly except I think Leland's going to be a good president for Rookery State. I think he's going to win out over the athletics. He's probably going to please the college administration in St. Paul. That's something else I got into in this book, the overall governance of colleges in the state. We go down to St. Paul and we have a look at the chancellor and so forth. As for the advertisers, he'll kick them off campus for a time, I think. In fact, I'm struck by how well things turn out in this novel. Probably one of my happier endings in a novel. What do you think, Joe?

Q. Yes, in fact, I was going to ask about that later. Among the last sentences in *The Dean's List* are these: "I have the blessing of a father at last" and "I have time then to write you a poem." I found these to be really upbeat and optimistic, and these ending sentences confirm that. I think you would agree that it is positive.

A. It is, yes. You quoted the last sentence there in the book. I had an editor one time, Bob Wyatt at Ballantine, who told me that the last word in the novel contains the novel. And the last word of *Rookery Blues* is "music" and the last word in this one is "poem."

Q. Jon, we talked about some of your humor already, and here are some examples that I just picked at random, and as you say, the dialogue is so witty it almost needs to be read aloud. Edna the philosopher's wife and Edna the New Woman are talking, and someone is introducing the two: "'Edna, this is Edna Kahlstrom, her husband's in philosophy.' 'Sorry to hear it,' says the New Woman, then adds proudly, 'mine was in plumbing.'" And a few lines down occurs this exchange: "'I hope you like Rookery,' says Edna Kahlstrom sitting down beside the New Woman. 'What do you think of the Hi-Rise?' 'Constipated at first'" (98-99). I always find your bits hilarious and also talented in exposing the gap between people in terms of background, education, and age, and you use this device often.

A. When the poet moves into the high-rise, I think that's certainly a collision, especially since the first person he meets there is Nettie Firehammer, who's out there in the cold winds, smoking a cigarette, and he has an exchange with her about how cold it is. I guess that'd be worth reading, perhaps right now. This is the poet entering the high rise:

> *'I happen to be out of cigarettes at the moment. . . . Would you have a spare one, Mrs. Firehammer, just until I unpack?'*
>
> *'Not on me.' She examines the mouth end of her filterless Camel, pulling out a stray shred of tobacco before handing it over. 'Here, take a drag off this.'*
>
> *'Thank you. Just one, until I unpack.'*
>
> *But it's several drags each, down to the tiniest butt. . . .*
>
> *'This isn't unusually cold for Minnesota then?'*
>
> *'I'm afraid not,' I [Leland] answer apologetically. 'Actually it's the wind today, rather than the temperature. . . .'*
>
> *'Real sting to it,' says Nettie.*
>
> *'Sting is exactly the word, Mrs. Firehammer.'*
>
> *Encouraged, she elaborates, 'Real icy feel to it.'*
>
> *He agrees. 'Icy, all right.'*
>
> *After years of sharing the lobby with such disagreeable men as Pyle and Hancock, she's obviously thrilled by his positive responses.*
>
> *'Real nasty,' she specifies further.*
>
> *'Nasty indeed, Mrs. Firehammer.'*
>
> *'Real . . .' She gropes. 'Cold.'*
>
> *'Yes, that too.' (184-185)*

I don't know where that comes from. I don't understand it, but it's funny. You explain it by saying it's a meeting of people from two different walks of life entirely.

**Q. I think much of it is opposites. Collision is also a good way to put it. Collision is what's funny. Let's talk more about Richard Falcon's poetry.**

A. Here's a poem that comes from my experience in Brandon,

Minnesota, when I used to go visit my grandmother. It's part of Richard Falcon's autobiographical poem.

> *A sultry night in Tipton Town,*
> *The moon climbing over High Street*
> *Like a ballooning bag of sweat,*
> *The stars Leo Gorcey and the Bowery Boys*
> *Projected on the west side of the grain*
> *Elevator, in 'Spooks Run Wild' . . . (178)*

> *That was a movie I saw there outdoors on a hot summer night.*
> *   the sound track moaning screaming*
> *hooting, frightening my ancient*
> *and unstable Aunt Patsy the other side*
> *of town, despairing on her deathbed . . . (179)*

You see, I made that up about Aunt Patsy, but my grandmother was home hearing these screams from downtown, and when I got home, she asked me what was going on. I remember that. I went to Brandon two weeks ago with my cousin George to the funeral of my last uncle who died there. It was his house I was staying at when I saw that movie. Yes, these autobiographical poems are interesting. Most of them I made up, but that's out of my life.

> *He's a quitter by nature,*
> *A solitary only child,*
> *A potential anchorite at twelve.*
> *He dreads the cheering adulation*
> *Of the vast holiday population*
> *So he quits the gunny sack race*
> *Two hops ahead and four from the tape.*
> *Too high-strung for first-string first base*
> *He retires, at sixteen, from the diamond*
> *Rather than face the beery fans*
> *Gathered gaudy and throaty in the stands*
> *Blurting and burping his name, 'Quitter,*

*Hey, Quitter.' They're the reason*
*His ardor ends before the season. (232)*


## THE NEXT DAY—December 27, 1997

Q. We already talked about this yesterday, but the descriptions that abound in this work are so striking and a few are priceless. I would like to quote "New Woman with the oxblood ears," and I think Corelli says, "I haven't seen skin like that since the last time I grilled cajun chicken," and these really amused me. Do you have any favorite descriptions in *The Dean's List* that you recall?

A. I'm very fond of my description of Mrs. Zastrow which was a continuation of how she was described in *Rookery Blues*. Mrs. Zastrow is that mysterious woman who's been around for twenty-five years and nobody really knows her. She enters the party; I'll try to find that and read it.

> *The stiff, unsmiling Mrs. Zastrow, wearing a brown suit with a stylish and very short skirt, keeps her eyes trained on Mother's feet as she allows me [Leland] to take her coat and allows her husband to steer her through the living room to the fireplace. In her twenty-five years among us, we have learned next to nothing about the soul of this eccentric woman whose expensive clothes are always of an inappropriate cut for a woman her age, and whose tanning-booth-blackened face is so thickly overlaid with cosmetics that you can't help imagining the hours of toil at her dressing table. Does she have a mind? The Corellis say yes, and I believe them because Angelo and Gloria are now and then invited to play Scrabble at the president's house. Does she have a voice? Yes, I have heard her utter words, though not sentences. Does she have a thirst for hard liquor? You bet. (90-91)*

There's this part where Leland goes outside and he gets away from the party and he looks around the neighborhood and he sees it's so Christmasy. I want to read that part, too. He just had an argument with Father Pyle who says: 'Bah! Shut your mouth.'

*I'm stunned for a moment, and then I laugh. My laughter hangs briefly in front of my face, a little moonlit cloud of dissolving steam. I'm immune to Father Pyle. I'm euphoric. It isn't entirely the brandy, as I've said; it's due in large part to the loveliness of the sub-zero night, so clear and bracing and still. Bells sound from some distant direction. Snow-covered houses stand about me like a calendar picture entitled* December. *Look at the Christmas trees in the windows. Look at the moonlit smoke standing straight up from the chimneys. Look at Mr. and Mrs. Cooper in their glassed-in, four-season porch across the street, sitting there in their accustomed chairs with their Franklin stove between them—an illustration by Norman Rockwell entitled* Serenity. *(105)*

Well, their serenity is about to be broken, because Father Pyle is going to drive into that room with his car which is based on something that happened in Brainerd, you know. It was actually a different radio hostess in those days. She had that strange name, Nordica Thabes. She lived across from my friend Chuck Pettit and had a Christmas party one afternoon. Chuck described it so well—he was sitting in his living room, reading his paper. A bunch of old folks came out, staggering out of the house having drunk a lot that afternoon. They got in the car, backed out into the street, backed up onto his yard, backed across the yard, and hit his foundation right under where he was sitting. And he described this, sitting there watching them come. Oh, that's funny. I never forgot that.

**Q. In line with the Christmas party, you often use social occasions to reveal character and plot, for example, the Thanksgiving dinner in *Dear James*. Could you tell about some of the social occasions and what you see as their function?**

A. Yes, well, in *The Dean's List*, I write about these big social occasions because I seem to be so good at it. I mean, they turn out to be so interesting, either funny or sad or something. But I have a talent, I discovered, for keeping the reader up-to-date on who's who. You know we've all read novels where there's a gathering of people and we've lost track of the people. I think I've figured out how to describe these people so that they're memorable, and you remember them even though you lose track of them. You move on in the party and you come back a little later and you recognize them, so I have fun doing that.

In this book I have, first of all, faculty meetings which are very brief, of course. And I have this long Christmas party at Leland and Lolly's house. In that one, of course, I bring together the high-rise people and the faculty, so that works fine, and that also gives Leland a chance to talk more about the poet who's coming to town. Then I have this two-in-one on that one Sunday afternoon. There's a huge gathering in the hockey arena, 4,500 people for the poet's reading, and, of course, that's the crux of the book. And following that we go immediately over to the gathering room at the Episcopal Church where we have Lolly's memorial service which she has because she wants to hear her eulogies before she's dead. And I got that from Father Illies in St. Cloud who told me about Mrs. Humphrey whom he used to know in St. Cloud. She was the wife of a chalice maker who did that one time, he said. She got sick and she decided to have her memorial service before she was dead so that she could hear her eulogies, and I thought that's exactly what Lolly would do. At this point Lolly was dead. She died in Omaha, you see, in this book on a trip during Christmas, so I brought her back to life for this memorial service, and she was so energized by it she survived the book. She's still living as far as I know. So she saved her life there. Those were the three biggest gatherings in this book. Oh, yes, there is another one at the end, and it's Inauguration Day, where we have Leland inaugurated as president and the gathering afterwards at the high-rise because there's no air conditioning at the college. They move it over to the high-rise. It's a cocktail party and that makes an interesting contrast, too, between the faculty and the old folks.

**Q. And that leads us to the next part. Do you see *The Dean's List* overall as more public than private? The characters are often at faculty meetings, committee meetings, social gatherings, the wake, the reading. Is that what you see, too?**

A. Yes, it sure is. It comes from my conviction that one can't leave the character alone for very long at a time. I get that from reading student papers. Every student begins the story with the main character meditating and about to act, and then around page 3 the action begins. I've always said to these students, "Throw away pages 1 and 2 because it's not interesting until you get people acting with each other." I have few solitary moments in my books now. Furthermore, Leland, I think, is a solitary man, and he'd be happiest if he were alone, and in those few moments alone he does meditate, for instance, fishing off the wharf and so forth. But those moments are so few because he's put upon by his many duties around this town and on the campus, and they involve other people, and if he were alone it wouldn't be much of a novel.

Q. Perhaps Simon in *Simon's Night* was the most solitary, who spent the most time alone of all your major characters.

A. Yes, he did, and I have a lot of people tell me that's their favorite book, too, so it's interesting, isn't it. He's a solitary type and he's alone quite a bit in that book and people like it a lot, yet I don't believe in leaving a character alone very much anymore. I guess I'm more concerned with plot now and keeping the action going.

Q. Will Rookery State and the actual colleges like that survive now as we approach 2000? How much diluting or compromising will education be forced to do, do you think?

A. Well, we're watching this happen in Minnesota now with a combination of community colleges and the trade schools, as you know. I think they'll come out okay because I believe Rookery is going to survive. And if Rookery survives, any place will survive because Rookery certainly is one of the least recognized schools—it's the smallest in the system and I think it's going to do fine. I'm not necessarily optimistic about the quality of the students we turn out, but I think the schools will continue to survive because a college education will be more important to people as time goes by.

**Q. That guarded optimism is refreshing to hear. This is more of a practical question. How do you write? I know that you use the computer, but could you estimate how many drafts you wrote of *The Dean's List*? The challenges that came to you in writing this novel?**

A. In retrospect, it seems to me to have been an easy novel to write. They all do, of course, after they're over. I think it was easier than some because I had established the characters of Leland and Lolly and several other people before I began. I didn't have to grope around for characters and personalities so that made it easy. I probably write the first chapter twenty times; as I try to get going, I try to imagine what's going to happen. Some chapters came off so smoothly. The trip to Omaha with Leland's mother to visit her relatives in the middle of this book, I think I wrote once or twice, and it came off just fine. It required hardly any revision. Other chapters required a lot of revisions. The last chapter I wrote over and over, of course, because endings are so hard. There's no formula for an ending, you have to keep writing it.

**Q. History, I noticed, often assumes a rather important role in your novels. Does history have any important role in *The Dean's List*?**

A. Well, I guess there's a reference to World War II when Leland was a boy. There's a reference to the late 40s when his father was killed by lightning and they bought the cabin. I guess history isn't very important here.

**Q. During World War II, since we're mentioning this, Leland's father sent a phonograph record to his family with the father singing "I'll Be Home for Christmas." This scene I found especially evocative. Could *The Dean's List* correspondingly be read as an upbeat, encouraging message to higher education that even with all of the apparent adversities, higher education would not only muddle through but eventually triumph?**

A. Yes, I think so. I think it's important to get the right people running it, you know. I mean, there are so many muddlers right now such as Zastrow, and most of the administrators I've worked for in education have turned out to be such dolts because once they go into administration, they become more interested in the budget than they do in educating people. If you get people like Leland in charge, I think it's going to be fine. And of course we will. I think we'll have sense enough to do that. School boards will choose better superintendents, regents will choose better presidents for their colleges, and in these unsettling times we'll come through fine.

**Q. I know some of the incidents in *The Dean's List* are based on actual events such as President Zastrow's toilet in his office, Incarnation Convent, the dual piano playing with Leland and Mary Sue. Would you like to identify any of these?**

A. Incarnation Abbey comes from Bismarck, North Dakota, where it's located. This is in the book because I went there a year ago last spring to give the commencement address. I was so charmed by the place, by the nuns, by the convent, by the room they gave me in which, when I turned down the quilt to crawl into bed, there was a handwritten note on the pillow saying, "When I made this bed this morning I prayed for whoever would sleep in it tonight." I thought, my, what a nice thing. Where in the world would you ever find this, where else in the world. So I have Leland find that same note there. And what else did you mention?

**Q. Leland's piano playing. Leland and Mary Sue.**

A. Oh yes. Well, my wife Gretchen and I have worked up some duets over the years. That's fun. And what else?

**Q. President Zastrow's toilet.**

A. The president of Saint John's put a toilet in because he had some bladder problems, I guess, at one point. So I put that in here. This was Father Colman, he's dead now, bless his soul. He was a great mind and a very amusing man, and Mrs. Weyerhaeuser came to the college one time to see about establishing a radio studio for public radio, the Maude Moon Weyerhaeuser Studios at Saint John's. She was a rich lady, of course, who came with an attendant, another lady, and they came into Father Colman's office. Father Martin, who was a little bit senile by that point anyway, was in the office, and they said, "Is Father Colman in?" and Father Martin said, "Yes, he'll be right out, he's just going number one."

Q. Maybe they found that charming.

A. Oh god. "He'll be right out, he's just going number one."

Q. St. Blaise's feast day is February 3rd, and he's known for healing throat ailments. One chapter in *The Dean's List* is entitled "The Feast of St. Blaise." I could see that healing takes place during the course of the novel, especially in Leland's life. Would you like to comment on that?

A. Well, here we get around to the basic theme. I write about it, I think, in most of my books. I put my characters through some tough times, but most of them come out healed in the end or better off at least, except poor Miles Pruitt in the first novel [*Staggerford*] who died in the process, but he's a sacrificial lamb and we'll talk about that another time. Yes, I see a healing process in most of these books, and I think it must be the reason people like them so well. I get letters from people who are sick or have been through troubled times, and they tell me reading my books helps them. I got an interesting letter from Maryland the other day from a man I've never heard of before who said he had been fighting depression all his life, and whenever his depression gets bad, he picks up my books and reads them and it helps him. Well, that's amazing. You see, I don't write as a cure-all, I just write to tell a story, and yet the trajectory of my characters must somehow inspire people.

Q. The writer as healer then.

A. Yes, right.

Q. Leland asked Richard Falcon, "Are you hungry, Mr. Father?" Leland seems to come to terms with the loss of his father as well as his son in the novel. Is this one of the things, accepting loss and moving on?

A. Yes, it is. And Leland's always had this empty spot in his life since his father died when he was fourteen, and then the poet comes in and he's an old man who loves him and helps him, and he feels he has his father again.

Q. You always seem to add a nugget of recognition in your novels. For example, one of Lolly's callers on her radio show is named Arne Carlson which coincidentally or not is the same name for the current governor of Minnesota. The new building on the Rookery State campus, Simon P. Shea Teaching and Learning Center, owes this name to Simon Shea of *Simon's Night*. I assume this is a deliberate reward to faithful readers?

A. Sure, it's fun to see that, and I think it's a reward to Simon for being such a great person, too.

Q. This probably is an obvious question. Who are your favorite characters in *The Dean's List* and why?

A. Leland, because he's so much like myself. He has all these problems to overcome and his will is so good. He tries to do his best by people. He's a kind guy, he's thoughtful. He knows his own limits, too. Remember when Angelo asked him to come to this burnouts committee meeting? He refuses to do it. He says he can't support burnouts, or he'll burn out himself. He has to go fishing instead. It's the only way he can keep going as dean. Then there's Lolly, of course, who became very dear to me in the process of writing about her. I didn't expect her to become so close to me. I like her a lot. The people in the high-rise I'm very fond of. Even Johnny Hancock, the dirty old man. He carries around this orange juice can in the middle pocket of his bib overalls to spit in. That's based on my friend Lee Hanley's father who did that and who was arrested one time for shoplifting because they thought he had shoplifted the orange juice, and they opened it and found tobacco juice in it. So that's a good story. I get more stories from Lee Hanley, I think, than anybody else. He was the one who told me about the cat who gave birth in *A Green Journey*.

**Q. This sounds like an essay test, I know, but do you have any least favorite characters in *The Dean's List*?**

A. Well, yes. You're talking about Laura Connor, I'm sure.

**Q. Yes. And Zastrow.**

A. Zastrow. Now Zastrow, he provides me with so many laughs. I like him a lot for that reason. And Laura, of course, I've seen her grow up. I've seen how deprived she was of love. I can feel for her, too. I can't say I dislike any of my characters even though they act awful.

**Q. That's a good, a really good, creator who loves his creation.**

A. I do, and furthermore, it's affected me in life. It's taken away my opinions; the more I get to know a character, the more I understand him even if he's bad. And so, it's happened in real life. I have fewer opinions as I write. Fewer political opinions, fewer opinions about people. I seem to be opinion-less these days.

**Q. That's a good point. One really gets to know someone and we often just see the tip of the iceberg, as it were, and seeing the whole complexity one would understand why a person is behaving in a certain way at a certain time.**

A. I hope so. I think it's probably good. I am more comfortable this way than I used to be when I was a hotheaded supporter of political movements and things like that.

**Q. Well, let's conclude our interview with a few personal questions if we may. You were diagnosed with Parkinson's disease in 1994, and I believe that this is the first time you have included a character with Parkinson's in a novel.**

A. Yes, it is.

**Q. This character found out from micrography, writing made small. How did you learn that you had Parkinson's?**

A. I was diagnosed by a friend of yours, Joe, as we had lunch in St. Cloud, you remember; her name is Rita Kirzeder. She is a physical therapist and she watched me put on my coat, she watched me eat my soup, she thought I had the symptoms. She told you and you wrote me and told me which forced me to face it. You see, up to that point I'd been denying it since I'd noticed a few little things, too, such as a stumpy walk, and a shaky way of raising my soup to my mouth, and so I faced it, and I was diagnosed then, and I've had it now for five or six years. Luckily it advances very slowly so I am still able to write and do most things. [Jon was later diagnosed with Progressive Supranuclear Palsy, which is related to Parkinson's. He died from PSP on March 20, 2008.]

Q. Did the character in *The Dean's List* exhibit any of your symptoms?

A. No, actually Richard Falcon exhibits the other kind of symptoms. Most people have what he has, that is, the tremors, and a lot of people get depressed with Parkinson's disease, particularly at its onset. Now I haven't been depressed, nor do I have the shakes. I have the rigid kind of Parkinson's so I can't say that he has my symptoms.

Q. This character increases his medication so that it does work and he can work, and he takes larger doses than are recommended. Do you think that would ever be a temptation for you in the distant future in order to continue writing?

A. I could see that, yes. I was wrestling with that very question for myself as I wrote about it. The doctor told him not to take so much because of the side effects, and yet he's willing to do it to get his writing done. When writing is as important as it is to me, I could see where I might be tempted to do that, too.

Q. Any thoughts about the appearance of the paperback version of *The Dean's List* in May?

A. Well, of course it's always exciting to get the paperback out there because it brings in a whole new audience. It brings in students and teachers. I mean, all my work was out of print in 1986, and then Ballantine began to bring out the paperbacks, and then my work began to be taught in the classrooms. Before that, it was impossible because it was all hardback and students don't buy hardbacks very often, not for literature courses, at least. So my paperback will go out and it will give new life to the story. It's fun.

**Q. I guess for a round-up final question. What are you working on now?**

A. I'm working on three books actually. All three are non-fictions for the first time in my life. The most important one is "Days Like Smoke, Recollections of a Happy Childhood." That's my memoir which I've been working on for two years. I hope to finish it in March this coming year [not published yet]. The second one is a book about teachers. *Stories Teachers Tell*, it's called, and it will be just that; it'll be a collection of fifty or sixty stories told by teachers [Nodin Press, 2004]. And a third is *My Staggerford Journal* which I'm going to publish because English teachers around the state of Minnesota found this interesting [Ballantine hardcover, 1999]. The journal I kept as I was writing the novel tells you what I was doing and how I was progressing through the book.

**Q. With that, then, we'll look forward to all of those. Any final concluding words?**

A. No, although I've had some thoughts about writing lately. One is that a book isn't finished until the reader reads it and brings his/her experience to the book and completes the act, and so I think unpublished work isn't really finished. I used to think differently. I used to think that even if I weren't published I would be writing and probably I would for the sake of passing the time, but it's important to me now to be published and have a reader read it. That completes the process.

**Q. I can see that being true for all art forms—the spectator, the observer, the reader, the theatregoer.**

A. I think so.

Q. Well, thank you very much. It's been a very insightful and revealing conversation. Good luck on your future endeavors, Jon.

A. Thank you, Joe. It's a pleasure.

PHOTO: CHIP BORKENHAGEN

JOSEPH PLUT received his bachelor of arts degree in English from Saint John's University, Collegeville, Minnesota, and his master of arts degree in English and Comparative Literature from Columbia University, New York. Plut met Jon Hassler in 1968 when both were in the English Department at Brainerd Community College (now Central Lakes College) in Minnesota. Plut taught English and humanities for thirty-six years at Brainerd.

The late JON HASSLER, Minnesota author, educator, playwright, and artist, began his writing career at the age of thirty-seven, completing fifteen works of fiction and two works of nonfiction. His novels include *Staggerford*, *Simon's Night*, *A Green Journey*, and *North of Hope*. Jon taught English in high school and college for forty-one years, ending his academic career as Regents Professor Emeritus at Saint John's University of Minnesota.